P9-CPV-668

Praise for *Elder Care Journey*

"After losing two siblings, Laura Katz Olson is left singularly responsible for her physically active and lively mother, Dorothy, a thousand miles away, both young at heart and eagerly bicycling everywhere, but increasingly limited by the normal process of aging. Being an expert on aging and health care, Olson is at first confident as she tries to let her mother 'age in place.' More than anyone, she believes, she should know what to do. Shuttling between Florida and Pennsylvania, Olson settles into a crushing routine, and with each visit she finds incremental downward change in her mother's health. Pulled by daughterly guilt at times, but also a wellspring of love, Olson is frank about the resentment she sometimes experiences.

"With a unique perspective that links the systemic flaws in our policy approach to elder care to real-world experience, Olson exposes the challenges we all face or are likely to face. More than a personal story, but nevertheless an extremely compelling one, the book should be read by those confounded and frustrated, and by those without direct knowledge of what quietly repeats itself millions of times a day."

— Miriam Laugesen, Department of Health Policy
and Management, Columbia University

"In *Elder Care Journey*, Laura Olson tells the riveting story of helping her aging, disabled mother navigate the system of long-term services and supports. A renowned scholar of aging and long-term care policy, Dr. Olson was nevertheless unprepared for the daily frustrations involved in confronting a bewildering array of obstacles, deceptions, burdensome and repetitive procedures and paperwork, and catch-22s, ranging from the annoying to the downright dangerous. She shows how well-intentioned policies can fall far short of meeting people's needs, especially for those in greatest need, in a system based on fragmented interests and private-sector profit maximization. Combining scholarly expertise with personal experience, she ends the book with a detailed but highly accessible analysis of the long-term care system and how it could be improved to the benefit of both taxpayers and beneficiaries. This book is a compelling read for policymakers and for students and scholars of health care and social welfare policy, highly recommended for undergraduate and graduate courses. The author's experiences also provide helpful advice to caregivers on what to expect and how to deal with it, as well as reassurance that they are not alone."

— Christine L. Day, University of New Orleans

Elder Care Journey

SUNY series in New Political Science

_____

Bradley J. Macdonald, editor

Elder Care Journey

A View from the Front Lines

LAURA KATZ OLSON

excelsior editions

State University of New York Press
Albany, New York

Published by State University of New York Press, Albany

© 2016 State University of New York

All rights reserved

Printed in the United States of America

No part of this book may be used or reproduced in any manner whatsoever without written permission. No part of this book may be stored in a retrieval system or transmitted in any form or by any means including electronic, electrostatic, magnetic tape, mechanical, photocopying, recording, or otherwise without the prior permission in writing of the publisher.

Excelsior Editions is an imprint of State University of New York Press

For information, contact State University of New York Press, Albany, NY
www.sunypress.edu

Production, Jenn Bennett
Marketing, Fran Keneston

Library of Congress Cataloging-in-Publication Data

Olson, Laura Katz, 1945– author.
    Elder care journey : a view from the front lines / Laura Katz Olson.
        pages cm. — (SUNY series in new political science)
    Includes bibliographical references and index.
    ISBN 978-1-4384-6073-4 (hardcover : alk. paper)
    ISBN 978-1-4384-6075-8 (e-book)
    1. Olson, Laura Katz, 1945–   2. Aging parents—Care—United States.   3. Children of aging parents—United States.   4. Older women—Long-term care—United States.   5. Caregivers—United States.   6. Older people—Long-term care—United States.   7. Frail elderly—Long-term care—United States.   8. Older people—Government policy—United States.   I. Title.

    HQ1063.6.O47 2003
    306.874084'60973—dc23   2015024109

10 9 8 7 6 5 4 3 2 1

For My Mother, Dorothy Zager Katz,
and Our Zager Clan

&

The stories in this book reflect the author's recollection of events. Throughout the volume, the names of some individuals and identifying characteristics have been changed to protect their privacy. Dialogue has been recreated from memory.

Contents

Acknowledgments

I owe a huge professional and intellectual debt to Deborah Stone who has so generously given me her time, support, and insights over the last several years. Her academic vitality, enormous intellect, and stimulating ideas have influenced my thinking considerably.

I have profited from my association with many fine people at New Political Science, an organization that has been an integral part of my academic life since 1973. They have assisted me in countless ways over the decades. There are too many individuals to name separately but I would especially like to thank Bradley McDonald for his backing of this book project at SUNY Press, along with Steve Bronner and John Ehrenberg for their help, encouragement, and friendship over the last several decades. I am also appreciative of the community of scholars I have met through the Aging Politics and Policy Group of the American Political Science Association, specifically Eddie Miller, Michael Gusmano, Bill Brandon, Cynthia Mara, Bill Weissert, Jim Brasfield, Miriam Laugesen, Christine Day, Tom Oliver, Colleen Grogan, and Frank Thompson.

I would like to acknowledge the millions of family caregivers who give selflessly to their care-dependent mothers, fathers, parents-in-law, spouses, children, and friends. The overwhelming demands on their life, finances, and emotional well-being cannot be overstated and must be more fully recognized by political leaders as well as the general public. In addition, during the long road traveled in the world of paid care labor, I have encountered many individuals who are bighearted and tireless, despite the paucity of sufficient financial and societal rewards. My special gratitude is extended to Julie for the tender care she provided to my mother in Florida, her unflagging commitment to us, and the ongoing love that we share. I am indebted to many of the hardworking and compassionate aides and nurses on my mother's NE 2 floor at Gracedale Nursing Home. A very special thanks to Jean, the charge nurse; LPNs Lisa, Debbie, Eva, Courtney, Arlinda and

Dola; nurses' aides Colleen, Janine, Charlotte, Jeanette, Tina, Sam, Jarett, and Tammy; restorative aides (mom's "walkers") Michele and Missy; and physical therapists Amy and Judith.

As my mother steadily became the center of my daily existence, I not only was preoccupied with her needs but also talked incessantly about the situation. The creation of this book, and my single-minded obsession with it, only intensified the tedium for everyone around me. My heartfelt thanks to my amazing friends and family who nevertheless stood by me with understanding, support, and companionship. I am especially grateful to Betty Webster Schaefer for her many visits to mom at Gracedale whenever I leave town for short periods of time. Anna Adams and my cousins Sharon Altman, Carol Brachfeld, Art Spar, who commented on various portions of the manuscript, also deserve special mention.

I have received the finest guidance from the knowledgeable and energetic people at SUNY Press. I have particularly enjoyed working with senior editor Michael Rinella, whose professionalism, interest in the project, and thoughtful suggestions contributed significantly to the final version of the book. Jenn Bennett, the production editor, proved to be both efficient and a pleasure to work with. I am also pleased that the manuscript is in the most capable hands of Fran Keneston, director of marketing and publicity, as well as copyeditor Sharon Green.

My daughter, Alix, has kept my spirits up with her lively sense of humor, laughter, and good sense. I am particularly thankful to her for being by my side during those last painful and challenging days in Florida when we packed up mom's apartment together. And my grandson Zinn's presence—even if mostly by Skype—has been a regular reminder that there is more to life than writing books. My sisters Denise and Anne are always there in spirit, sitting on my shoulder and second-guessing every decision I have made regarding our mother.

I have also benefited from the anonymous reviewers who painstakingly evaluated the manuscript and gave detailed comments and suggestions that contributed materially to the final product. The book is much improved because of their feedback. Of course, the opinions, conclusions, and errors are mine alone.

I want to thank Lehigh University for funding the databases that allowed me to research the power structures of the several nursing homes and home care agencies. As usual, I am appreciative of Pat Ward, our conscientious librarian who ensures that the articles and books I need are ordered and delivered as expeditiously as possible.

I couldn't have written this book without the enthusiastic and unstinting support of my husband George who read early drafts of the manuscript and inspired me through our many conversations about elder care. He also did far more than his share of household duties while I was consumed with writing and revising the manuscript. My greatest gratitude goes to my mother, to whom this book is dedicated. She not only taught me to make lemonade when life hands you lemons but she has now given me an opportunity to love her in a new and meaningful way.

Prologue

For over thirty-five years, I have studied aging policies in the United States and the social, economic, and political structures they are grounded in. Despite the significant and steadily rising percentage of national, state, and local budgets devoted to the elderly, we are not meeting many of their ongoing and pressing problems. My studies, including a recent analysis of the Medicaid program,[1] has revealed how existing institutional arrangements and ideological boundaries have fostered government strategies that serve entrenched private-sector interests at the expense of the older population, especially the most disadvantaged among them.

Elder care, one of my main concerns, is possibly one of the more striking policy failures in our market economy. Billions and billions of public dollars annually are poured into and enrich a host of for-profit enterprises while conspicuously failing to care for vulnerable seniors. It is also largely an invisible issue since there tends to be a conspiracy of silence surrounding long-term services and supports (LTSS). There are more and more dependent people at advanced ages and growing numbers of relatives burdened by their care, yet it is an issue that few people openly discuss. There seems to be some invisible boundary between those of us performing care labor and the outside world.

My previous books on the frail aged, their caregivers and social welfare policies, however rigorous and straightforward, were academic approaches to the subject matter, with the inevitable objectivity and detachment required. They relied on aggregate data that described and analyzed systemic concerns and their social and structural determinants. Although heartfelt, these investigations were in retrospect about other people, abstract ideas, theories, and findings. They certainly were not about me—or my mother, Dorothy Katz. After all, she was a healthy and strong older athlete.

Then, unwittingly, I was steadily drawn into mom's everyday life and her growing dependency needs. Since she lived over 1,200 miles away, I was thrust into a long-distance caregiving role that was neither chosen nor particularly desired. In actuality, it could hardly be escaped, even had I endeavored to do so. There is a distinct irony, of course, in the fact that an actual person inconveniently interrupted my scholarly inquiries on the topic.

As Dorothy Katz's story became intertwined with mine, my rational notions as a researcher increasingly clashed with the reality of the caregiving experience. Investigating societal issues is one thing; personal relevancy is another. Now that I have a front-row seat, it is obvious that my previous work had just skimmed the surface. It is as though I were now witnessing the access, cost, and quality questions of health and long-term care through a magnifying glass.

There are various ways concrete, real-world events clarified and deepened my understanding of old age social programs and provided a more nuanced view of them. In traversing the elder care terrain, I encountered myriad "Aha!" moments. A number of these insights revealed hidden aspects of a situation that shattered earlier convictions and exposed the absurdities of many government strategies, along with the half-truths and hollowness of much of the official rhetoric.

The recent political noise about rebalancing Medicaid funding for care-dependent elders away from nursing homes and toward home-and-community-based services (HCBS) is one of these, something that I had previously advocated for, without reservation.[2] The underlying assumption is that it is simultaneously preferable and less expensive to allow seniors to "age in place." It soon became apparent, however, that the main reason Medicaid in-home services save money is because there are so few caregiver hours offered in most states.[3] Undoubtedly, cost-cutting is the main goal of public officials. Given that an elder must not only be poor (and prove it!) but also frail enough to require a nursing home level of care, the stark reality is that burdens are being shifted to relatives, particularly women—and this meant me. It is sheer nonsense to argue that a seriously disabled senior in dire financial circumstances can maintain an independent lifestyle with a maximum of only ten hours of assistance per week, as was the case with my mother. And she was among the privileged poor since we managed to "jump" the long Florida Medicaid Waiver waiting list.[4]

When I was finally forced to move mom to Pennsylvania, I fared even worse in my attempts to secure public services for her, and later, for my mother-in-law. Given my prior knowledge of the Area Agencies on Aging, I expected at least some assistance for them. Even its national website boasts that they are the foremost vehicle for organizing and delivering supportive services to older people and their caregivers.[5]

Nevertheless, in my actual encounters with two county Area Agencies on Aging, the extensive list of services on their brochures proved to be mostly illusory. At best, they inform, refer, and assess their needy clients for services that are either unavailable, have long waiting lists, or are of such limited quantity that nearly full-time family assistance is essential anyway. The arduous and protracted enrollment process, in the case of my mother-in-law, involved reams of paperwork, untold amounts of documentation, and two in-home assessments, altogether gobbling up over six months; the end result in the level of help was barely worth the effort. In view of the paucity of direct services, it seems as though much of the government funding for Area Agencies on Aging is used to feed administrators, social workers, and customer service representatives.

The United States is enmeshed in a dysfunctional, high-priced system of long-term care for chronically ill and dependent older people. The costs—whether for home and community-based services, assisted living facilities (ALFs), or nursing homes—outstrip the ability of the vast majority of seniors to pay for sufficient assistance. Even those with modest savings can easily exhaust all of their resources within a short period of time.[6]

Single older women of all races tend to encounter the most precarious economic circumstances. Indeed, over a third of women age seventy-five and over are classified as poor or near-poor.[7] Their average Social Security benefits are not only far lower than couples age sixty-five and over, but a significant percentage of them rely on the program for all or nearly the entirety of their income.[8] In my mother's case, her bare-bones Social Security check was $946 per month, a sum under the official poverty threshold.[9] At the same time, women at advanced ages are more likely than men to be living alone and to require formal long-term care services.[10]

Clearly, there is a disparity between the economic situation of frail elders and their ability to pay privately for the LTSS they may need, thereby forcing them on Medicaid. Nonetheless, as I found out, the state programs generally have such insufficient in-home services that the only real option is institutionalization or family care.

The sizeable "gaps" in government-funded home care services, whether because of limited supplies or an inability to access them, took on new meaning for me—it meant that I would have to find a way to provide them. Given that there are so few public dollars available for the vast majority of care-dependent individuals, it is no wonder that over 80 percent of elder care is provided by kin.[11] As Lynn Feinberg puts it, becoming an unpaid caregiver to one or more parents has become the "new normal" for their adult children.[12] At present, there are 43.5 million Americans assisting older people; the computed cost of such unpaid care is valued at between $450 billion and $522 billion per year.[13] Still consisting mostly of women, more men—similar to my husband—are being drawn into the world of "informal" care labor.

Roughly five to seven million of these individuals are, like me, long-distance caregivers. In my previous writings, I had seriously underestimated the complications of caring from afar. Yet, as with others in my situation, I had to visit frequently; help with everyday tasks; arrange for paid help; navigate the medical and LTSS systems; arrange for meals, transportation to doctors and other necessities; manage finances; and perform other vital chores, as needed.

Some adult children, including myself, contribute financially toward the purchase of in-home services as well. Many of us hold jobs and have to rearrange our schedules, miss work, or take an unpaid leave of absence.[14] In that regard I was quite fortunate in having a flexible schedule as a university professor. Even so, I inevitably had to short-change my other commitments.

Caring labor at a geographical distance can be all-consuming and psychologically overwhelming. For the most part, one is likely to be out-of-control over situations that arise unexpectedly—and many of them do. Among other unforeseen events, as my elder care journey makes clear, there may be a constant cycle of falls, hospitalizations, and post-acute care.[15] It became clear to me that a frail older person receiving medical and rehabilitative services, either in a nursing facility or at home, should have an on-site advocate to protect against poor treatment—and that entails unforeseen travel, especially if there are no other relatives close by. I just had to muddle through everyday issues as they arose.

Contending with already problematic situations from afar was further complicated by certain needless government and private-sector policies. Not the least of these was the 1996 Health Insurance Portability and Accountability Act (HIPAA) that, despite its well-meaning goals, became the bane of my existence.[16] Intended to protect patient privacy and rights, it actually hampered, complicated, and slowed down my every effort to help and protect my mother. HIPAA forced me to fax a Durable Power of Attorney document far and wide in order to obtain any information or benefits for her or to find out about her medical condition, even when she was taken to the hospital emergency room.[17]

It was also an unwelcome discovery that the Durable Power of Attorney document that had been so difficult for me to obtain is not accepted at either the Social Security Administration or the Department of Veterans Affairs. The VA won't even speak to a relative without a notarized copy of its own separate form allowing representation. Social Security Administration agents refuse to talk to you at all unless the beneficiary is there, in person. That surely complicates long-distance caregiving!

I learned, too, that intellectual awareness of the relentless streams of paperwork is quite apart from the actualities and the toll they can take on you. As a low-income older person in need of public help, my mother encountered ongoing demands for excessive, at times hard-to-acquire documents. We were drowning in convoluted rules and regulations for every piece of assistance she required, ranging from the rationed personal care services through Florida's Medicaid waiver program,[18] HUD section 8 rent supplements and AT&T Lifeline credits for her telephone bill, to Pennsylvania's Medical Assistance payments toward her nursing home care. Each of the onerous forms regularly resurfaced, in spite of the fact that nothing in mom's financial situation could possibly have altered. I am still facing grueling recertification burdens to hold onto my blind mother's nursing home assistance. It is a veritable bureaucratic merry-go-round.

Programs also tend to operate as functional silos, with separate eligibility levels, recertification cycles, and requirements. The social welfare system is so complex that it is not feasible for anybody to negotiate it on their own, least of all people with physical, functional, and cognitive disabilities. Despite my alleged "expertise" in the field, it is astounding how ill-prepared I was for dealing with the rigid barriers imposed at every turn. Even with so many academic tools in my arsenal, I often felt overwhelmed and rudderless. When faced with impersonal officials and their formalities one is downright helpless, regardless of his or her know-how. At times, I was besieged with rage at the unwarranted hurdles that prevented my mother from acquiring vital services in a timely manner.

As a senior citizen, I had signed up effortlessly on line for my Social

Security pension which, since then, has appeared regularly in my bank account every month for several years. No muss, no fuss. Not so for economically disadvantaged people, even if they are physically and mentally ill elders. For receipt of their benefits, they have to incessantly prove that they are truly poor through protracted, demeaning procedures. The social welfare system is teeming with social workers as well. In Florida, mom endured countless people poking around her apartment to assess her condition and financial resources but in the end relatively few direct services were forthcoming. They were often just acting as gatekeepers to ensure that she was not exploiting the system.

To be sure, the multiple obstacles to obtaining publicly supported services serve a clear purpose: to safeguard against people taking advantage of taxpayer money. The underlying concern is that households may acquire more than they are entitled to. The LTSS system for individuals with limited income is set up to be punitive, off-putting, and stingy so as to discourage people from applying, minimize enrollment, and control government outlays. Mom and I jumped through countless and pointless hoops that were both enervating and demoralizing.

The dizzying number of consumer choices overwhelmed me too. I stumbled through decision after decision, never quite sure that I had opted for the most appropriate one. Yet, program guidance is at a premium; the ubiquitous agency "help lines" are generally better at sucking up your time and taking you in circles than in providing meaningful information. Whether attempting to contact federal departments (e.g., the VA, SSA[19]) or state agencies in Florida and Pennsylvania, I was recurrently subjected to automated systems and their countless options; long waiting periods, sometimes up to an hour; innumerable "security" constraints; and ill-informed and robot-like customer representatives who were clueless about overall agency policies or your particular case.

Then again, it was surprising how constricted the nursing home choices actually were for us. The much touted "Medicare.gov Nursing Home Compare" website,[20] which grades nursing homes, was not particularly helpful since the higher-rated facilities, typically nonprofit places, are generally only available to people who are capable of paying directly out of pocket. For low-income elders like my mother, as I found out, "choice" is an empty promise. Certainly, none of the five star facilities in my area in Pennsylvania were willing to accept her as a Medicaid-funded resident unless she first paid privately for a year or two, a cost well beyond her means.

Moreover, post-acute care placement decisions are generally made by case workers and hospital discharge planners who just want to track down a bed in any facility that will admit the patient, especially in an emergency.[21] The "Nursing Home Compare" website proved to be useless because there were no decent options when mom was hastily discharged from two Florida hospitals. Make no mistake about it—when you are looking after a physically and/or mentally incapacitated person of advanced age nearly every such decision is an emergency.

My personal involvement as a caregiver added emotional force to my scholarship in other ways. It provided me the opportunity to truly grasp the financial drain, everyday demands, crises, dangers, agony, stresses, and consequences of having a parent totally reliant on you. The full extent of the selflessness required is way beyond what I had envisioned. Likewise, although I have no young children at home, the term "sandwich generation" became more real as I forever balanced mom's ever-present needs with those of my job, husband, adult daughter, grandchildren, and friends. There was no space for myself. Certainly, the experience tested me and how much I was willing to give up for mom.

U.S. long-term care policies are largely based on unrealistic expectations about what adult children—or spouses—can or should do. And, as the total number of years devoted to frail older people increases so does the age of the caregivers. I am now sixty-nine; my husband, an only child assisting his ninety-nine-year-old mother, is seventy-three. So much for the baby boomers' "golden years."

Relying on such unpaid work or offering programs aimed at "shoring up" families are ignoring the realities of the twenty-first century. That traditional expectations of adult children are still in force, even for supplementary caregiving duties, attest to how out of touch our political officials are. According to historian Stephanie Coontz, "The most common reaction to a discordance between myth and reality is guilt," subsequently followed by anger.[22] I grapple with both in full force. My husband has only the anger.

In addition to weighing down families, our policymakers have displaced social responsibility for seniors to the market. Public LTSS for older households in the United States generally rely on public-private partnerships (PPPs), an arrangement whereby the private sector delivers the services that are subsidized by taxpayers. Primarily consisting of commercial entities, the goals of these LTSS industries tend to be far removed from the needs of the people they serve.[23]

To be sure, formal elder care services are big business in this nation. Concomitantly, quality of care suffers, at times substantially, as nursing homes, home care agencies, assisted living facilities, health insurance companies and the like seek ever-increasing profits to the detriment of frail older people and their paid caregivers.

Having studied nursing homes over the years, I consider myself somewhat knowledgeable about them. I've read a good number of government documents, scores of research papers, and newspaper exposés, nearly all of which depict pervasive low-quality care. My own work on the subject is equally scathing. All the same, I was unprepared for the squalor and appalling conditions I witnessed in the two Florida nursing homes my mother stayed in for post-acute services. The assistance she received from several home care agencies was scarcely better.

In chapter 14, I move from the personal to a larger perspective by investigating several of the specific companies that provided services to my mother. Many of these companies, as with LTSS industries overall, are owned by private equity firms or multi-chain conglomerates trading on public exchanges. Despite extensive dependence on Medicare and Medicaid for their revenues, there is an out-and-out dearth of accountability and transparency. Thus it was tricky to penetrate their inner workings or lay bare the dizzying layers of control and spread of earnings flowing among them. In some cases, however, it was possible to juxtapose the adequacy of my mother's services against the gains of the government-funded establishments providing her care. The evidence suggests that the goals of these proprietary enterprises are patently at odds with the needs of their frail clients.

&·

Notwithstanding our discouraging experiences, mom and I encountered people along the way who caringly and effectively serve older people in need. The foremost individual in this regard was my mother's devoted aide who took charge when I was not there and rendered my long-distance caregiving achievable for a long while. Mom's caseworker at the Florida waiver program, too, ensured that she had as much assistive paraphernalia as possible, despite funding shortfalls.

When I was at wits' end over the improper withdrawal of one of mom's benefits, a paralegal at Florida's Legal Service of Broward County stepped in with invaluable pro bono assistance. We also benefitted from a sympathetic agent at my local Social Security office who facilitated the recovery of Dorothy Katz's stolen pension checks when nobody else would assist us, not even the federal Social Security Administration. Mom was also fortunate to stumble upon Chen Medical Center, whose doctors pay careful attention to the medical needs of their patients, making the diagnosis of her Parkinson's disease finally possible.[24]

And then there is Gracedale, the county nursing home in Pennsylvania where Dorothy Katz currently resides. The facility and its hard-working, attentive nurses and aides are providing decent enough care so that I am no longer fearful for her health, safety, and well-being. My long-distance caregiver journey has ended here; I am now a nursing home daughter. And it has been a surprisingly rewarding experience. Once there was relief from the overwhelming and crushing emotional and financial burdens, my mother and I have been able to forge a healthier, more affectionate relationship. I am forever grateful for that.

Although Mom and I are at the center of this narrative, it is not entirely about us. In the end, the story belongs to two generations: care-dependent older people striving to remain at home and their beleaguered adult children attempting to assist them. The intention is to show how our private odyssey is linked to the larger social, economic, and political policies and structures. Rather than convey the issues confronted by at-risk seniors and their families through facts and figures, this book is a firsthand look at what's behind the statistics and the consequences for real people. Such personal involvement not only has augmented my research on LTSS but also serves as a counterpoint to any professional judgments and findings.

There are a number of memoirs that document the emotional, psychological, and at times physical challenges in caring for a frail aged parent or spouse. They relate moving stories and provide insights and practical advice.[25] However, few of them address the compounding and often overpowering problems faced by elders with limited financial resources and who are reliant on government funding for their basic care. My account makes clear the demands and stresses of caregiving as well as the manifold indignities perpetrated by the U.S. social welfare system. Hopefully, it will elucidate the struggles confronted by other families who are attempting to navigate the complex and sorely inadequate programs serving the low-income elderly population.

The Precarious Situation
of the 1950s Woman

When I entered her apartment, my mother was seated in her lift recliner, the latest addition to the arsenal of enabling paraphernalia. When appropriately pressed, the small remote control would gradually raise her to a standing position, where she could grab onto her cane. She was having trouble locating the proper button on the device, and, increasingly, from removing it from the side pocket.

The chair, covered in a greenish-brown tweed, was situated in the corner of her small apartment. It was the center of mom's life. Her aide, Julie, had placed a few items within reach—lozenges, tissues, a water bottle, a peeled orange—but mom still hadn't gotten the hang of using her hands for eyes. Tissues were all over the floor, along with orange slices. She was facing a blaring television that she could no longer watch. On her small, white, round table sat another remote control with more useless buttons.

Mom could no longer see me clearly but as soon as the door opened she beamed her "I'm so glad to see you" look. The warmth of her smile usually was infectious but I was too distraught to reciprocate. It had been a few months since I'd visited and her deteriorated condition hit me anew, like someone punching me in the stomach. How could this be? Dorothy Katz, my sturdy, resilient, and spirited mother, didn't even have the energy to get up and greet me.

❧

I eyed the hybrid bicycle that my cousins had given mom for her 75th birthday. It was a well-worn deep blue, with twenty-one gears, probably overkill for the endless flat terrain of Hollywood, Florida, where she lived. She already had a racing bicycle and a mountain bike crammed into her tiny apartment. During her youth in New York City, Dottie had always delighted in the freedom of riding around the neighborhood, hair blowing in the wind. She wore a helmet only in her later years.

As a child of poor Eastern European immigrant parents, and the youngest of nine siblings, she had never actually owned a bicycle. But my ever-resourceful mother told me that she often "borrowed" one for the day. When I asked her to clarify, she just chuckled. "In those days we often 'borrowed' things." She particularly relished pedaling to her favorite basketball court and watching the boys play. Occasionally she would "borrow" one of their balls and practice her shots. "I was good," she said. "I rarely missed. They were surprised that a girl could play so well." Later on, some girlfriends would join in and they even challenged the boys. Mom and dad had met on the basketball court when she was sixteen.

She gave up riding after Denise, Anne, and I were born. "Too busy for bicycles," she told me recently. "Taking care of three children was a full-time job." She promptly added, "No, four. Your dad was always so needy."

Nevertheless, she had bought a bike for me, basic black with no shifts. Mom would periodically use it to cycle up and down the sidewalk of our apartment building in the Bronx. At nine years old, I had been too embarrassed to notice the elation on her face. I'm not sure if anyone else censured her but I knew that none of the other respectable middle-class mothers rode bicycles. After all, it was the 1950s.

Dorothy Katz, like others of her ilk, conformed to the mores of the day. She nearly always wore dresses, sometimes a skirt and blouse, even when vacuuming, washing and drying the dishes (which she did without our help), cleaning our rooms, and making the beds. Our family had a "magic spot," a clothes hamper, where we dropped our dirty garments—they presently appeared clean and pressed in our drawers. Since we didn't have a washer and dryer, mom hauled everything to the laundromat once a week.

In the evenings, while the family sat around one of the first television sets in the nation, she ironed our clothes. Mom even pressed our sheets, something I never appreciated until I crawled into the wrinkled bedding in my own first apartment. She shopped every day and cooked our meals. She never packed a lunch box for us. Similar to many other mothers, she always had food and snacks waiting for us at home; few young children stayed at school for the midday meal.

We had lived in a tiny three-room apartment in the Bronx until I was thirteen. The three girls squeezed into one bedroom, whereas the living room served as my parents sleeping quarters. The family had been ecstatic when we graduated to five rooms in the same building. As the eldest I now had my own space, which my sisters forever resented. Even then we were cramped but didn't realize it.

My mother had dreamed of moving to Levittown, in Long-Island, and my uncle drove us there a few times to check out available places. We didn't have a car. The mass-produced, identical dwellings in this suburban development, complete with white picket fences, small manicured front lawns and modern kitchens, had looked like heaven to my sisters and I. And dad qualified for a VA loan guarantee under the GI Bill. But he balked, probably because he dreaded the responsibility of homeownership. Dad was the head of the household and that was that. Only years later did his three daughters, attired in jeans, tie-dyed T-shirts, and high leather boots, dismiss these tract housing as bourgeois, namely Pete Seeger's "Little boxes made of ticky-tacky . . . little boxes all the same." To say the least, we were much less disappointed about having stayed in our tiny Bronx apartment.

Although a stay-at-home mom for many years, Dottie had not exactly been a June Cleaver. She obeyed most of the rules of her era but had a rebellious streak. Her dresses were selected mostly for comfort rather than style, even during those infrequent occasions when my parents went out together. Instead of the fashionable high-heeled pumps, mom preferred saddle shoes.

At five feet, eight inches and roughly 170 pounds, with broad shoulders and ample breasts, she was sturdily built. Mom had beautiful greenish-brown eyes that were nearly always covered with plain Cat-Eye glasses. She never powdered her face, wore eye makeup, or polished her nails, though she did apply the obligatory lipstick. She rarely went to the beauty parlor or used curlers. My mother generally just brushed through her medium brown wavy hair and let it fall into place.

Dad had been more conventional, both in appearance and attitude. An electrical engineer, he wanted to fit in. Sol Katz epitomized the "IBM look," a company he eventually would work for during the last year of his life. I remember an occasion when I met him at his office, probably around 1966. Every one of his coworkers looked alike: dark pin-striped suits, white button-down shirts, striped rep ties, and shiny wing-tipped shoes. His hair, prematurely white, like the others was cropped close to the scalp in a crew cut.

By then, my sisters and I were haranguing him to let his hair grow longer but dad was too much of a traditionalist. He was not very political but his response to protesters of the Vietnam War was typically die-hard patriotic. "Love it or leave it," he would say to my college friends, chanting the conservative slogan of the day. Mom was more supportive of the demonstrators, probably because she liked to be in tune with her children. She was highly responsive to our growing radicalism. However, I don't ever remember her reading a newspaper or even watching current events on TV.

For most of my high school and college years I was in constant combat with dad, often over my unconventional outlook. Much to his consternation, I immediately absorbed the progressive views of my classmates at the High School of Music and Art, in Manhattan, which I attended from1959 to 1963. It was not mainly the politics, however, that irritated him. Rather, it was my stocking-less feet, sandals, wide bell-bottom jeans, casual T-shirts, and work shirts, although such attire increasingly appealed to mom. Even so, she continued to conform to the stodgy dress code of the day.

My father and mother fought as well. He had a raging temper that could be triggered by the smallest incident. They argued over everything, especially mom's attentiveness to us. I think he sometimes felt left out, like a little kid barred from an exclusive club. I could hear them at night, spitting anger at each other. Dottie was not a pushover, which probably escalated dad's fury.

In spite of everything we were a tight-knit family because my mother would have it no other way. Every weekend we took long walks to the Botanical Gardens or some other park, where we devoured the generous assortment of deli sandwiches, pickles, coleslaw, potato salad, and desserts that she conscientiously packed for the excursion. I drifted a bit in high school and even more in college, even though I lived at home during those years.

My father's modest income had been expected to support the whole family—and it did. There were a few extras, such as music lessons, but the budget was tight. Mom controlled the money, which he dutifully handed over to her every payday. He worked hard, car-pooling to Long Island five days a week. When he arrived home in the evening, exactly at 5 o'clock, dad expected his dinner to be ready, which my mother supplied in ample portions. And we were required to be at the table as well, although that was more likely to meet my mother's needs.

When my youngest sister, Anne, was in third grade mom found a part-time job, first selling *World Book Encyclopedia*s and later *Parents Magazine*. She worked for "pin money" we were informed, a commonplace symbolic gesture intended to reinforce the father's role as family breadwinner. Yet dinner was still always punctual as were the expectations for us to be there. Mom rushed in at 3:30 and, after soothing herself with a hot shower, prepared the meal. The extra money, though relatively negligible, allowed Dottie to indulge her girls with a few "nonessentials."

Then in 1967, my senior year of college, dad suddenly died. He had been having heart palpitations for a while. When we went for a walk together he had to stop, rest, and regain his breath. My boyfriend's brother, a physician, had given me the name of a cardiologist and, with great persistence, I convinced dad to make an appointment. The doctor gave him a prescription for nitroglycerin, the only makeshift remedy available during those years. Every time he felt the excruciating pain across his chest, which was more and more often, he would grab for the medicine. Unknowingly to us, it treated just the symptoms, and his heart disease progressed unabated. One Saturday night, while I waited anxiously in bed for my parents to return home—it was 4 o'clock in the morning—mom arrived, sobbing. His death was fast and painless, something I later learned to be grateful for. My father was only forty-five years old.

We now had no income except for mom's "pin money" job. Even worse, my parents had spent dad's retirement pension, to make ends meet, when he was unemployed during 1965. After over a decade of working for the Sperry Rand Corporation, he was laid off because his division had lost a lucrative government defense contract. The company gave him his retirement accumulations, just enough to sustain the family for a year. Nothing was left. There wasn't any life insurance either. Insurance salesmen had periodically come to our apartment but my parents said they couldn't manage the high monthly premiums. I rather think that dad had been superstitious and was afraid that if he did buy a policy he would die.

Mom grieved pretty hard. Sol had been her companion since she was sixteen and now she was on her own, with two teenagers and me. Yet she didn't have the luxury to let her anguish interfere with the realty of our financial situation. As with many women of the 1950s, mom was intelligent, in a street-wise sort of way, but had no marketable skills. She barely completed high school before getting married.

Dad's current employer, IBM, gave us $3,000 as a death benefit. Dottie was forceful and decisive: the family would use the money to piece together a counterculture shop in order to engage her girls. We rented an empty store and called it the "Out of the Way" place; nearby retailers dubbed it "The

Mud Pie"! My sisters, our respective boyfriends, and mom purchased inexpensive wooden crates, painted them black and white, and designed displays. We had to use countless coats of paint since, unbeknownst to us, the crates were porous. Denise and Anne, though only sixteen and fourteen, respectively, were both talented artists and produced much of the initial inventory: earrings, crepe paper flowers, decorations, tie-died T-shirts, peasant blouses, beaded necklaces, head bands, hand-painted posters and cards, and brightly colored candles. As money trickled in, mom acquired a huge glass counter and gradually purchased a wide variety of avant-garde items, including silver rings and necklaces.

My mother mourned dad's death for years while simultaneously blossoming in her own right. Her dresses and skirts gave way to jeans, and the button-down blouses to T-shirts. She began wearing sandals, love beads around her neck, and the lipstick vanished. She became "mom" to an entire neighborhood, it seemed; young people dropped into the shop just to confide in her. She always had such a "sunny" disposition and optimistic outlook that I dubbed her "Pollyanna."

Dottie decided to take a second chance at homeownership now that she no longer required her husband's permission. After rambling from house to house for a few weeks, real estate agent in tow, she spotted what she viewed as the perfect place. She was excited but nervous and asked me to go with her to the bank. She had already filled out the forms and had the required documents in hand. Managing a house by herself wasn't going to be easy and I admired her spunk in taking on the challenge. What we hadn't foreseen, however, was the loan officer's out-of-hand rejection of her mortgage. After hemming and hawing around for several moments he informed us that they don't lend money to single women. She needed someone with sufficient resources, clearly not me, to cosign for her. I protested. After all, mom had saved enough for the requisite 20 percent down payment. It soon became clear, after trying a second bank, that my mother would not get a mortgage without a cosigner. Adamant about not relying on her sisters or brothers, she abandoned the effort.

But she managed to purchase a new car, paying for it outright. She traded in the bronze Plymouth Belvedere, which Dorothy and Sol had bought on time payments during the last year of dad's life. It had been an exciting experience for my parents since neither of them had ever owned an automobile before. But it was mom who loved being behind the wheel and, despite the usual norm, became the sole driver; dad navigated. Her new car, which she chose on her own, was a first-rate, ultra-safe bright red Volvo, unlike the low-end, conventional Belvedere her husband had preferred.

The "Out of the Way Place" remained a diamond in the rough for the entire twelve years my mother ran it. Still, it was an appealing store that permeated with a powerful blend of aromas. As soon as customers opened the door they would catch whiffs of lemon, lime, chamomile, lavender, spice, peppermint, cinnamon, and sandalwood oozing from candy sticks, incense, and multi-shaped candles, spread everywhere. They were also assaulted by a dazzling display of vibrant colors, like a kaleidoscope, everything bursting with the energy of my sisters' creative touches. Mom had special clients who regularly bought odds and ends and, overall, she sold just enough merchandise to support my siblings, both of whom worked part time in the store for several years. They eventually drifted away to lead their own lives: Denise to Colorado and Anne to Brooklyn.

Having mostly withdrawn from the shop soon after it was established, I finished college, travelled, went off to graduate school in Colorado, married, had a child, and started my career as a professor at Lehigh University in Bethlehem, Pennsylvania. My main contribution in the later years of the store had been to periodically bail mom out when it was robbed—which occurred more and more often. Eventually she had to give it up and, at age fifty-six, headed to Florida in the Volvo, with her bicycle attached to its rear.

2

Athlete to Cane

The Elusive Search for a Disease

Dorothy Katz's long, winding medical odyssey began in August 2006, just a few months after her 83rd birthday. It was a disturbing crusade as she desperately struggled to find out why she was so worn out all the time. My mother, who was rarely ill and who complained about her health even more infrequently, was particularly ill-suited for negotiating the health care system. She'd never had patience for sickness; as a young child, I rarely stayed home from school unless I was seriously ill, preferably with visible signs like a rash. And aspirin had been unthinkable. "You don't need to put any pills into your body," she would insist. "Your body will ease the pain on its own."

Now in her early eighties, she was forced to wade through ambiguous diagnoses, obscure medical jargon, swamped and impatient physicians, and contradictory test results. Unable to afford the out-of-pocket expenditures associated with traditional Medicare and its indispensable companion, Medigap insurance, mom also confronted the controls, restrictions, and stringent regulations of her Humana Medicare Advantage plan.[1]

Her three daughters were somewhat removed from her day-to-day existence and had taken a hands-off approach to mom's medical issues. And my self-sufficient mother had made it clear to us that she wanted it that way. "I would like to enjoy my children," she said. "I don't need directors." Dottie had always been incorrigible; she was on her own in the search for answers, updating us regularly.

Concerned but not unduly alarmed, I phoned mom once a week, something I had been doing consistently for over forty years. She shared her progress and setbacks with me at a distance, punctuated by her regular trips "up north." I flew to Florida from time to time but she mostly came to stay with us. Driving was one of her abiding pleasures, a penchant we definitely didn't share. She would hop in the car and camp her way up to Pennsylvania, then on to New York to see her siblings and Anne. On a few occasions my husband George and I met her at a campground in Florida, where she would pitch her tent next to ours. She always arrived with a cooler full of nutritious provisions. Unlike me, mom was a vegetarian and only consumed natural and organic foods. "My body is my temple," she would say. She was so very careful about her eating habits.

At other times, mom arrived at our house by plane, alternating between my airport and Anne's. I must admit that over the years my sister had initiated these trips way more than me. She would say, "It's time for another visit."

I would breathe deeply, anxiously tallying my work load. I mostly begrudged the time taken away from my writing projects. "Wasn't mom just here?" was my usual retort. But I always ended up buying the ticket; Anne could never afford it.

꽃

My mother's symptoms had begun with an increasing loss of energy and shortness of breath when she exercised. The doctor sent her for a cardiac evaluation. "Everything is normal," the cardiologist declared after reviewing the diagnostic tests. "You can continue with your usual activities."

Mom's "usual activities" consisted of strenuous physical workouts. She recently sent me her silver medal for winning the local Senior Olympics bicycle racing events. She had taken up competitive riding in her late seventies, challenging herself to go faster and faster. She worked her way up from bronze and was rightly gratified by the achievement. The swimming competitions consistently earned her silver or gold, as did the basketball competitions. I had always been too busy to come for the actual tournaments.

Dottie was a much admired figure in her circle of competitors, including much younger men and women. They considered her a first-rate athlete, a person who trained diligently. She woke up at 4:30 a.m. every day to swim laps. "The pool is too crowded later on," she said. "Only my mother would get up at that hour to exercise," I replied, shaking my head with a mixture of awe and disbelief. I hid my head under the pillow when the alarm went off during my visits.

Her biking was just as impressive, occasionally surpassing me in endurance and speed. During one of our cycling excursions in Pennsylvania, my eighty-year-old mother had left George and me in the dust—we were both veteran riders. I needed to rest periodically; she obligingly but impatiently waited for us. She was a dynamo.

But it was her basketball skills that I had always admired most, even during my childhood. One summer, in 1955, my parents had rented a bungalow in Rockaway, and would spend the evenings on the boardwalk. "Hey, sir," the person manning a basketball booth called out to my dad. "Don't you want to win a pretty little stuffed animal for your girls?" We walked up to him, dad paid the quarter, and proceeded to miss all three shots. On the second attempt he put one ball into the basket. After trying a few more times, mom nudged him to move on. The operator of the stall grinned at us. "Tell you what I'm gonna do," he said. "For the lady only. Sink two out of three balls and you win the prize."

Everyone knew, of course, that the hoops at these places were higher than usual, and the rims, which were bent to make them appear larger in the front, were smaller than regulation size. Nevertheless, my mother had taken the ball deftly in her hands, focused on the basket, and canned three in a row. We amassed a closet full of stuffed animals that summer. At the end of the season, the booth's owner gave my mother the basketball.

Six months after the initial onset of symptoms, mom became deeply concerned about her progressively worsening fatigue, intermittent dizziness, and subsequent heavy rectal bleeding. She drove to the Emergency Room of Memorial Hospital. They admitted her. She received comprehensive, and costly, diagnostic procedures: a colonoscopy (for possible cancer of the colon and large intestine); a CT scan of the brain (for assessing the dizziness); and a series of blood tests.

After reviewing the results, mom's physician informed her that she had anemia, which he attributed to bleeding hemorrhoids. "Everything else," he pointed out, "is normal." Along with a prescription for iron pills, he recommended the removal of her hemorrhoids. She agreed, eager to have her strength restored.

Even though she diligently took the iron supplements, the condition worsened. Her legs, in particular, were losing strength. She became alarmed by her progressive sense of unsteadiness on the bicycle and, with great reluctance, gave up riding.

Dottie used her bike to travel everywhere, including shopping, no matter what the distance. "It's easy parking," she said airily. "And there are no gas costs." But I suspected it was the exhilaration she experienced, the steady rhythm of pedaling. Prior to retirement, she had cycled twenty-four miles round-trip to her job, where she drove a bus for a private elementary school. She told me, "No matter how worn out I was at the end of the day, the bicycling invigorated me." Parting with her bicycle, even temporarily, was a considerable loss since it had become such an essential piece of her everyday life.

Her arms, too, were failing and she soon was forced to abandon swimming as well. "It's only until I find out what's wrong," she assured her increasingly worried daughters.

Mom began having difficulty in all of her activities, including shopping. "I'm always wiped out," she said to me during one of our weekly calls. "And my fingers are so stiff and clumsy. At times I can hardly write." She soon became concerned about the undue effort it took for her to operate the computer. She had joined a special program for the elderly, which gave its participants a new Dell PC, together with group lessons at the nearby senior center. She had been pleased with her newfound ability to send e-mails and bombarded everyone she knew, especially her granddaughter and daughters, with daily missives. Typical of Dottie, ever the Pollyanna, her e-mail address was Havefun418 (her apartment number).

This time the physician diagnosed Carpal Tunnel Syndrome. Accordingly, she headed off for rehab sessions, assiduously exercising her hands and fingers. After a few weeks there was no improvement. She had to quit, in any case, because she had reached her insurance company's maximum allowable sessions.

By now, mom was telling us, "I feel foggy in my brain. I can't think straight anymore." She went for more blood tests. Everything came back "normal." Two years later, in 2009, my mother switched physicians.

The new doctor promptly diagnosed her as merely "old." Just as unhelpfully, he further identified her as "depressed." Mom had been outraged when she reported the conversation to me but couldn't say anything to him. Her generation of women didn't contradict medical professionals, at least to their face.

Confined to the insurance company's limited list of participating physicians, my mother searched for another general practitioner. Yet again, she stated her ongoing medical situation: She felt shaky on her feet and had numbness, pain and tingling in her hands. She said, "I am walking around like a zombie. My head is in a fog." She insisted, however, "I am not depressed. Just sapped of energy."

The doctor examined her thoroughly in an attempt to figure out what was wrong. After sending her for more blood tests, he referred mom to a neurologist. The specialist gave her a battery of tests, including nerve conduction studies and an MRI for memory loss and weakness. Except for determining, yet again, that she had Carpal Tunnel Syndrome in her right hand, the results were negative. The neurologist concluded, in his evaluation report: "I think the major issue here is depression." He gave her a wrist brace, and a prescription for antidepressants, the latter an apparent fallback for when a medical professional couldn't figure out what was wrong with a frail elderly woman.

Nevertheless, his assessment of my mother's condition gave me pause. I knew, of course, that she was brokenhearted—after all, she was still grieving the death of her youngest daughter the previous year. Unexpectedly, in the fall of 2007, my feisty and robust sister Anne had started coughing up blood. Her doctor soon determined that she had lung cancer. And it was the type that spread rapidly.

Mom had flown to New York to be with her but both of them were too debilitated at that point to be of much use to each other. I watched how precariously mom climbed the steps to Anne's bedroom. She could not stay. It would be too much of a burden for my brother-in-law, who was by now caring for his wife full time. My sister succumbed to the cancer in July 2008, shortly after mom left.

As the unfathomable reality of Anne's death sank in, she fell into a deep malaise. Any mother would be devastated—there weren't too many occurrences in life that were worse than losing a child.[2] We all cried separately and together, my daughter Alix, mom, and I. The three of us had been shocked and shattered by our loss. But the fact of the matter is, regardless of whether or not mom was depressed, the mounting evidence suggested to me that Dorothy Katz had some type of degenerative disease. And I had to help her find out what was wrong.

I was a bit wary about stepping in since my previous intervention in her affairs had created havoc. It was in 2006, when Medicare recipients had to sign up for their Part D prescription drug coverage. A knowledgeable student of the subject, I had agreed to take charge. Mom was appreciative of my help. After diligently perusing a variety of websites and assessing individual stand-alone plans to complement her current insurance, I signed her up for what appeared to be the "best" one. Unbeknownst to me, that triggered an automatic termination of mom's Medicare Advantage plan and, with it, all of her health care benefits. Evidently, you couldn't have both. It had taken me days to clean up the mess, during which time my mother was without any medical coverage. So much for my "expertise."

Nonetheless, given the circumstances I decided to give it another shot. And, once more my efforts weren't terribly productive. I began with my suspicion of Lyme disease, which previously had been put on hold in deference to my family. "Mom does not have Lyme disease," Anne had insisted when I first raised the topic. "You just want to blame everything on me." I was at a loss as to why she had taken it so personally.

My mother, too, had been resistant. "Since when did you become a doctor?" she had accused me. "None of my physicians think I have the disorder. Leave it alone." I had backed off.

Now I was determined to seek answers. By this time I had read six books on the subject. Indeed, when confronted with any predicament, my first response was to study it to death. Perhaps it gave me a sense of control, even if it's mostly illusory. In any case, the research had convinced me that mom's symptoms were consistent with the disorder. Besides, they had begun shortly after visiting Anne, who lived in an area covered in deer ticks. My sister and her husband had had bouts of Lyme disease themselves over the years so, in my view, it certainly was a promising diagnosis.

I took mom to my brother-in-law's infectious disease specialist in New York, who handed us a prescription for a comprehensive Lyme disease screening, a prescription for doxycycline to treat the ailment, and a bill for $300, which I had to pay out-of-pocket. The verdict came in two weeks later. "Your mother has Lyme disease," the physician reported. "She should start antibiotic treatments immediately."

Next, I searched for a Florida specialist within Humana's Medicare Advantage service area. Much to my astonishment, each geographic area had its own restricted group of participating physicians, even within the same plan. And, even more disturbing, her coverage didn't include any Lyme disease specialists. I petitioned the insurance company and, after days of phone calls, received permission for a few sessions with an appropriate doctor in another area. At least we could get her treatments started.

Mom took the New York report with her to the first appointment. "You definitely do not have Lyme disease," the Florida specialist said.

In disbelief, I phoned the doctor. "The test results are clearly negative," she confirmed. "I'm sure of it."

Still not persuaded and desperately wanting a solution to my mother's deteriorating condition, I couldn't let it go. I took her medical information to another infectious disease specialist, this time near my home in Pennsylvania. "*What do they know about Lyme disease in Florida,*" I told myself. "*They don't even have deer ticks there.*"

"Negative," the Pennsylvania doctor confirmed, kindly refusing any payment.

I was at a loss. Mom was now slightly over eighty-seven years old but, in my view, her swift degeneration had to be more than the typical aging process.

℘

Mom attempted to schedule another visit with her primary care doctor, whom she both liked and trusted, but discovered that he had been dropped by her insurance company. Perhaps he gave too many referrals and tests to the detriment of Humana's financial bottom line?

No diagnosis. No physician. And my mother's condition was steadily declining. At this point she required a cane to walk and even then she seemed unsteady. Serendipitously, she fumbled her way into the Chen Medical Center, a recommendation from her card partner, and met Doctor Ana Apaza.

The Chen Center turned out to be an oasis of responsiveness and attention, not the usual medical whirlwind of overextended physicians who couldn't remember their patients' names. In the past years, my mother had been merely a folder, sitting outside her doctors' office doors, which they cursorily reviewed before entering the examination room. And the actual person they soon encountered was, to them, a feeble, depressed old lady. Some of them summarily dismissed her; others were willing to employ a panoply of dazzling and expensive technical equipment. But none of them had ever taken the time to hear what Dottie was experiencing or actively involve her in their evaluations.

This place was different. Concentrating its medical practice strictly on the aged, its primary care doctors and specialists—nearly all of whom were on-site—didn't have rigid time limits per patient. They actually listened to their clients, who were not viewed merely as passive consumers of services.

When I first walked into the spacious waiting room, humming with people of varying races and nationalities, I immediately spotted the generous, complimentary array of healthy snacks, coffee, and hot chocolate. One elderly woman was contently slipping a treat or two into her jacket pocket, something that most likely was commonplace. The indulgent staff regularly re-stocked the provisions.

The ease of the check-in procedure took me by surprise. After only six months the receptionists knew my mother and bantered with her. "So, this is the daughter you're so proud of," one of them said. She turned to me and smiled. "We all adore your mother here. She has such a sunny personality." I sighed, reassured. At least they wouldn't be giving her antidepressants.

The Chen Center was impressive in other ways. Taking into consideration the needs of its patients, the facility offered wheelchair-accessible vans, free of charge, to pick up individuals for their appointments. It was a convenience that served mom well, later on, when she no longer could walk on her own. And she had constant doctor visits these days, including acupuncture for her recent pain. It provided some relief, if only temporarily. I never asked how these countless treatments were being paid for, or whether the Chen Center was in constant battle with her insurance company over what had to be astronomical costs. Despite my usual personal and professional curiosity over such matters, I just didn't want to know. My mother finally was receiving the medical care she required and deserved.

At the first visit, which mom had gone to alone, Dr. Ana read her history carefully, including the letter I had sent, "An Introduction to Dorothy Katz." In it, I related her athletic prowess and achievements prior to the illness. I was so tired of everyone dehumanizing my mother and I didn't know what to expect from her latest physician.

As it turned out, Dr. Ana would have taken my mother and her condition seriously without my meddling. Almost immediately, she had referred her to one of their neurologists. "I was pretty sure what was wrong from the start," she disclosed to me. "But I wanted to verify it."

The neurologist, too, recognized mom's affliction straightaway, even before any of the test results materialized. "You have Parkinson's disease," she had informed her. "I could tell from your shuffle when you walked in."

Strangely, despite the devastating diagnosis, I was relieved. Mom's condition had a name.

3

The Reluctant Long-Distance Caregiver

As my mother's Parkinson's disease progressed, her health care odyssey became mine as well. I was steadily enmeshed in her life, responding to situations as they arose, regardless of any other demands on my life. And issues surfaced relentlessly. Having previously given short shrift to the notion of long-distance caregiving, I was now confronted with its harsh reality. As the days turned into months, it was like being at a carnival, replete with merry-go-rounds, roller coasters, water slides and bumper cars. Without warning, there were unforeseen predicaments and crushing bureaucratic nonsense. Unbeknownst to me, however, this was merely the lull before the storm.

I was drawn in piecemeal at first. Mom informed me, rather matter-of-factly, that she had received a notice that her annual application for the Medicare Savings Program had been denied. She had been receiving payments for Medicare Part B through the Qualifying Individual (QI) Program for low-income elderly.[1] She wasn't quite sure what that implied. In the past, Gail—the social worker in her building—had assisted with routine paperwork. Apparently, this was beyond the scope of Gail's duties. "Can you check into it?" mom asked me.

This was the beginning of my education as a consumer rather than a researcher of services for the low-income population. And, much to my endless frustration, it was a steep learning curve. Just contacting anyone for assistance was a formidable, often exhausting task that could devour a client's energy and crush her willpower. At times, it certainly taxed even my customary fierce resolve.

In this case, I dutifully attempted to call the Florida Department of Children and Families (FDCF), which had rejected mom's renewal application, and quickly discovered that speaking to an actual human being was

17

quite problematic. After dialing the Customer Call Center and pressing a sequence of obligatory buttons, a robotic voice directed me to the agency's website. If the client really had to speak to an agent, the machine said, she could select zero. I proceeded. Again, the automated system referred me to the online tool but this time I perceived exasperation in its mechanical voice, as though it couldn't believe that I was still pursuing a real person. Then it transferred me to another place, where I was told, "because we are experiencing high call volume, the wait is approximately twenty minutes." I called again later and the delay was even longer.

Making up my mind to get in line, I now had to listen to a programmed voice on the other end haranguing me over and over again to use its website instead. In a misguided attempt to multitask, I worked at something else simultaneously but missed my turn and was unceremoniously disconnected. After several days of desperate but determined dialing and re-dialing, an agent finally materialized. However, she advised me that nothing could be done until my mother filled out their form designating me as her official representative. And that form could only be found on their website.

I had jumped into the bureaucratic bumper cars but didn't realize, at the time, that I had bought a multiyear pass. My life, from now on, would be suffocated in telephone Muzak, communicating with computerized voices, hearing that a place was "currently experiencing a high call volume" or that "representatives are working hard to take my call as soon as possible" (they were also at times "sorry for the inconvenience"), enduring constant busy signals (beep, beep, beep) and dealing with inadequately trained representatives. Then, in order to receive even basic information, there would be demands for Social Security numbers and special codes. After a while it wouldn't have surprised me if someone demanded the promise of my firstborn grandchild in exchange for information!

It was unclear to me why some government agencies even bother to have a call center since the individuals on the other side of the line were generally ill-informed about both agency policy and individual cases. They had a script to read and did so without deviation. I was always told to "have a good day," despite the fact that I was seething with rage at their inability to help me.

I learned, too, that the HIPAA privacy rules, much touted for their protection of patient rights, would obstruct nearly everything I sought to accomplish on my mother's behalf. Confidentiality and government safeguards, from the perspective of an adult child attempting to oversee the needs of her frail, dependent mother, translated into gobbledygook. Even in emergencies, there were always special permissions for Dottie to sign and this was not only challenging but often impossible to achieve in the context of long-distance caregiving. At times, I couldn't even find out if my mother was hospitalized or how serious her condition was.

Having no alternative, I downloaded the requisite document allowing the FDCF to discuss my mother's case with me and faxed it to them. Back to the interminable dialing! Reaching its call center in due course, I found out the service representative didn't have a clue as to why my mother had been turned down for the Medicare Savings Program except that this year her income was over the eligibility limit. How could that be?

My tenaciousness served me well. After repeated phone calls and speaking to similarly evasive operators, I somehow managed to reach a supervisor willing to discuss Dorothy Katz's case with me. My satisfaction at the achievement was short-lived. In a no-nonsense tone she told me that because of mom's recently obtained VA benefit, her income was now too high for the QI supplement.

This explanation took me aback since my mother had applied for the low-income VA widow's allowance only to acquire a few hours of caregiving a week. Without telling me, she had hired an aide, through a home care agency, to help her with cooking, cleaning, and laundry. No longer driving, she also wanted someone to take her shopping. I shook my head in disbelief. The VA had provided a small stipend to my frail mother that then triggered the withdrawal of her Florida QI Benefit. It was a "Catch-22."

In fact, I discovered that mom was signing the entire VA check over to the home care agency and was several thousands of dollars in debt to it. Apparently, a social worker, who had facilitated the arrangement between her and the company, arranged for the caregiving to begin nearly a year before the VA money had been actually granted to her.

It became an effort in futility to clarify the situation to the supervisor, who didn't budge. I then added that it would be a severe hardship for mom to lose Florida's QI support. "Those are the rules," she said, not backing down. "There is nothing that I can do." She seemed utterly indifferent, like a parent stonewalling a child's demand for more sweets. "By the way," she warned me. "Your mother's ineligibility is retroactive. Her next Social Security check will be $300 less than the usual amount."

As it registered that mom's already bare-bones income was scheduled for reduction, I incurred spasms of panic. A one-time loss, a drop to $614 the next month, would render her incapable of paying her bills. My mind was racing. Her sole monthly funds was a meager $946 Social Security check and the permanent loss of the $100 QI benefit would be a devastating dent in her finances. Florida was so stingy in serving the poor that mom had not even qualified for traditional Medicaid, or help with the full array of Medicare out-of-pocket costs.[2] Now the state was after the limited subsidy it did offer her.

After several restless nights I awoke with a jolt at 2 a.m. "*I need to contact Legal Aid,*" I mumbled to myself, half asleep. Somehow my inert brain conjured up Lyndon Johnson's "War on Poverty" program which had been discussed in my Presidency seminar several weeks earlier. Finally having a plan of action, I fell back to sleep, calmed.

꿎

The Florida Legal Service's office was overflowing with people, young and old, all in desperate need of assistance. With mom at my side, we waited in the stuffy room with mounting weariness. Poorly lit and somewhat shabby, the place did not inspire confidence. Would an underfunded agency so burdened with requests for cost-free aid help us? Or, for that matter, would their beleaguered lawyers be capable of providing sufficient help. Whatever my doubts, they were immediately eradicated by Renee, the straightforward paralegal assigned to Dorothy Katz's case. She took charge at once, reading through the cancellation notice, my summary of conversations with the supervisor at the FDCF, mom's bank statements, and other material I had brought with us. Renee thoroughly explained mom's "rights" in the situation and outlined the steps she intended to take to address them.

The key to the problem, she counseled me, was to obtain a letter from the VA indicating what portion of mom's newly acquired pension was an Aid and Attendance Allowance, which under Florida law should be excluded from my mother's total income. According to the paralegal, the rest of the VA pension could be discounted as unreimbursed medical expenses. Sounded simple. Renee would fill out the various forms and appeal mom's case for us. She was certain that my mother would have her QI benefits restored without a serious battle. Yeah, right. The Department of Veterans Affairs, not exactly known for its user-friendly practices, proved to be a stumbling block. Predictably, nobody at that agency would talk to me without a formal, separate form, signed by mom, authorizing me to act on her behalf.

Even after faxing the document I encountered innumerable hurdles, not least of which was locating the appropriate office to send it to. Their customer service representatives were neither friendly nor helpful.

We ultimately acquired the coveted piece of paper and, six months later, won the appeal; my mother's VA benefits were not counted as income. At least for this year. Would we be embroiled in legal action every May, when the Medicare Savings Program renewal was due? What did I get myself into?

❧

By mid-2010, my trips South increased since it had become too challenging for mom to fly by herself. It felt strange to land at the Ft. Lauderdale airport and not glimpse her, waiting to greet me. She had always been larger than life, becoming even grander when welcoming her children. I could envision her waiving excitedly, her radiant face framed by curly snow-white hair, as soon as I approached the terminal. She would utterly enfold me as I took in her familiar scent. After a long embrace, we would walk arm-in-arm toward her car, mom dragging my suitcase in the other hand. She had always insisted on carrying my luggage, uncomfortable when any of her girls were burdened down.

On this particular stay, I negotiated my way, alone, to the shuttle bus, waited on the long line at the rental car counter, placed my GPS on the vehicle assigned to me, and headed straight to mom's place, a tedious ritual that before long became routine.

Mom had left the apartment door open. As I entered, she struggled out of her chair to welcome me, first grabbing the carved wooden cane that I had bought for her on my last visit. It was dismaying to watch her stooped body shuffling across the floor. Dottie had always stood tall, all 5' 8" of her. At the moment she appeared frail and small. It unnerved me.

The five-day visit was tense. Her slouch grated on me and I harangued her over it. "Straighten up," I said repeatedly, as though it were her fault. "You're being careless about your posture."

She threw her shoulders back, determined to accommodate me, but quickly slumped again. "Do you think I like bending over like this? I work at it but there's nothing I can do." Her voice was a mixture of resignation and reproach. I shrugged my shoulders.

When we shopped for groceries she insisted on Whole Foods, an organic market that was not only far away but sold what I viewed as overpriced goods. In the past I had acceded to her penchant for expensive "natural foods." Besides, she had always been the one at the wheel. Now I was forced to drive the long distance in a rented car. I paid for the high-priced items irritably.

There was a persistent edge in my voice as I found myself ever more intolerant of quirks and habits that used to amuse me—they had made Dottie the unique person that she was. Her long, drawn out stretches in the bathroom obsessively brushing her teeth, the orange that had to be cut in a certain way, the endless water bottles (she refused to drink water from the tap), all now ticked me off.

I was particularly impatient with her foundering capacities, constantly urging her to try harder. We toddled around the block twice a day and I warned her that she had to do this regularly or she'd end up in a wheelchair. Mom nodded assent, her face tense, but I knew she was lying. She wouldn't—couldn't—take such long walks on her own.

Dorothy hadn't entirely lost her customary optimism, a trait I had grown accustomed to, but at the present time seemed inane, out of place, given her situation. She even dressed as though she was ready to hop on a bicycle, which grated on me even further.

The tension, and conflict, was mutual—mom could still throw her poison darts. Even during my childhood, I had endured regular stinging remarks, seemingly out of the blue. She would hold in her disapprovals for a long while and then, without warning, hurl them at me all at once. The barbs during this visit intensified as she reciprocated my unkindness. She was critical of the constant rushing around, my unkempt hair, the glasses of wine she didn't think were good for me, the way I probed her, everyone, and everything, with questions.

᠅

Before returning home, I bought her a new, easy-to-put-on bathing suit, and suggested that we go for a swim. Mom demurred at first, protesting that it would be too taxing for her. I insisted and she relented, obviously seeking to please me. We hobbled to the YMCA next door, where she still had an annual pass.

Because there weren't sufficient handrails she was forced to depend mostly on me to ease her into the water. It was awkward and physically demanding for both of us. She was obviously extremely hesitant but I kept at it, ignoring her mumbling protests. She was now waist deep and I egged her on to swim.

"You can do it," I said. She just stood there. "Come on mom. Just a short swim." She didn't move. "What's wrong?" I was exasperated.

"I can't move my legs," she finally said.

"Please try," I said, beseeching her.

"I can't. I can't. I can't." My mother sputtered the words, with a pained expression on her face.

I stopped short and, for the first time, really looked at her, so weak and vulnerable. In a flash it became clear that it wasn't her eccentricities that had been unsettling me but rather my fears for her, for us. Over the last many months, I had been deluding myself, unwilling to face the stark reality that she was no longer capable of caring for herself with the limited help that she received.

The heartrending decline of her body and the gradual loss of the mother I had always known were terrifying. Longing for her to stay exactly as she had been, always there for me, I was like a two-year-old having a tantrum. Yet, the truth was that I also dreaded the future upheavals in my own life, the specter of my mother's ever-growing needs taking over my carefully calibrated existence. Unduly self-disciplined and goal-oriented, I always incessantly scheduled, organized, and paced out my time, like a bee colony building its nest. Watching mom now, her legs temporarily frozen—a typical symptom of Parkinson's disease I later learned—forced me to grudgingly accept that we were on a joint venture. And, my life would be out of control in the coming days ahead.

I hadn't asked to be in charge of my mother. Yet it was thrust on me. The future seemed uncertain as I faced the full weight of my responsibility for her.

I gently guided her out of the pool, murmuring soft words of encouragement, and rubbed her down with a towel.

§.

Upon returning home to Pennsylvania, I sought more personal assistance for mom. She already had Julie, the aide from ResCare, the agency that mom had engaged with her Veterans Pension. Originally from Haiti, the caregiver was a stroke of luck. She was sturdy, with broad shoulders, similar to my mother. Her broad lips, covered in bright red lipstick, regularly broke into a beaming smile, accentuated by dimples tucked into coffee-colored skin. Julie's hair was always carefully coiffed and she dressed impeccably, regardless of any drudgework ahead of her.

She was inordinately attentive to mom, treating her as though she were her own mother. She shopped with Dottie, driving her once a week to Whole Foods and, unlike me, without complaint. Twice a week, Julie cleaned, did the laundry, took mom to the doctor, and prepared breakfast, sometimes leaving tasty dishes in the refrigerator for lunch.

They had become fast friends, despite the fact that my mother could hardly understand her garbled English. They seemed to communicate in their own way, reacting to each other's facial expressions and gestures. During my visits, I often had no idea what Julie was saying but had warmed to her kind heart.

It was clear that Julie was quite a special person, a gem really. There were boundless stories of long-distance caregivers, like myself, who spent their days anxious over aides who didn't show up, were habitually late, quit without notice, did a slapdash job or, even worse, pilfered from their unsuspecting clients. Families were regularly interviewing caregiver after caregiver, often at a moment's notice. Julie had never missed a day, even when her beat-up car broke down—despite her miserable wages she had taken a cab to arrive on time.

But Julie's ten hours—on Tuesdays and Thursdays—wouldn't suffice anymore. After checking into hiring her for additional hours, I realized that mom simply couldn't afford it at the $16.50 an hour, plus travel, that ResCare charged. Even more dismaying was the discovery that the agency paid Julie only $9.00 an hour (and some small undisclosed amount for gasoline)! That revelation, picked up from the aide, left a bitter taste in my mouth. Despite her full-time, physically and emotionally challenging work, she received no sick days, paid vacation, or health insurance. It was hard to envision how she supported her three daughters but somehow Julie managed, and without rancor.

"Sweethot, iz gut," she said. "Don worry."

The weight of the exploitation, and our complicity in it, troubled me. Nevertheless, mom still needed extra help and it was my duty to figure it out. Despite my in-depth knowledge of social welfare programs, especially Medicaid, I felt like a neophyte, treading on unknown territory. It was one thing to pore over data, articles, and books for scholarly purposes, and quite another to seek urgent, concrete information for one's own mother.

My expertise afforded me a certain advantage, the least of which was the knowledge of where to start. Concentrating on services for the elderly in Florida, and opting for a "Medicaid Waiver" program, I perused the tiniest details of Florida's website, eventually reaching the Department of Elder Affairs. It had a number of possibilities but Dottie was only eligible for the Channeling Project Waiver, which provided at-home services to frail older people. Although it only served two counties, one of them was Broward, where my mother resided. Eureka!

My elation turned to frustration over the next several months as I jumped through long-drawn-out, time-consuming hoops to complete the application process. To begin with, the form itself was confusing as were the massive documentation requirements. That began my online relationship with Richard, an Intake Social Worker with a lot of professional credentials after his name, who guided me, more or less, through the process.

After painstaking, protracted effort, I finally completed the paperwork. Yeah, right. Three weeks later, after not hearing from him, I requested an update. "Hey Laura," Richard e-mailed me, in response. He always began with that salutation. "I'm not sure when we'll be submitting your mother's application. There are stacks of them ahead of hers."

My heart was racing but that only spurred me on. I called Richard on the phone to plead mom's case. Surprisingly, I actually reached him, and even more remarkably the personal appeal worked. Dorothy jumped to the head of the line. Was it the desperation in my voice?

For a month and a half, I badgered him with countless messages regarding the status of the application. It was on my daily to-do list: "E-mail Richard." (I suspected he was sorry he had given me his e-mail address!) Finally, he wrote back, insisting on a list of additional documents. He said that my mother's packet could go forward only if I faxed the materials to him by the next day. Otherwise, it would sit in the agency's unattended pile for an undetermined amount of time.

Sure thing. I would ask my eighty-seven-year-old mother, who was in dire need of home care services, to ferret out her Social Security and Medicare cards, driver's license, *original* Social Security award letter, last three bank statements and other assorted documents, run to the nearest copy machine, and then immediately fax everything to him.

Needless to say, mom balked. "I can't do it," she said. "And certainly not by tomorrow."

"You must," I said. "I know this is daunting but without more caregiving hours you won't be able to live at home anymore."

"I can't do it," she repeated, nearly in tears.

"You must." My voice was firm but tender.

Later in the day she called me, sounding weary. "It's done," she said. "I found everything." I heard a hint of pride in her tone. "Gail just faxed the materials to the number you gave me." I was sure the social worker had been annoyed at the short notice, so it was a relief that she helped out.

"Great job, mom," I said, meaning it.

Two weeks later Richard officially submitted the Channeling Project Waiver application to the Department of Elder Affairs and, in another two long months, it was approved. Meanwhile, with only the limited help that Julie could provide, Dottie struggled with her everyday chores.

Even with the authorization from the agency, it was too early to waive the victory flag: Richard informed me that mom still had to be assigned to a case manager, and then wait for a home visit by a social worker, who would draw up a care plan for her.[3] The home care services, which presumably would follow, were like the elusive prize at the end of a treasure hunt.

In due course, the social worker—Steve—arrived at mom's apartment and, after assessing the situation, notified me that she was eligible for two hours of caregiving per night, five days a week.

"That's not enough," I said. I could hear his forbearing sigh at the other end of the phone line.

"Sorry," Steve said. "I know she requires more but I'm granting her all I'm allowed to at the moment. Our budget is severely stretched." He paused. "You're lucky you know. There's a long waiting list."

I had another one of those "Aha!" moments, a self-revelation that would occur regularly over the next years. In my books on elder care I had written pages about the growing unmet need for at-home care, the dearth of affordable help in the United States, and growing queues under state Medicaid waiver programs. Right now, these "gaps" in services were more personal. What it meant was that *my* mother wouldn't receive anywhere near the assistance that she required. Only ten hours a week? The implications were staggering. Did the Channeling Project Waiver assume, then, that despite her vulnerability she could stay in her apartment entirely on her own most days? Or, that mom's caregiving needs would simply vanish on weekends?

My first reaction was to lash out at Steve, make him recognize the absurdity of what his agency was offering us, to other dependent older people. I thought better of it, especially because he actually seemed apologetic. Besides, did I really have a choice? At least it was ten hours more than we had before. It would have to do for the time being. I thanked Steve, if not profusely then at least with sincerity.

4

Coping with Blindness

My mother's gradual loss of sight had started in 2004, with blurriness in seeing road signs. "It's hard to tell where I am," mom told me with a tentative chuckle. "They should make those signs bigger. How are old people going to find their way around?" She was eighty-one at the time.

A few months later she said, "Perhaps I need stronger lenses." She made an appointment with her optometrist and purchased new glasses. It didn't help. The optometrist changed the prescription again. It still didn't help.

The eye doctor referred mom to an ophthalmologist, who diagnosed her with glaucoma. The pressure in her eyes was high but the condition seemed to be relatively mild. He gave her a prescription for eyedrops and told her to come back in a year. She diligently applied the medication. Dottie always followed her doctor's orders meticulously.

My involvement in her vision problem, as with her weakening health, had mostly been at a distance. I knew about the glaucoma and that she was taking medication for it. But I didn't realize how rapidly her vision had been deteriorating. During one visit to Florida I became somewhat nervous in the passenger seat of her car. She was veering back and forth, however slightly, across the right side of the line on the road. All of a sudden, the woman who relished sitting behind the wheel—who had contentedly chauffeured a school bus for many years—had turned into a precarious driver.

Before long, people became more shadowy to her. Her driving was increasingly uncertain and she relied more and more on Julie for doctor appointments and grocery shopping. Soon mom relinquished her license for good. She gave Julie the Toyota.

Up until now I had not been terribly concerned about mom's glaucoma. After all, it was a controllable disease and she was under the care of an ophthalmologist. Nevertheless, several months after receiving approval for the Medicaid Waiver, I noticed, with alarm, that she was having trouble changing the channels on the television. I watched her fumbling with the remote control, searching randomly with her fingers for the correct button.

"Mom," I said. "What's going on?"

"I don't know," she said, her voice trembling. "I can't seem to do anything anymore."

I berated myself. Had I really been too busy to think about what was happening to her vision? Had I been neglectful for not visiting more often? My intrepid mother had always taken charge of herself. Should I have interceded earlier? Would it have made a difference? I'll never know.

With a heavy heart and some trepidation, I telephoned Dr. Ana. "I think my mother is going blind," I said. "I'm not sure she's receiving proper treatment." My tone was frantic.

Dr. Ana referred her to a new ophthalmologist. However, by this time it was too late. She had severe damage to the optic nerve and was suffering such a significant degree of vision loss that the doctor classified her as legally blind. In the summer of 2011—Dottie was now eighty-eight years old—the ophthalmologist performed laser surgery in one eye, successfully preventing her from succumbing to total darkness.[1]

Increasingly disabled at this point, mom was now reliant on a walker. The Parkinson's disease and vastly diminished vision proved to be a lethal combination, generating countless anxieties for both of us. The complexities in mom's daily existence multiplied like wild animals whose natural enemies had been wiped out. Consequently, not only did my trips to Florida proliferate but they became all-consuming. On each visit I endeavored to help her cope, generally with unsatisfying results.

One of the more pleasurable pastimes for my mother in recent years had been playing Crazy Rummy with her neighbor, Lillian, which they pursued for hours on end, five times a week. Despite the fact that they were only wagering pennies, both of them were highly competitive. Mom always hauled a small container of coins down to the building's activities room in a basket attached to her walker.

"It's pretty heavy today," she said, chuckling smugly across the phone line. "I won four days in a row. Lillian is furious."

I'd watched them play several times and even joined them occasionally, bringing my own rolls of pennies. It's a complicated game and when I played they always replenished their stockpiles at my expense. It was one of the few diversions that my mother had left, so I was rattled when she called to tell me that she might have to give it up.

"I can hardly tell one card from another," she said. "I'm losing nearly all of the time."

"Mom," I said, in a teasing tone. "The point is to have fun, not to win." Luckily, she couldn't see the pained look on my face.

On my next visit I brought along ten packs of jumbo size, large print playing cards. It prolonged their game for several more months. Eventually she had to quit—she could no longer even distinguish red from black.

As my mother's eyesight deteriorated, I fixated on empowering her so that she could continue to live on her own. I pored over websites, methodically seeking optical aids. The special magnifying spectacles, which arrived shortly, didn't even remotely suffice nor did the more expensive high-power magnifying visor I purchased next. The headgear was unwieldy and it proved too challenging for mom to focus the device. She gave it a half-hearted try but she mostly seemed indifferent. The paraphernalia took their place among the growing pile of useless items under her desk.

ॐ

Because I squeezed the Florida trips into my school breaks, they were inevitably brief. Therefore, we had to communicate more than our customary weekly phone calls and, just as important, mom needed to touch base with me or family and friends at will. Her nephew Jay, who adored her and resided only an hour away, could be counted on in a crisis. Nonetheless, since he already had a full plate—family, job, and his own disabled, blind mother—I considered him as a backup that shouldn't be taken advantage of too often.

Mom's impaired ability to see had made it difficult for her to operate the cell phone, which sat on a small round table adjacent to her recliner. Several years ago I had added her and my mother-in-law to our Verizon family plan in case of an emergency. As with the rest of society, both of them eventually began to rely on their mobile device for everyday use.

In order to simplify the process, I decided to store several special numbers on speed dial—911, Esther (her only surviving sister), nieces and nephews, Lilian, Julie, Alix, myself, and a few others. Painstakingly writing the numbers and their attendant names on a piece of paper, using a thick black magic marker, I hung it on the wall near the phone. Despite the fact that the large, bold markings nearly jumped out at us, she could barely decipher them. Even worse, she couldn't distinguish the digits on the phone's keypad. We went over the procedure repeatedly, with limited success. Her face was tight with determination as she worked at it but, after several days, we were forced to give up.

The next tack was to voice activate the phone. Since I was not exactly tech-savvy, the setup was tricky for me. After several tedious hours my perseverance produced results. All she had to do was flip open the phone and call out the name of the person she wanted to dial.

Surprisingly, Dorothy was relatively comfortable with the procedure, even if the system at times misunderstood her command.

"Say 'call Laura,'" I directed her.

"Call Laura," she said into the receiver.

"Do you want to call Lillian?" the activated voice said.

Mom attempted to clarify her instruction to the machine but it was obvious that mix-ups were going to be inevitable. I was concerned about the potential havoc of wrongly dialed numbers, especially an inadvertent 911, but shrugged my shoulders in resignation. At least she could call people on her own.

❦

During yet another trip, I targeted the remote control. Mom had given up trying to change channels, listlessly allowing the TV to drone on. Although the images were blurry, I hoped to set up the device so that she could enjoy listening to her favorite programs.

After positioning Day-Glo flagging tape on the appropriate buttons, yellow for the power, orange for volume, green and purple for channel controls, I was stunned to discover that she couldn't differentiate among the colors.

"Press the bright yellow one to turn the TV on," I said over and over again, growing increasingly impatient.

"Where is it?" she said, fumbling around.

"You can't see it?" The color blazed.

She shook her head no.

Later in the day I piled on the tape in tiny, thick layers and placed raised guides on the side of the remote. I steered her index finger to show her how to find the various buttons. She couldn't feel the tapes. I built each one up higher. She still couldn't identify them. My exasperation rose with each new layer.

"Enough," mom said. "Julie will change the channels for me when you leave." She was exhausted. We both were. I was overcome with sadness and frustration, in equal measure. She had lost both her capacity to see and to touch.

As I worked at solving the problem, the painful irony of the situation struck me. Sitting in front of a TV was so antithetical to my mother's very essence. Even after her husband died, Dorothy had such a zest for life, always filling up her spare time with activities. She was forever on the go. As a young widow, she had worked full time in her store. Nevertheless, in the evenings she would play cards or mahjong, visit with one of her four sisters, assemble yet another family photo album, take in a movie, read a novel, or ride her bicycle.

Later, at age fifty-two, she bought herself running shoes and began jogging for the first time. The shop was overly confining for a free spirit like Dottie. She enjoyed the clientele but needed an outlet for her bursting energy. Sometimes, in the middle of the day, she would shut the place temporarily and go for a run at a nearby park. My mother had informed me, more than once, that she functioned by "mood." Unlike my highly regimented self, whatever she pursued depended on how she felt at any given moment. She rarely, if ever, sat in front of a television.

There had to be an alternative to the television. Accordingly, before my next visit I purchased a portable DVD player, headphones, and a subscription to Audiobooks. After querying mom about her taste in books—it was surprisingly unknown to me—I ordered two female detective stories, chosen after consultation with friends who were aficionados of the genre. In my fanaticized vision, mom would take the small device outside, push the walker to her favorite bench, and immerse herself in the delightful stories. At least it would be far more stimulating than TV.

It didn't quite work out that way. No matter what I glued on the DVD's start and stop buttons to enhance tactile contact—beads, Velcro, coarse sandpaper—she couldn't locate them. She appreciated the book-on-tape well enough but just couldn't control the device.

I pushed her but she resisted. "Try harder, mom. I know you can do it."

She became irritable. "Leave me alone," she said. "I'm through."

"Then sit in front of the television all day long," I spat out, feeling my anger at her intensifying.

With pursed lips, mom closed her eyes.

Strong-willed like my mother, I didn't give up easily. At home I perused other possibilities and discovered that the National Library Services for the Blind and Physically Handicapped delivered cassette players and tapes, free of charge. This discovery roused me to action. I applied for the machine, diligently picked out tapes from their voluminous menu, and had them sent directly to mom. When I arrived in Florida, the packages were sitting on her desk, unopened. Julie told me, somewhat apologetically, that Dottie had been adamant about waiting for me before unwrapping them.

Undeterred, I ripped open the boxes and set everything up. The machine appeared to be relatively simple to use.

"Press the large, round protruding button," I said, guiding mom's finger to it. "There are just two of them. On and Off." There were also a few other functions but that would only have confused her.

We forced down on the button together and the tape began to whirl. "Now you do it," I said.

She groped every which way with her fingertips. The two buttons were jutting out like the Empire State Building, yet she couldn't find them. We tried for a half hour, to no avail. She abruptly abandoned the effort.

☙

Despite the failures and disappointments, during the fall of 2011 I continued to track down ever more gadgets. It was crucial to facilitate mom's adaptation to her declining abilities if she was to live independently. I explored additional websites for ideas, and at times, conjured up more of my own Rube Goldberg contraptions. It was difficult to sleep as I lay wide-awake most nights ruminating about options.

Not surprisingly, nowadays, when I opened the door to my mother's apartment, she greeted me with, "So, what did you bring this time?" She was both grateful and overwhelmed.

After poking around my suitcase, I retrieved two packages. "Ta-da."

In one was an analog talking watch that not only announced the month, day, and time with the press of a button but also set itself automatically. The second parcel contained two small talking alarm clocks, one for each room. These, too, uttered the time aloud.

The website where I found them, along with several others, introduced me to an entirely new realm of technology. It featured a mélange of impressive tools available to cope with acute vision loss, even blindness. Among the ingenious items were talking calculators, liquid level indicators that provided warning beeps when fluid reached the top of a cup, and guides for signing documents. I'd had a sense of anticipation as I perused the specialized products. Now I was giddy with excitement as we tried out the two items I picked out.

The watch and clocks were relatively easy-to-use devices and I patiently showed mom how to work them. Again, her lack of coordination, along with an impaired sense of touch, impeded her from accomplishing the tasks. My composure crumbled.

"Even the totally blind can do this," I said, petulantly. I was being unreasonable but the words leaked out. Mom shut her eyes, a signal that it was time to stop. It worked.

Still enthralled with the possibilities that technology could offer, as soon as I returned to Pennsylvania I continued in my search for assistive gadgets. I decided next on a Talking Money Identifier, clicked on the item, and added it to the Lighthouse International virtual cart. At this point there was considerably less optimism on my part.

Yet this time I hit pay dirt—mom not only appreciated the device but was determined to use it. She had been feeling particularly demoralized these last several weeks because she couldn't deal with money anymore. I had been leaving five hundred dollars of various denominations in an envelope so that she wouldn't feel penniless. But by my next visit the entire amount was gone, largely unaccounted for. Most likely she was handing out bills willy-nilly; that obviously could not go on.

She tried again and again to slip the corner of a bill into the money identifier. It clearly was daunting for her but eventually she was rewarded with a sound: "One dollar," the machine announced. Mom was delighted, like a child playing with a sought-after toy on Christmas morning. She ran more bills through the device. "Five dollars." "Ten Dollars." "Twenty Dollars." She would be able to maintain at least some semblance of financial independence.

&

As mom's world steadily imploded, she seemed to be resigning herself to it in stoic silence. Her small pleasures, like the regular Senior Center trips to the theatre or to the casinos, where she delighted in the slot machines, had faded away like the daily Crazy Rummy games with Lillian. I nudged her not to give up on the gambling, but she interrupted me.

"I can't even climb the one step onto the senior center van," she said, clenching her teeth.

Resolving to take her to the Casino myself, I changed the subject.

Tedious routine tasks, along with my assorted gadgets, consumed our limited days together. The pace was so slow that it was hard to cram in more pleasant diversions. Breakfast, followed by her interminable medications, absorbed the entire morning.

I had taped a list of her drugs on the wall, with directions given to me by Julie, just in case the aide was away for a day or two and the agency had to send a substitute. At this point, Julie was responsible for mom's morning medications and eyedrops. If truth be told, I not only relied on the instructions myself but also trusted in Julie to keep the information up to date.

The several eyedrops, some of which were administered twice daily, others in the morning or evening alone, had to be dispensed at no less than five minutes apart. Glancing repeatedly at my watch, I periodically let out an audible sigh.

"You should have let Julie do it," mom said. "I don't understand why you need to take over."

I wondered that myself.

Particular precaution had to be taken with the white, milky Xalatam drops, for which Humana would authorize refills only at certain intervals. Recently, Julie had called me in Pennsylvania from CVS, complaining that the druggist was demanding $100 for the tiny bottle. Frantic rounds of long-distance telephone calls with him and the insurance company came to naught, and I grudgingly had to surrender my credit card number. After all, whatever was left of my mother's vision had to be preserved.

There was quite a collection of pills as well. Julie left the Sinemet, which required three daily doses, within mom's reach. I fingered the L-Dopa tablet, grateful for the relief it had accorded her from the Parkinson's disease. Although her leg and arm muscles were still uncomfortably stiff, she no longer trembled as badly. It was unclear as to whether the trembling bothered her as much as it did me.

The sheer number of medications on her shelf appalled me—it was yet another sharp divergence from the mother I had always known. During my youth, she only reluctantly gave me so much as an aspirin when I was sick. If memory serves, she had never taken any pain relievers herself.

"Your body is your temple," she would say. "You don't want to pollute it with drugs." Surely mom must have been ill in the past, but I can't actually recall a specific incident other than a brief bout of Bell's palsy that left her face with a slight droop on the left side. I guess she suffered through many ailments in silent agony over the years. I, on the other hand, became a pill junkie, gulping Tylenol, Advil, or whatever else was stocked in my cabinet, at the slightest headache or pain.

Each day I tried to fit in at least one outing, even if it was only for a short period. My usual rented economy car had morphed into a more expensive SUV to accommodate the walker. By now it had become a ritual to dine at Red Thai and Sushi, mom's favorite restaurant, with her former card partner Lillian. Sometimes, when Lillian found out that I was in town, she made her presence known lest I forget to invite her. My lips curled into a satisfied smile at the pleasure Lillian took in the unaccustomed glass of red wine and lavish meal her low-income budget didn't permit. Both she and mom especially savored the nearby ice cream parlor afterwards.

Our favorite excursion was to the boardwalk, where we reveled in the gentle breeze of ocean air mingling with the agreeable warmth of the Florida sun. Navigating the walkway was laborious and we rested repeatedly on one of the conveniently located benches. At the end of our stroll, enticing whiffs of knishes, French fries, pizza, popcorn, and hot pretzels inevitably drew us in. At times, we indulged in dinner at one of the outdoor tables, our light conversation competing with the boardwalk chatter and ocean roar.

There was also a scent of regret in the air as I closed my eyes and replayed the not-so-long-ago past, especially our customary bicycle rides to the beach, with mom generally leading the way. Although I was an ardent cyclist myself, mom was far stronger from her long, daily workouts and, later on, the Senior Olympics training. At age seventy-nine, she had set her sights on a Triathlon with one of her fifty-something friends, but wisely thought the better of it.

We also peppered our days together with shopping expeditions, whenever possible, in an attempt to replenish worn out sneakers and socks, outgrown shorts and slacks, and ever more tight-fitting T-shirts. A large-framed women with an even larger appetite, my mother had always kept her weight in check through vigorous physical exercise. Nowadays, her sedentary lifestyle was leading to a steadily expanding waistline.

She was surprisingly particular about style and color, even though she had only limited ability to see the clothes and few opportunities to venture outside. My inclination was to purchase elastic-waist garments and Velcro-strapped shoes that would boost her ability to dress herself, but inevitably indulged her preferences instead.

Less understanding of her penchant for walking around in backless rubber clogs—she had nearly ten pairs of them—I made clear that they were too dangerous in her current condition. Despite my repeated insistence, she ignored me.

Still feisty, my mother remained steadfast about where she shopped for groceries. In peeved silence, I drove her to Whole Foods to stock up on the overly expensive organic foods. Paying $50 for two small pieces of fish, I wondered whether it was an organic salmon. She ate it with relish.

🍂

A certain incident from that fall of 2011 stands out, never failing to bring joyful tears to my eyes. Earlier in the year, my husband and I had installed a pool at my home in Pennsylvania, most likely inspired by mom's lifelong passion for the water. Taking immense pleasure in long swims over the next several months, I ached for her to share it with me. The fantasy of actually bringing her for a visit built up, lap by lap, into an unqualified commitment.

Not under any illusions about the challenges, I constructed a full-fledged plan. Julie was enthusiastically on board, willing to enable the trip at her end. Excited but anxious, my mother was packed, suitcase by the door, a week before the journey. Despite strict security regulations, the aide managed to navigate mom through the Ft. Lauderdale airport and deposit her charge right at the gate. And as I eagerly awaited her arrival at the airport in the Lehigh Valley, Pennsylvania, a beaming Dorothy Katz slowly emerged, walker in hand, ambling down the ramp and into my arms.

Notwithstanding the cool September day, the pool was ready, a steaming 83 degrees. Despite the steep expense of the free-flowing propane, the opportunity to let her swim, to watch her swim, was just too important to concern myself with the cost. Tentatively stepping into the water, holding tight to the rail with one hand and clasping mine with the other, mom's lips were pursed in eager concentration. Whatever apprehension she may have had dissipated abruptly as she plunged into the water. She effortlessly glided back and forth, mostly using her fingertips for eyes when she reached the end of the pool. Mom's endurance, of course, had waned since her heartier days but she kept at it. Head tilted to breathe, face back in the water. In and out, in and out, the soothing rhythm of breaststroke.

Mesmerized, I stared at the white bathing cap as it bobbed in the water. An unbidden image emerged, the same white cap slowly disappearing into the horizon as three little girls—her daughters—had gazed nervously from the ocean shore. We huddled together until her return, our mother blithely unmindful of our concern over sharks, dangerous undercurrents, drowning.

She was still blissfully oblivious of the outer world as she propelled her body across the pool nearly every day at my home for a week. It almost seemed as though the Parkinson's disease had vanished until it was time to climb out, an ordeal for mom, George, and myself. Afterwards, she collapsed into a chaise lounge with an exhausted grin. "Wow," she said. "This has been amazing." It was the last time mom swam in my pool—or anywhere else.

5

From Crisis to Crisis

More and more responsibilities tumbled down on me. There were always stacks of envelopes awaiting me on every visit. At this point, mom didn't even open the mail. Julie extracted the letters from the mailbox, and piled them up for me. They spilled over everywhere—on the desk, kitchen table, couch, dresser. The aide's limited proficiency in English prevented her from reading the correspondence to my mother.

I had taken charge of the bills, most of which were somewhat straightforward once I disentangled them. Sometimes my payments were not in sync with a particular company's billing cycle so mom incurred late charges. However, after putting her banking online, and managing the payments at home in Pennsylvania, everything became more or less organized. Only the home care agency's records were impossible to keep straight. Its billing department was so chaotic that charges appeared twice for the same date of service. Figuring out the statements, with my now well-worn calculator, and unfathomable monthly explanations by phone with the company's representatives in Georgia, kept me busy each month.

There were other billing snags, but it was impossible to review the transactions with mom's bank since its customer agents were not allowed to discuss anything with me. They wouldn't even answer some basic questions without Dorothy Katz's explicit personal approval. We had several convoluted three-way conference calls until, ultimately, mom handed over "Durable Power of Attorney" to me. She seemed relieved to legally cede control over her affairs.

Not me, on the other hand. I was often dazed and sometimes downtrodden as we moved from crisis to crisis. For the next year-and-a-half time marched on in a dull blur. There weren't many tears, neither mom's nor mine. It was as though we were both empty, dried up. Mostly functioning

41

on automatic pilot, I never lost control or had a temper tantrum. It was as though I were numb most of the time.

But occasionally there were moments of self-pity, questions about why there was nobody else to step in. How had I become an only child? How could my two sisters have left me alone with our mother's messy, engulfing problems? Anger at them crept up unawares, leaving me dejected, lonely, and depleted. Of course there was too much ahead of me to indulge in such misplaced resentment for long.

⚬

As December 2011 turned into the New Year, I was forced to fax the Durable Power of Attorney document all over the place. I purchased a fax machine. Still, there were more than a few ongoing "privacy" obstacles that complicated my ability to handle Dottie's pressing affairs. In Florida, my attempt to cash a check for my mother at her bank elicited a request from the branch manager to see the Durable Power of Attorney certificate, even though mom was along with me. Then she demanded the original copy, to retain at the bank for their records. Needless to say, I refused to relinquish it to them. Straightening out the situation wasted an entire afternoon of valuable time.

My dealings with the Social Security Administration (SSA) developed into a much larger fiasco and a potentially more devastating setback. It initially caught me off-guard when mom's Social Security pension didn't show up on her monthly bank statement. The money generally appeared like clockwork on the first Wednesday of each month. In my gut I knew something was amiss but let it go for a few days.

My head whirled in panic as I ultimately attempted to call SSA. Since there was only one contact number for nearly fifty-five million people receiving benefits, it wasn't surprising that my attempts to connect with the agency sorely tested my patience. There were the usual rituals of automated instructions and information, interspersed with bids to redirect me to its website. In this instance, when the chattering automaton eventually transferred me to a wait line, a mechanized voice told me that it would be an hour.

I tried again several times but in due course braced myself and hung on. After fifty-five minutes of inane announcements, accompanied by tedious tunes, an actual person surfaced.

"Sorry," the consumer representative said. "We only speak to the beneficiary." He didn't sound very apologetic to me.

"I have Durable Power of Attorney for my mother," I said. "I'll fax it to you."

"Sorry," he said again. "Social Security does not accept Power of Attorney. The beneficiary must call herself."

"My mother is eighty-eight years old, blind, has Parkinson's disease, and can't dial a telephone," I screeched into the phone. "Her Social Security money has vanished and she needs help."

"Sorry," he said yet again. "Tell her to call us."

The nonsensical response jolted me, like a trapped animal caught unawares. Seething with anger, I chewed and bit at the cage seeking a way out. Without the Social Security check my mother not only wouldn't have funds to pay her bills, but also might have to give up Julie.

I rummaged through my professional toolkit. After all, I had worked at the Social Security Administration for a year as a researcher and had written a number of articles about its benefits structure. Nevertheless, my experience proved useless in resolving mom's predicament.

Nobody at my mother's local Social Security office would discuss the issue with me either. I called the federal SSA number again, protesting that Dorothy Katz was incapable of contending with her missing check. She needed me to do it for her. The agent responded with the scripted, patronizing "Sorry."

I wasted days agonizing over the dire situation. Raging anger contended with my rational self, thwarting my ability to act. There was sufficient indignation for myself, for mom, and for all other vulnerable people who were forced to fend for themselves. Despite my academic know-how, I was virtually defenseless.

Out of desperation I called *my* district's Social Security office in Pennsylvania. After giving a garbled, tearful account to an agent, I anticipated the usual "I'm sorry but I can't help you." Instead, a sympathetic individual jotted down the essential material, and told me to call back in a few hours.

Although I dutifully wrote down Paul's name, there was no particular reason to be encouraged. Yet, he actually made inquiries and discovered that somebody had re-routed my mother's check to a private account at another bank. It was stunning that a random person actually had siphoned off mom's money while I, as her authorized representative, couldn't even acquire basic information about it. We talked several times that week as Paul pursued particulars on the case.

After concluding the investigation, he told me that he wasn't allowed to resolve the problem, or even furnish any data related to the offender. Even so, he quietly divulged the name of the con man's bank and the illegal transmission number. He also mentioned offhandedly that the embezzlement of Social Security funds in such a manner wasn't uncommon. The powerlessness of unsuspecting, at-risk victims was chilling.

In due course, with the information Paul had provided, I untangled the mess. Mom's measly Social Security check was back in place and I moved on to new, unbidden battles.

❧

Interspersed among the mounds of mail—advertisements, catalogs, solicitations, and bills—were annual recertification documents. At least one of these menacing notifications caught me by surprise on each trip to Florida. I eyed the return address on certain envelopes guardedly and sometimes closed my eyes, wishing them away. But the offending items sat there, mocking me, until I ripped them open in such haste that I inevitably tore pieces of the pages inside.

Every now and then, an ominous looking letter deceived me and contained benign communications, or even sheets of colorful, personalized stickers. Mom's drawers were overflowing with them. Apparently, she had been contributing to scores of "causes," with a donation of $5.00 each, and was rewarded with more Dorothy Katz labels than she could ever possibly use.

More often, however, my trepidation was borne out and a letter greeted me with a message of looming disaster. At times, it declared that my mother would lose one of her vital benefits if she didn't renew expeditiously, usually within a week or so. On occasion, the deadline had already elapsed. In either case, there was a barrage of demands for proof of this and proof of that. It seemed as though I had hopped on a carousel of seemingly never-ending, frustrating paperwork. It was mindboggling that the various agencies supplying my mother with financial and other assistance hadn't figured out that a blind person couldn't read these renewal notices. Or, for that matter, that the incessant documentation requests were overly burdensome for someone in her situation.

On one occasion mom had to verify that her income was still under $16,755 to continue receiving AT&T Lifeline Credits toward her telephone bill. Did anybody really suppose that an aged, incapacitated woman had suddenly acquired such a profusion of resources as to render her ineligible? Did she find a job, perhaps? I sorted through her bank statements and completed the form.

The AT&T renewal was relatively uncomplicated compared to the obstacle course of other reauthorizations. Unbeknownst to me, Mom had been providing exhaustive information about her income and expenses annually, for nearly thirty-five years, in order to retain her HUD, Section 8, rent supplements. To my dismay, the task was now mine.

I scurried around for original physician receipts (they didn't take copies so each of her medical providers had to be called individually) and a host of other verifications. Then, unexpectedly, the building manager informed me that my mother was hiding assets. Apparently, he had poked around at her bank and found a wealthy Dorothy Katz. It turned out to be another person with the same name. Unfortunately, his misplaced snooping cost me days of unmitigated grief.

Several months later, I stumbled upon a large packet from mom's Medicare Advantage plan. It wasn't particularly troubling since the insurance company, thus far, had not impressed me with its regard for trees. Given Humana's unceasing flow of trivial communications, usually lauding itself or its products, the envelope was almost thrown out, unopened. Luckily I caught myself. It warned mom that if she didn't verify her address shortly she would be disenrolled from the insurance plan. After several wearisome phone calls, and the transmission of a Durable Power of Attorney fax, the customer service representative informed me that there had been an inexplicable misunderstanding and mom's insurance was not in jeopardy. There were no apologies.

The Medicaid Waiver recertification notification was almost overlooked as well. I'd written an entire book on Medicaid that included pages lambasting the program's oppressive renewal process for needy families. It was yet another "Aha!" moment as it dawned on me how much easier it was to convey the laborious process conceptually than to experience it personally. The struggle to complete the forms, and the complications encountered, were beyond easy description.

Gathering the material for these various renewals overwhelmed me and would have been inconceivable for mom to achieve by herself. But even more problematic was the demeaning aspects of the process, the not-so-subtle assumption that you were attempting to receive something you weren't entitled to. "You are innocent until proven guilty" in our legal system is turned on its head when dealing with the social welfare system: the burden of proof is on the applicant, even one who is poor, aged, and disabled. As I filled out form after form and collected masses of information and documentation on my mother's never-changing sparse income, nonexistent assets, and escalating disabilities and needs, I was forced over and over again, year after year, to confirm that she was not cheating the government.

§.

As my mother's eyesight worsened, she struggled to perform even the most basic tasks. Without notifying me, and without considering the cost, mom had hired Julie for additional hours, off the books. She and the caregiver had entered into a mutually satisfying arrangement whereby Julie arrived every morning for two hours on the five days not scheduled by the agency.

They had developed a ritual that attended to my mother's essential needs but also indulged her idiosyncrasies. Julie tenderly washed and powdered Dottie prior to helping her get dressed and then served breakfast, on a tray. As mom sat comfortably in her special chair, the aide brought the food precisely in the manner and order she craved. An orange, cut exactly as she used to do it herself, always started the meal, followed by oatmeal with cinnamon, bottled water, and hot chocolate.

Mom's growing dependence on Julie elicited a mix of relief, irritation, and foreboding. To a certain extent, there was less worry because of the caregiver's competency and affection for her charge. Their bond seemed strong and enduring, an observation that was reinforced later on, when Julie was no longer on our payroll. Nonetheless, I was troubled that the more Julie did for her, the less my mother would achieve on her own. That Julie was now feeding her was particularly disturbing. It appeared as though Dottie had regressed to childlike behavior.

As a rule, most of the hands-on care during the five or so days of my visits was done by me. Much to my mother's displeasure, I would give Julie a paid vacation for much of the time period that I was in town. To a certain extent it was because of my guilt at Julie's paltry wages but, truth be told, there was also a need to feel useful. Mom preferred her aide's gentle hands to mine. I worked hard at duplicating Julie's every move but knew that my exertions would always fall short. It was such grueling labor that every so often I asked Julie to return a day early—she always readily complied.

At these times, my gratitude and appreciation of her were coupled with a heightened sense of what care labor truly entailed.

By the third day of providing full-time care I became testy. One evening, in the middle of my cooking dinner, mom shouted out for a tissue, from the box on her nearby table. Walking into the living room with arms crossed, I snapped: "Can't you get it yourself?"

She tilted her head in my direction. "It's hard on me," she said.

In actual fact, by spring 2012 my mother required more help, not less. "I'm hungry all day," mom said during one of our phone conversations. Even when Julie left a salad for her in the refrigerator, she didn't eat it. I demanded to know why.

"I can't find it," she said. There was a long pause. "Everything falls out."

It turned out that whenever mom rummaged through the refrigerator, she knocked all the food to the floor, plates and all. The last time she had attempted to retrieve Julie's lunch she left glass everywhere. She eventually called Lillian, who swept it up for her. My proud mother was not going to do that again.

"Maybe we can ask Julie to stay all day," mom said. She sounded hopeful.

We'd already stretched her budget to the absolute limit, including covert monthly supplements from me.[1] After calculating the cost of full-time care, I rejected the idea. I considered a number of alternatives for the midday meal, each with sufficient drawbacks to squelch the plan.

Meals On Wheels in her area didn't have vegetarian choices, even if mom would eat its food. "Yuk," mom said, when the subject was broached. "I'd rather not have anything."

I pored over the Internet for frozen meals that were vegetarian, organic, and salt free, mom's basic requirements, or so I thought. Needless to say, the frozen food sites were not brimming with such options. Amy's Kitchen popped up and I cautiously read the details on its products. Mmm. Only a few of its items were salt free. Then again, everything was vegetarian *and* organic. I decided to go for it anyway, especially because a supermarket near mom's building stocked the product. Triumphant, I read the selections off to mom, ready to make a grocery list for Julie. Cheese Enchilada, Garden Vegetable Lasagna, Macaroni and Cheese, Pizza.

"I don't eat macaroni and pasta. Too much starch," she said.

"Mom, the food looks yummy." My stomach clenched in disappointment. "The company even uses filtered water," I added lamely.

She was unmoved.

My mother's insistence on shopping at Whole Foods, the cases of bottled water cramming her tiny apartment, the dogged vegetarianism, obsession with scrubbing fruit and vegetables, all swirled in my head. A lifetime of strict attention to every single morsel that she had consumed seemed downright at odds with the current degeneration of her body. Why hadn't Dottie's healthy eating habits protected her?

Infused with senseless resentment at her, the Parkinson's disease, the blindness, I lashed out. "Then figure out how to get your own meals."

Back to the drawing board. Perhaps someone could be hired to prepare lunch. After compiling a long list of agencies, I proceeded to call each of them. "We don't send our aides out for less than four hours at a time," was the usual refrain. The few places that would agree to the two-hour stint charged such exorbitant fees that the idea had to be discarded.

❧

I spent a considerable amount of time worrying about how long my mother would be able to manage with the limited hours that Julie provided, and her lack of resources for more paid help. The evenings, too, had become problematic. After going through several caregivers from the Medicaid Waiver program, mom now had Monique, an affable if not particularly hard-working aide. Nobody, of course, measured up to Julie.

She cooked dinner during weekday evenings, generally with a Haitian touch that didn't always appeal to Dottie's rather narrow sense of taste. Even so, mom liked her well enough to overlook the shortcomings. I was fond of Monique as well but couldn't shrug off the uncompleted tasks as easily. Not surprisingly, mom could no longer see the crumbs under her chair or flecks of dust everywhere. Ever solicitous Julie attempted to compensate for the other caregiver's underperformance but she was already overextended.

We desperately needed more assistance than mom could afford. I turned to Steve, the caseworker at the Medicaid Channeling Project. Despite my initial disappointment at the limited help he offered us, he'd been some- what responsive to mom's ever-growing needs in other ways. He visited her monthly, as required by the regulations, noting in his discreet questioning if anything was amiss. Every so often, assistive devices and other articles mate- rialized unsolicited, at least by me. Julie could possibly have been behind at least some of these developments.

The first object to turn up was the mechanical-lift recliner that had become indispensable to mom. With the press of its sizeable control switch she was gradually lifted to a standing position, allowing her to readily grab her walker. The plush chair, which blended in unobtrusively with the rest of the livingroom furniture, had become the center of my mother's daily life—it was where she ate meals, greeted visitors, took catnaps, listened to television, and often just sat, listlessly. Most importantly, the ease of standing up prompted her to walk more, to move around.

The walker, itself, had appeared shortly after mom became too unsteady with the cane. The transition was challenging at first, but she adjusted. For months, I had been coaxing her to stroll around the block, hopeful that it would slow down the deterioration of her muscles. It was now my mantra. During every phone call I said, "Mom, have you taken your walk yet?" It seemed less an option than a necessity for keeping her legs strong.

Now that she could maintain her balance with the walker she was more game to do so and it gratified me. That is, until I witnessed her jaunty trek across the parking lot, oblivious of any moving cars.

On one visit, I spotted a medical alert pendant on my mother's dresser, courtesy of the Medicaid Waiver program. It was surprising since she had forced me to return the expensive one I had bought her. When questioned, mom was noncommittal. "Steve wants me to have it. I couldn't say no."

"But you can reject mine," I countered. "Anyway it won't do any good on the bureau. You must wear it around your neck." We spent the next several months sparring about the whereabouts of the panic button.

Steve shipped other beneficial items to her as well, especially the boxes of adult diapers (though an insufficient monthly supply), raised toilet seat, and bath bench. Julie lobbied for a wheelchair but, fearful that my mother would no longer walk even short distances, I vetoed the suggestion. In my mind, Dorothy Katz's strong, athletic legs had to be prevented from failing completely.

It was an ordeal getting my mother in and out of the car for shopping and doctor appointments. And, Julie was not shy about making requests of Steve during his monthly inspections. "I tell Steef and he do it," she said. But I was determined to keep my mother out of a wheelchair and Julie gave me a weak, but genial, "Ukay, sweethot. Dat's goot.

Steve was sympathetic to my requests for more caregiving hours. After all, he had observed my mother's dire need for additional assistance firsthand. All the same, he had to refuse me, mumbling that the agency didn't have sufficient funds.

Aware that the main purpose of the Channeling Project Waiver was to avert nursing home placement, I pressured him by insisting that mom wouldn't be able to remain at home without more help. "Can't you at least extend our two evening hours through the weekend?" I pleaded. "I'm concerned for her safety when there's nobody to check in on her at night."

Although he agreed to confer with his supervisor, the denial was a foregone conclusion.

 ֎

Julie had her own solution to the problem. Once I cut through her mispronunciations and thick Creole accent it became evident that she wanted to leave the home care agency and take on even more hours with us, off the books. It was tempting, given that ResCare, in my estimation, was fleecing her—and us. I calculated the cost of a range of hours at various wages, in addition to benefits. Although Julie was unconcerned about Social Security, worker's compensation, health insurance, sick days, and the like, I couldn't in good conscience disregard them. After all, both professionally and personally I have advocated for the rights of women, especially low-wage workers.

Almost immediately, however, my principled intentions were at loggerheads with pragmatism as I confronted the massive, complicated paperwork. The Social Security agency's "Employer's Guide to Filing Timely and Accurate W-2 Wage Reports" alone was forty-five pages long. Even with one worker, an employer must fill out a raft of forms every year: W-2 (wage and tax statements); W-3 (transmittal of wage and tax statements); I-9 (citizenship verification); W-4 (amount to be withheld, if Julie requested a wage deduction); and Schedule H on my own 1040 (indicating the amount of wages that had been paid to her). Additional forms were required for federal unemployment taxes, state unemployment taxes (renamed reemployment assistance in Florida), and worker's compensation insurance. And, in order to file the documents, it was necessary to apply for an Employer Identification Number (EIN). Whew.

Bewildered and enraged, I struggled to puzzle through the maze of red tape, rules and regulations, worksheet computations, and countless warnings about potential errors. It felt as though I was being sucked into a black hole, its gravitational force tugging hard and strong. I drew back, unwilling to be consumed by such senselessness.

I returned to my catalog of home care agencies, tucked into one of the many files that were piling up every which way in my home office. Interspersed with my professional work, the mounds of material for mom were creating chaos in my customarily well-ordered room.

Julie had indicated willingness, indeed an eagerness, to switch agencies if I couldn't hire her off the books. Reality jolted me once again. Most of the companies charged anywhere between $12.00 and $16.50 an hour, with the aides paid only $9.00 to $9.50 of that amount, and nearly always without any coverage of health insurance, vacation, or sickness. When questioned about the lack of benefits, the customer relations' voices sang in unison, "Our aides are independent contractors and not agency employees."[2]

By the summer of 2012, I still had not found a solution. Concerns about my mother's situation seeped into my sleeping hours. I agonized about her well-being and safety, as well as money. How much more could I afford to pay toward her care? Despite my so-called professional expertise in long-term care, I had no idea what to do. I made the decision by simply choosing not to decide, my willful blindness matching mom's actual blindness. That is, until her first fall several weeks later.

☙

Tumbling out of bed in the middle of the night, mom couldn't pull herself up. Julie found her the next morning lying on the floor, bruised, bleeding, and scared. Her 180 pounds was too much for the aide who immediately pressed Dottie's medical alert pendant, which as usual was lying inaccessibly on her bureau. Thus began a revolving door of emergency rescues, hospital ERs, and home care nurses.

And it was the start of the endless, terrifying phone calls. Perpetually on standby, I swapped my soothing but difficult to hear "Sparkling Mist" cell phone ring for the more urgent "Jungle Drums." The booming sound shadowed me everywhere, from my early fall bicycle rides and workouts at the gym to business meetings and student appointments. The merciless demands for my attention invaded my life, every so often rousing me from a deep sleep. Dreading each time the cell phone rang, I once turned it off for a full day, disregarding the consequences.

Catastrophe impended with every call, each generating daunting dilemmas and, at times, necessitating immediate decisions. There was a 1,250 mile distance between us, rendering it impossible for me to jump in a car. My job, of course, prevented me from hopping on a plane at a moment's notice. And this was not counting other priorities or people in my life—husband, daughter, cousins, and friends. My stomach lurched at the cell phone's summons, triggering a mix of lumpy emotions, like poorly mixed hot cereal. And it tasted as bad.

Long-distance caregiving was even more confounding, even life-shattering, than my academic writings had conveyed. It was a further "Aha!" moment gleaned not from an intellectual landscape but through real-world experience. Such supervision from afar, I starkly discovered, could become both all-consuming and psychologically crushing. Regardless of the actual situation, it stirred up your mind to imagine the worst.

On this particular occasion, the Hollywood Fire and Rescue medics, the on-call emergency squad at the other end of mom's panic button, notified me that my mother was in the Memorial Hospital emergency room. That was all they could tell me. Details were only available through the hospital itself. With my heart pulsating wildly, like the "Jungle Drums" beat on my cell phone, I called the contact number that popped up on Google search.

"I'm seeking information on Dorothy Katz," I said.

After several transfers, I finally reached my mother's ER nurse. "Sorry," she said. "I can't discuss her medical condition without your Durable Power of Attorney document."

Beads of sweat trickled down my neck as adrenalin surged through my blood vessels. "Please," I said. "Just tell me if my mother is okay."

"I'd like to," she said. "But I can't violate the privacy laws." She paused for a moment. My hands were so clammy at this point I could hardly hold the phone. Then, in a whisper, she added, "Your mother will be fine."

I took slow, deep breaths. "Thank you," I said. "I'll fax the form straight away."

My mother's bruises from the fall were not severe but I rushed to Florida anyway. Mom, as usual, was sitting in her chair, waiting for me with a broad, welcoming smile. The massive swathes of gauze wrapped around her right arm and leg caught me unawares. They had been carelessly applied and the surgical tape was peeling around the edges. It later turned out that there were deep gashes underneath, with sizeable black-and-blue splotches surrounding them.

Apparently, a nurse from a home health agency, paid by Humana Medicare Advantage for post-acute care, had been coming to the apartment erratically to clean and dress the wounds. She never called, just simply showed up. Even worse, my mother disclosed with irritation ringing in her voice, she arrived without adequate supplies.

"We'll have to buy more gauze, bandages and dressing," mom said. "The nurse has used up most of mine." Dorothy Katz, ever the Girl Scout troop leader, always had a bulging first-aid kit in her apartment. Needless to say, the depletion of my mother's emergency materials was bewildering.

On my second day in Florida the nurse appeared unexpectedly. "You're lucky to find us in," I said testily. "You're supposed to call." I had called the agency to find out when the nurse would be arriving next and had been told that their nurses *always* telephoned in advance.

She was very busy, the LPN told me—and, worked only part time. Couldn't always predict her schedule. People like my mother were always home anyway. She had trouble understanding why it was such a big deal.

When questioned about the lack of medical provisions, she was equally unapologetic. "The agency doesn't furnish me with sufficient supplies," she said. "So I do what I can." She dipped again into my mother's dwindling kit and changed the wounds mechanically, as though on an assembly line. Clearly in a hurry to move on, the nurse finished the job and then disappeared, barely acknowledging her patient. We had no idea when, or if, she would return.

The next time she landed in my mother's apartment, I was in the shower. By the time I stepped out, the nurse was gone. Not only did my mother receive a quickie wound dressing but this time it seemed calculated to escape encountering her ticked-off adult daughter. The fact of the matter is that Medicare was paying mom's insurance company big bucks to subcontract for the agency's shoddy treatment.

The injurious fall should have been a wake-up call for me. Instead, I embarked on my next series of projects, single-mindedly focused, as usual, on maintaining the status quo. Each tactic confronted the immediate emergency at hand, a particular problem that needed addressing. I was blindly following a GPS without providing it with a destination. I should have known better.

On my next visit, in quick succession from the last, we picked up the bed rails that I had ordered on the Internet. Mom was adamant against them, braying that she was not a child. In anticipation of her disapproval, I had selected short but sturdy ones rather than the institutional-like bars that slide down the whole length of the bed. Those, most likely, would have been more suitable.

While I struggled to stretch the straps under her Queen-size mattress, in the 90 degree, humid August weather, she was still resisting. "I won't fall out of bed again," she said, adding "This is too hard for you anyway."

Mercilessly abusing every muscle in my body, I was even more determined to get the taut straps snapped. I yanked harder at the obstinate cords while simultaneously attempting to lift the substantial mattress. I kept at this balancing act, unwilling to give way. Click. Then fifteen minutes later another click. I was jubilant, like a child proudly showing off a solid "A" report card.

Mom was unimpressed. "I don't need rails," she insisted. "But I'll try them out for you."

"Thanks, mom," I mumbled, collapsing onto the bed.

After I returned home, she told me how useful they were—she was grasping the rails to get out of bed easier. Mom had conveniently forgotten our fierce struggle over them.

***

By the end of August it was time to surmount my self-imposed indecision and expand Julie's hours. Still unsure of how it was going to be paid for, I steeled myself for yet another hit on my wallet. I was brimming with unproductive ill will—anger at my mother for her lack of resources, bitterness toward my two sisters for abandoning me, and self-reproach for having these feelings in the first place.

The computations were complex as I weighed what I could afford against what my mother required, while at the same time attempting to compensate Julie fairly. Again, there were calculations and recalculations for various lengths of time and alternate pay levels. My high standard for what was a "decent" wage steadily crumbled in the face of the harsh reality of my pocketbook. Despite the evenhanded balancing act, I experienced lingering guilt that Julie deserved more than I eventually offered her.

My discomfort at the proposed pay scale wasn't matched by Julie's delighted response. It was not only more than her current wages, but there wouldn't be an agency to siphon off some of the daily mileage fee that she could now fully take for herself.

Although the extra time wouldn't be nearly enough for mom's needs, we settled on nineteen more hours per week. Yet, it was everywhere evident that I was still stamping out brush fires with buckets of water. Pushing and pulling against a move to Pennsylvania, I continued to carry out stopgap measures even though, in retrospect, it should have been apparent that relocation would be inevitable. I was barely containing the blaze.

❧

We continued to move from crisis to crisis in the space of the next five months. In early September, a mishap occurred during the three days that I was visiting my daughter Alix in Massachusetts. Since there was so little time to spend with her, the trip had been eagerly anticipated. I had barely walked in the door when my cell phone started ringing. As its ominous jingle clamored, my chest muscles tightened. Sensing the unease, Alix eyed me curiously.

"It's about grandma," I said. "There's always something these days."

"Aren't you going to answer it?" she said.

Shrugging, I reluctantly pressed the dreaded key. As anticipated, it was Julie, who told me that mom was in the emergency room again. Still unable to decipher her words through the thick accent, I had no idea what happened. All that could be untangled from our conversation was that Dottie had been picked up by the medics and taken to the ER.

I devoted the next several hours to figuring out why my mother was in the hospital and, most importantly, ascertaining that she had not been seriously hurt. These weren't easy tasks given that my Power of Attorney document was not with me. Nor did I have easy access to a fax machine, in any case.

Apparently, mom had fallen into the bathtub during the night, having taken a wrong turn on the way to the toilet. Predictably, she didn't have her emergency call button around her neck and had to lie in the tub until morning, where Julie found her. Alarmed and unable to lift her out on her own, Julie had again pressed the panic button.

Mom spent several days in the hospital for observation, where they scanned her bones for breaks and administered the customary sequence of other tests, necessary or not. Julie stayed by her side for a significant number of hours, not wanting Dottie to face the ordeal alone. Needless to say, I was not only grateful but made sure that Julie received compensation for every extra hour. Ka-ching.

Cutting short the stay with my daughter, and disregarding accumulating work obligations, I headed yet again to Florida. As disquieting thoughts raced through my mind, I slowly and cautiously turned the key to my mother's apartment. She was sitting in her usual chair, unperturbed, seemingly indifferent to the disruption in my life.

"Hi mom," I said, my relief mingled with vexation. "You're looking good."

She gave me a drowsy, satisfied smile. Clearly pleased to see me, she said, "Come here and give your ole mother a big hug." She put out welcoming arms as I bent down on my knees to embrace her. My head nestled against her chest like a child seeking assurance that everything would be all right.

But it wasn't. Almost immediately a sharp deterioration in mom's condition became apparent, especially in her ability to walk. Her legs were more unsteady than previously and the gait slower. I watched with alarm as she stumbled, walker in hand, toward the bathroom. I had become somewhat used to her hunched back but now the spine curved even further.

During Dottie's three-day hospital stay she had remained in bed, contributing to the weakened condition. Nobody had helped her walk, even briefly, down the hall. Although she was entitled under Medicare to physical therapy at home, she was forced to wait two days for a nurse to assess the situation. After the evaluation it took another two days for the therapist to arrive, while mom languished even further.

Ta-da! The therapist turned up on the fifth day, during my stay in Florida, toting a small, entirely inadequate, portable pedal exerciser bike. I stared at the puny machine and then at my mother's size eleven shoes.

"What's that?" I muttered, shaking my head.

"It will work fine," she assured me. "We'll have your mother up and about in no time."

I regarded the item skeptically as the therapist positioned my mother's sneakers between the grips and nylon strap. Was this the full extent of my mother's rehabilitation program?

Mom began pedaling, pleased to be moving her legs. Round and round, slowly, steadily . . . when suddenly, the therapist announced, with a broad smile, "Time's up. Good job, Dorothy."

Time's up? It was only fifteen minutes. "That's all my mother gets?" I said. "She needs more than that."

"Sorry," the therapist said. Humana only pays for a half hour of my time per therapy session. But I'll be back."

She returned twice a week for a month to provide the sorely lacking restorative care.

§

Although actual services were in scarce supply, there was no shortage of evaluators. Over the last several months, various types of social workers had arrived uninvited and often unannounced at Dottie's doorstep, to poke and question her. They floated in and out. For the most part, she had no idea who they were or why they were there. The reason they appeared, of course, was to verify her ongoing eligibility for whatever services they offered, to ensure that she wasn't cheating the system or "misusing" benefits. We needed help, not visiting vultures attempting to cut her out of the little I had managed to secure.

This tangled web of "assessors" included the insurance company, under the banner of HumanaCares, a misnomer to be sure. There was a veritable team of people, ostensibly to manage her chronic conditions, but they had not provided one single tangible benefit, at least for mom. During one visit in August 2012, when mom urgently needed more personal care services, Humana's nurse left a phone number for me to contact. It turned out to be a non-profit agency with the same number as the Broward County Elder Helpline that I had already ascertained was just smoke and mirrors. The agency didn't provide any direct services and there was a six-months to a year waiting list for whatever limited care it could refer me to.

The Waiver program, too, had several professionals who regularly checked up on mom with probing questions and, except for Steve, delivered nothing of consequence. Then there were the nameless people from the home health agencies who had to assess mom before authorizing the post-acute services she was entitled to. Their major contribution, besides the reams of paperwork they left in their wake, was to delay any actual rehabilitation or medical care Dottie critically required.

6

The Bottom Falls Out

I closed my eyes and tipped my head toward the warmth of the September sun, allowing myself a few moments to breathe it in. The balmy Florida air soothed me, like an after-dinner brandy. There was no time to bask in it, however, to ignore the tedious chores ahead. I had only a few days to accomplish the most important task, to procure an ID card. Mom's driver's license would expire soon and she desperately required a replacement. Without it, she couldn't purchase food or other necessities with the credit card, or even board an airplane for Pennsylvania, if necessary. My last attempt the previous month had been aborted because the Florida Department of Motor Vehicles (DMV) refused to allow her unexpired driver's license to serve as proof of identity. Grimacing, I remembered the arduous trip to its local office that would now have to be repeated.

Again, the intractable bureaucratic complexities turned what should have been a routine procedure into a nightmare. For starters, Florida required an applicant to obtain the ID card at the nearest DMV, *in person*. The state wouldn't allow me to drive to the office by myself or obtain it through the Internet. So, we had to maneuver my mother into the rented car, no easy task in her weakened condition. Everything was in slow motion. After she abandoned the walker to me she inched her way alongside the car to the passenger door, which I had left open, windows down. Clutching the side with two hands, and turning her buttocks toward the seat, she steeled herself for the ordeal of lowering her body into it. Because of her long legs, it was difficult for Dottie to use whatever strength she had left in them to push and pull herself up and down.

I tried not to glance repeatedly at my watch as my type-A personality wrestled with the drawn-out process, a routine that we invariably went through these days. Instead, I acted the cheerleader, encouraging and reassuring her at every step of the way. Nevertheless, I found myself fidgeting and pacing, much to my mother's annoyance. And, because of her sizeable weight, it was difficult for me to assist to any great extent, although I periodically struggled to do so. In due course, Dottie plopped down in the seat and we drove thirty miles to the nearest DMV office.

Exhausted by this time, we confronted a long line that mom clearly couldn't endure, even with the walker. Collapsing on a crowded bench, she looked up at me beseechingly. "I won't be long mom," I promised. "You stay here and I'll take care of everything as quickly as possible." Yeah, right.

While waiting in the seemingly interminable queue, I extracted the necessary paperwork from its folder. In order to prove your identity for a Florida ID card, you must have extensive documentation that seemed nonsensical to me, especially for someone of my mother's age. The state required a passport or an original birth certificate; *and* a Social Security card; *and* two out of three other credentials to verify that you were a resident, including a signed rental agreement, voter registration card, and a copy of your tax form. Apparently, a picture card driver's license wouldn't do!

My mother's options were rather limited since she wasn't required to pay taxes (her income was far too low) and she had never had a need for a passport (the furthest mom had ever travelled was to Georgia, in 1945, when dad was in the Army). Riffling through her belongings once more, this time searching exhaustively, I had located her birth certificate. Pleased with myself, I flashed a complacent grin. This time we had everything we needed to satisfy the authorities. Or, so I thought.

"Our department can't accept this birth certificate," the clerk said, when I finally reached the head of the line, mom now at my side.

"It's the original," I said, pointing to the raised seal.

"But it says 'Female Zager,'" she said, narrowing her eyes. "It doesn't provide her first name." She handed the document back to me in a dismissive motion.

"Perhaps my mother's parents didn't have a name for her at the time. I don't know." I shoved it back at the clerk.

"We can't accept this," she said again, this time more firmly.

At this point I was straining to control my temper. "Look," I said. "It's the only birth certificate my mother has and the only one she will ever have."

Ignoring me, the woman said, "Doesn't she have a passport?"

"No."

"Then you'll have to get a letter from Social Security verifying her birth date. She'll have to go to the agency, in person."

We went round and round for a while, she with the power and I with the worthless, now barely contained, rage. After her feigned politeness faded and she waved us away, I gave up.

Again, in slow motion, mom maneuvered into the car, I programmed the GPS, and we headed to the Social Security office. For a second time that day, we faced a room full of people and an unconscionably long wait. Shortly after she was seated, my mother suddenly threw up her slumped head and said, in a defiant voice, "I'm hungry . . . and thirsty. And I have to go to the bathroom." This was not one of our better days.

꽃

Although still not willing to uproot mom, nor was she willing to leave, I brooded over what would have to be done to bring her to Pennsylvania. One main holdout was Dottie's connection to her aide. By this time they seemed inseparable and tugging them apart, in my mother's view, would be like taking away her only lifeline. Julie was a daily presence, unlike me who randomly and periodically dropped in and out of her existence. My long-distance caregiving, although onerous, was mostly unseen.

Then there was her attachment—and mine—to Doctor Ana. It seemed inconceivable to me that we could replace her or the Chen Medical Center. Dotty relied heavily on its highly competent on-site specialists, the easy coordination of care for her complicated and interconnected disorders, and the free-of-charge, convenient transportation. Her very well-being depended on the first-rate health care she was finally receiving. I wasn't convinced that it could be duplicated in Pennsylvania.

All the same, I couldn't let go of a possible relocation to Pennsylvania. A vast array of concerns about such a move danced in my head, and then leapt onto paper with dizzying speed. The worry list was daunting as things to do, numbers to call, places to visit piled up on my yellow pad—housing, health insurance coverage, prescription drugs, aides, doctors, Medicaid, special diets and, as always, money.

Perhaps it was my need to feel in control that propelled this irrepressible urge to pave the way—just in case. Options. I craved options, like a trapped woman escaping a rapidly approaching, menacing flood. In-between other time-consuming obligations in my life, I confronted the list bit by bit.

That low-income housing was the starting point suggested a lingering illusion on my part that mom could still live on her own in Pennsylvania, with the assistance of a part-time aide. After all, I would be nearby to fill in when necessary. In retrospect, I must have been in LaLa Land, a place my mother generally inhabited.

In any case, it proved to be a nonstarter. Before anyone could even submit an application he or she had to fill out a pre-application *for placement on a waiting list.* According to the Bethlehem Housing Authority, that could take from six months to a year. So much for an emergency landing from Florida. And, if she were not ready to move in immediately when her name rose to the top of the list, she would lose her place. That obviously would precipitate a quick relocation. So much for any long-range planning.

Even more discouraging, however, were the irreconcilable documentation requirements. Dottie would have to prove residency in Pennsylvania through receipts and notarized letters. An inhabitant of Florida, she was not eligible for low-income housing in another state. I considered the possibility of furnishing my address on the pre-application, but then realized that she would have to provide her Florida ID card. Beyond that, the other mandatory papers showed that mom still lived in Florida. Just as worrisome was the fear that establishing a Pennsylvania residency for her could lead to the loss of mom's current government-subsidized apartment prematurely, rendering Dottie homeless. I moved from LaLa Land to Catch-22 Land.

≈

After fully grasping the situation, I ditched the low-income housing idea, at least for the time being. After all, this was merely a pave the-way "just-in-case" scenario. It could be dealt with later, if necessary. There were other alternatives, I assured myself.

Still a bit anxious, I made an inventory of assisted-living facilities near my home, and inspected two of them. The most promising, at least from outward appearances, was Mrs. Bush's. The small, homey place sat on top of Blue Mountain, surrounded by patios and gardens, with a picturesque view of the valley below. Absorbing the scene with a growing sense of calm, I conveniently overlooked the fact that my mother was nearly blind.

Its social calendar was not only jam-packed with activities, but the home also maintained its own buses to transport residents for special events, shopping, and shows. And, the owners were willing to prepare special vegetarian meals, relieving me of that concern. With cautious optimism I discussed rates with a member of the staff, including extra charges for the highest level of services that my mother most certainly would require. I suppressed an "ouch" from bursting out of my mouth upon learning the total monthly charge. Much to my alarm, far more of the costs would have to be shouldered by me than I had initially anticipated, even for a semi-private room with a shared bath. My body felt heavy as I thanked the woman for her time.

Still, I trudged on to Walden 11, an assisted-living facility less than four miles from my home. I immediately warmed to the director, who owned and operated the residence with his wife. Not as plush as the previous place, and with fewer amenities, the comfortable looking sixty-five-bed facility nevertheless appeared quite serviceable. Besides, mom wouldn't be able to see the threadbare rugs and scruffy furniture. By now I had discarded any possibility of obtaining a single room with a private bath.

Walden 11 had a wooded setting, 24-hour supervision, some personal assistance (at an additional cost), and a decent if not extravagant recreational program. The daily lunch and dinner menus consisted mostly of meat and chicken but the owner said that he would serve mom special meals, both vegetarian and organic. There were two small dining halls where everyone sat together for meals. Watching residents traverse the public rooms on their own, nearly all with canes or walkers, I conveniently ignored the obstacles my mother would encounter because of her limited eyesight.

Satisfied that this was a viable option, and slightly less susceptible to sticker shock, I'd mostly reconciled myself to taking on a greater financial burden if mom relocated to Pennsylvania. But how much extra would I be willing to spend? Although the expenses at Walden 11 were lower than Mrs. Bush's place, the monthly fee still would be a severe financial strain. Fidgeting in my chair, and with a queasy stomach, I told the director that I'd get back to him. Reluctant to commit even to the waiting list, I tucked the literature he handed me into my bag.

Determined to have several Pennsylvania standbys whether or not we actually took advantage of them, I checked out nearby nursing homes as well, albeit reluctantly. Ever the diligent researcher, I immediately perused Medicare's online Nursing Home Compare site for guidance. Seeking a comparatively first-rate facility willing to accept Medicaid, I winnowed my search results down to a few options.

Jackpot. Moravian Hall Square, which had received a "Much Above Average" rating in every aspect of its evaluation—health inspections, staffing, quality, overall care—was only seven miles from my house. And, the facility had an agreeable feel to it: spacious sleeping quarters; two comfortable sitting rooms, replete with leather couches, plush rugs, elegant furniture, and chandeliers; a fully-equipped library; and more. It met my smell test as well—no distasteful odors. I felt optimistic.

My enthusiasm faded when the chirpy admissions director apprised me of the price tag. I should have known better, of course, but winced anyway. What is more, flashing a cold smile, she informed me that the facility only admitted residents who could pay out-of-pocket for at least six months, a cost way beyond Dottie's means (and mine). With obvious distaste, she added, "If the client subsequently runs out of resources only then will we accept Medicaid."

I yearned to chastise her for the false advertising but, instead, slinked out of the place feeling surprisingly and absurdly humiliated.

Dispirited, I ceased my search for a few days. But there was too much in front of me to flounder for long. I was driven by a compulsion to lay out future possibilities. That fall I periodically toured a few other nursing homes that had decent ratings on Nursing Home Compare. However, none of them accepted Medicaid either, despite their marketing claims to the contrary. It was obvious that my expectations would have to be seriously downgraded; the expenses of the relatively better-rated institutions proved to be prohibitive.

Frowning over my dwindling list of barely acceptable facilities, I categorically rejected the county nursing home, Gracedale. Even though it accepted Medicaid and was only a few miles from my home, it seemed unimaginable to place her there. What's more, its "Below Average" overall rating on the Medicare website suggested substandard conditions. My chest tightened at the thought of allowing my mother to reside at such a place.

Slumped over my computer, I settled on one more nursing home to inspect. Upon entering the facility I was overcome with the stench of urine intermingled with the even more odious smell of disinfectants. The halls were lined with wheelchairs, with its occupants either staring blankly ahead or hanging their heads catatonically over armrests. Regardless of the nursing home's appalling conditions, its monthly costs were astronomical. I again consoled myself with the thought that mom most likely would stay in Florida.

Replaying the limited alternatives in my mind, every so often I toyed with the idea of keeping her at home with George and me. That began my online search for home care agencies. They tended to have catchy names like Home Care Angels, Keeping Seniors Independent, Attentive Care, and

Care Bearers. Although there were scores of them, I had difficulty getting in touch with anyone. Invariably reaching voice mail or an answering service at each one, I engaged in days of unproductive phone tagging despite making myself available for large blocks of time.

Once I obtained actual hourly rates, which were far higher than in Florida, I abandoned the idea. Needless to say, the total cost of services, even accounting for my own participation in her care, was simply too large a hit on my bank account. Full-time help was, of course, out of the question. But even for barely adequate assistance, I would have to supplement mom's income by at least $2,000 per month just for the aide, and countless more money for food, medical care, and other expenses.

Chin cupped in my hand, I sat brooding but ultimately decided to explore Pennsylvania's Medicaid Waiver programs to ascertain if any of them offered personal assistance for the low-income aged. The Department of Public Welfare's help line seemed a promising way to start the search. Unsurprisingly, it had an automatic voice that offered nine options, none of them pertaining to Medicaid. The final alternative allowed you to hold on for an "advocate." Nonetheless, after choosing to wait, I was told by a pre-recoded voice, "We are currently experiencing a high call volume. We are sorry for the inconvenience. Please call again later. Goodbye, and thank you for calling." The machine then hung up on me. I tried this for several days, and ultimately was transferred to the Department of Public Welfare, which was closed for the weekend.

A heavy sigh escaped my lips. Perhaps the link to the Aging and Disability Resource Center, an information and referral service sponsored by the Pennsylvania Department of Aging, would be of more assistance. An actual person answered, startling me. However, not only did she have limited information but her only referral was to the Northampton Area Agency on Aging (AAA).

"*Okay, that agency is next,*" I muttered to myself. Putting aside even more of my other commitments, I perused its website. Among AAAs many offer-ings were a number of waiver programs, along with other supportive services, that were exactly what I needed for mom. With a sense of relief, I dialed the number and was immediately transferred to "intake," where a customer rep-resentative notified me that nobody was available at the moment. Somebody would get back to me. My cell phone remained close at hand all day.

Two days later, Nadine returned the call. Her organization didn't have any direct services, she told me. It just served as the focal point for the

Department of Public Welfare, which had only one waiver program for the frail elderly. The AAA's role was to assess client eligibility and determine the allowable number of caregiving hours each participant was entitled to.

My stomach clenched as Nadine conveyed the particulars. Even if mom was deemed qualified, and that could not be established until she actually moved to Pennsylvania, the maximum assistance the agency could grant was two or three hours a day for three days, and that would be considered very generous for the PA waiver program. Although there wasn't a waiting list at the time, the assessment process itself would take at least two months.

As this discouraging information sank in, Nadine warned, lowering her voice, "The family needs to keep a watchful eye on the aides. They have been known to steal from their precious charges." She told me that although the Department of Public Welfare paid for the services, private agencies actually delivered them. The AAA sent every client a list to choose from.

"Don't you vet the home care agencies?" I asked.

"No," she said. "But they are bonded." Then she added, in a confidential tone, "We contract with the ones that have the least expensive hourly rates. They obviously aren't going to have the most qualified workers. You have to be careful."

Nadine moved on to other available "services," none of which her agency provided or, for that matter, we could afford. It appeared that all roads led to the Area Agency on Aging but all it could do was inform, refer, and coordinate. Publicly funded, concrete in-home services for older people were a rare commodity in the state. So many taxpayer-funded help lines, so little help.

Evidently, the political noise about rebalancing Medicaid funding for care of the frail elderly away from nursing homes and toward home-and-community-based services was more rhetoric than anything else. In order to meet the criteria for Medicaid-subsidized at-home care you had to be both extremely poor and nursing home eligible. How would such a vulnerable person of this description, then, live alone with so few hours of government assistance? How could they afford to pay for more on their own? Clearly the Medicaid Waiver program was spread too thin.

I hadn't made much headway in clinching fallbacks for mom in Pennsylvania. Despite being a knowledgeable researcher on long-term care issues, I couldn't figure out how to work the system to the benefit of my own mother. I wasn't panicked, of course, because these endeavors had merely been to pave the way for a situation that most likely wouldn't occur. Yeah, right.

Julie had become ever more valuable now that I fully grasped the restricted and seemingly inadequate choices in Pennsylvania. All the same, my mother required additional assistance in Florida. I decided to see if Julie was still willing to quit the home care agency and add those hours to assist mom "off the books." It appeared to me as the only feasible alternative at this point.

Julie jumped at the opportunity and resigned from the home care agency. "They no goot," she said. "I now wit Dodee and Lorwa."

By the end of October, she was entirely on my payroll at $10 per hour, for six hours every day, plus a daily $10 reimbursement for gas. She wouldn't receive any benefits other than paid vacations whenever I came to town, which left me feeling somewhat queasy. Nonetheless, even with the ten-hour Florida Waiver hours, mom would require more help than Julie was going to supply. Was I still in a fog of denial?

Toward the end of October I rushed to Florida for yet another short stay. I had been hearing hesitation in Julie's voice during the past few weeks—even if her words were mostly incomprehensible to me—and felt that something was terribly amiss. When notified of my imminent visit, she had released such a palpable sigh of relief across the phone line that I should have been prepared for the steep decline in mom's condition. But I wasn't.

Over the next few days, Julie would take the paid "vacation" we had agreed on, her eyes dancing with delight, but she insisted on staying for the first morning. The aide tenderly washed, oiled, massaged, and powdered Dottie before dressing her and fetching the walker. Mom appeared shakier than ever as she plodded her way to the living room recliner.

Although Julie always took pride in her appearance, today she was all gussied up. Wearing a long red, gold, and blue floral short-sleeve blouse over flowing black crepe pants, a light blue tinseled scarf around her neck, and two sparkling hair combs tucked into her dark hair, her appearance contrasted sharply with my mother and me. We were both attired in our usual shorts and T-shirts, mine rumpled from the long trip, mom's neat from Julie's careful upkeep. A baseball cap covered my unkempt hair. I complemented the aide and she flashed me a shy, pleased smile in return.

Julie moved to the kitchen to prepare mom's breakfast, serving her in the painstaking order that Dorothy Katz expected. Folding my arms across my chest, I listened as my mother, in rapid succession, asked for water, tissues, and slippers. Julie seemed nonplussed, unlike me who generally responded to these demands with a sharp, "I can't do everything at once. I'm only one person."

The air conditioner was turned on, which cut through the damp, stuffy air. Mom had instructed Julie to start it an hour or so prior to my arrival, a new development that surely gratified the aide. Dottie was like a rattlesnake, thriving best in sweltering heat. In the past, we had been at odds over the stifling apartment, its windows wide open, the temperature often over 90 degrees in the summertime. Feeling uncomfortably sticky, with sweat trickling from every pore, I finally had stipulated that I wouldn't come back to Florida unless she agreed to use the air conditioner during my visit.

Despite the steady droning sound of the cooling unit, I hadn't entirely won the argument. "Julie, could you get me a jacket," mom said, with a sly smile.

I took the bait. As the aide wrapped her in the fleece jacket, I burst out, "It's at least seventy-five degrees in here. How could you possibly wear that?"

The drenching rain that afternoon kept us in the apartment, adding to my testiness. Julie was now gone, and wouldn't return until the morning of my flight. Alone with mom, I gave her a long, steady look. She seemed more weary than usual, as though every movement was a struggle. And her bronzed, wrinkled face was tighter. Sitting in her chair with a pained stare, she was also less talkative. The unfamiliar long silences between us became oppressive.

Most alarming, though, was the way she teetered and tottered from chair to bathroom and back. I stayed close to her at these times, even though I couldn't possibly catch her full weight if she tripped.

"I'm okay," she said. "Don't worry about me so much." Yeah, right.

At night, I couldn't sleep, in fear of her falling during the invariable trips to the bathroom. Hovering over her each time, an unseen shadowy presence, I held my breath until she was safely back in bed. Observing her exceedingly stooped posture and precarious stagger, a crushing sadness swept over me, as though I were seeing my mother's diminished state for the first time. Mom blithely shuffled to and fro.

I glanced around the apartment, hugging myself uncertainly. Was it really safe to leave her here? I brushed the unspoken answer aside. My emotional self was reigning, not the sensible, clear-eyed Laura who should have been in charge. I so desperately longed to figure out a way to keep her at home—that's what my mother wanted, and planned on. How could I snatch her away from sunny Florida? From Julie? Mom needed her aide. We both needed her.

Evenings were challenging, especially bath time. Climbing over the high tub into the shower chair had become trickier with her growing instability. I held my mother's hand tightly, and when she was seated, passed her the hose. Dottie's face, upturned, slowly relaxed as the gushing hot water spread over her body. For most of mom's life, she had taken at least two nearly scalding showers a day, always washing her body vigorously, as though scrubbing away all concerns. The water both calmed and rejuvenated her; it had been her therapy. These days she had to resign herself to only one.

Tonight I prepared a Swiss cheese omelet and sweet potato for dinner, one of my mother's favorite meals. For the first time, I had bought groceries on my own, both of us in agreement that a trip to the supermarket would be too onerous for her. My lips curved into a guilty smirk. Instead of the expensive organic vegetables, fruits, canned goods, and fish at Whole Foods, I had slipped into Publix. Not only was it closer but the total cost was nearly fifty percent less than usual.

Later, unable to sleep, I flipped through one of mom's photo albums, selecting it at random. Barefoot baby Alix, wearing only a diaper, beamed back at me, tufts of hair on her otherwise bald head. Page after page documented her granddaughter's progression, from crawling, to walking, to her first day at school. Soon an eight-year-old Alix appeared, wearing the same broad grin but who now boasted a long, wavy blond mane. I was sure other albums covered the rest of my daughter's thirty-seven years.

Mom had always preserved treasured moments. Indeed, each inch of wall space in the apartment bore witness to a piece of her life: the husband, children, grandchild, sisters, brothers, nieces and nephews who embraced Dorothy Katz's little world over the decades. They were papered in batches, lovingly fashioned for her pleasure alone.

Taking it all in, I realized that there were no recent pictures of her or of us together. In the past, we had photographed every visit. Was it because, unlike the documentation of my daughter's wondrous maturation, we would now only be recording mom's steady deterioration? Were memories of descent into fragility worth keeping?

I glanced in the direction of the two absent bicycles that used to crowd the tiny area outside her bedroom. The vacated spot had been replaced with a walker, cartons of adult diapers, and boxes of prunes and fiber supplements. The lovely, engraved cane I had bought her, rendered obsolete, was tucked into the nearby closet. More recently, a folding wheelchair had arrived, courtesy of Steve and the Medicaid Waiver program. Julie had won me over on the need for it. She couldn't easily handle mom anymore on their shopping trips or for doctor appointments. Despite my reluctance, I had to be considerate of the aide. I consoled myself with the thought that at least my mother could still walk and they would use the wheelchair sparingly.

Tears unwittingly appeared at the corner of my eyes. Trickling at first, they soon started to gush out uncontrollably, like a rain-swelled dam that had finally burst. Muffled sobs wracked through my whole body for a long while. Until this evening, I had not really had a good cry over what was happening to her, to us. Perhaps I was finally mourning the loss of the person my mother had been. Maybe I was just tired of being in charge, and wanted my mommy back. Or could it be both? I poured myself a glass of white wine.

ॐ

Tending to Dottie's every need as conscientiously as Julie drained me, but I kept at it. At times, it seemed as though I were in competition with the aide, wanting mom to reward me with an "attaboy" for each wearisome task.

"Am I doing as well as Julie?" I asked, as we went through the morning routine on the first full day we spent alone together.

"It's okay," she said. "But why did you send Julie away?"

I wished that I hadn't.

Collapsing into mom's comfortable recliner on the third night, October 27, I watched the weather report, with growing concern. Tropical storm Sandy, aimed at the Northeastern Coast of the United States, had restrengthened to a Category 1 hurricane. I stared at the TV in disbelief, leaning forward to catch every word. New Jersey had joined five other states in declaring a state of emergency.

The situation only worsened. The next day all flights to Newark Liberty International Airport were cancelled.

My jaw clenched. "No!" I shouted at the television. "No!" I'd already begun counting the days until departure, when my real life could resume again. Only one more to go! To tell the truth, I'd had enough of mom and her seemingly endless needs. Having performed my daughterly duty, I was more than ready for Julie to take over again.

Steve had agreed to have a bedside commode delivered to the apartment within the next few days. My mother wouldn't have to walk to the bathroom at night anymore. The situation was under control, at least temporarily. She would be safe, or at least that was what I told myself.

Then, on October 29th, the largest Atlantic hurricane on record slammed into the Northeast, inundating infrastructure and downing trees. Millions of people in the region were left without power. Not only was the Newark airport shut down, but the Superstorm had knocked out my electricity in Pennsylvania. Even Lehigh University was closed.

"Entire trees, branches, and poles are scattered every which way in our area," George reported from his ninety-seven-year-old mother's house, to which he had escaped. "Electrical wires are sagging and many have snapped. I'll be stuck at my mother's for a while." He paused. "You're probably better off in Florida."

I listened in exasperated silence, shaking my head. "No," I muttered. "I'm coming home."

By the 31st Newark airport had limited service. And the stretch of roads in Ft. Lauderdale that had been closed because of the storm, including the route from mom's house to the airport, re-opened. Although Sandy mostly bypassed Florida, it had left severe flooding in its wake.

I spent the entire day on the telephone in an attempt to squeeze onto a flight, with mom cheering me on. It was not entirely clear as to whether she was commiserating with me or if she, too, was anxious for me to leave—and to have Julie back.

The representatives at United Airlines reported that nothing would be available for at least a week. Every other carrier was similarly booked up. Dogged in my pursuit, as I tended to be when single-mindedly focused on a goal, I called the airline continuously. During one call in the late afternoon an agent advised me that they were periodically getting cancellations. Did I want to "hang on" just in case? I remained on the line for over an hour, my cell phone tucked between my shoulder and chin, while intermittently attending to mom. Lunch. More water. Tissues. Slippers. Hot chocolate. Fruit. Eyedrops. Medicine.

"Anything yet?" I grumbled into the phone from time to time.

"You're in luck," the agent suddenly said. "One seat to Newark just became available. For November 2nd."

"I'll take it," I said, even before she gave me any details. I had secured the coveted seat to Newark. Just two more days in Florida and then home.

è.

Home, of course, meant staying at my mother-in-law's place until the heat and electricity were restored at our house. It also entailed over an hour's commute to work, since the university had resumed classes. It seemed as though electrical energy was humming everywhere except for my neighborhood. I settled in at my mother-in-law's house for the long haul.

Yet, almost immediately another storm erupted, this time a personal one. The disconcerting sound of "Jungle Drums" thundered on my cell, demanding my attention. It was Julie. She was at the hospital with mom, who had fallen on the way to the bathroom. Julie had found her lying on the floor in the morning. Seemingly, mom had decided to ignore the portable commode, situated next to her bed.

I listened numbly, the anger at mom muted by my complicity, the pretense that she could continue to live on her own. I had been sleepwalking into the future.

Bracing myself for another juggling act between obligations in Pennsylvania and those in Florida, I was once again entangled in an endless stream of phone calls. I took over my mother-in-law's house, with her quiet acquiescence.

After finally attaining information about Dottie's condition from reluctant hospital officials and nurses, who as usual invoked the HIPAA privacy law, I telephoned Walden 11, the assisted-living facility here in Pennsylvania. It was time for the waiting list.

In retrospect, this time period was a foretaste of things to come. From November 2, 2012 onward, the situation in Florida would be like riding a roller coaster that plunged down but never climbed up again. Henceforth, nothing would be the same. It was as though a dark shadow had been cast over us.

7

From Bad to Worse

Rehabilitation to Debilitation

Mom had been delirious in the hospital for several days and we couldn't communicate at all. Julie—kind Julie—was with her several hours a day (paid of course) but she, too, couldn't get mom to say anything. And, as usual, I didn't understand Julie's broken English. Needless to say, the situation was alarming.

"Julie," I asked over the phone. "What are the doctors telling you about mom's inability to speak?"

"[Unintelligible], okay, honeh," the aide typically responded. Julie was patient as she repeatedly gave me the same indecipherable report every day.

The hospital was of no assistance either. The various nurses that I conversed with—a new one appeared at every shift change, of course—didn't have a clue as to what was wrong with mom. "Ask the doctor," they told me. Yeah, right.

I later found out she had a urinary tract infection (UTI) that, in the elderly, could cause confusion, agitation, and other mental instabilities. If only I had known that before the deeply disturbing phone call from her. Apparently mom had suddenly regained some awareness because, out of the blue, she demanded that Julie dial my number.

"You've broken my heart," my mother screeched into the phone. "You've broken my heart," she said again, this time sobbing. "How could you dump me in a nursing home?" My heart was broken too.

Mom had heard that she was being discharged to a nursing home, which I reluctantly had agreed to. My preference had been for her to head directly home but was advised that she could not be on her own yet, even

73

with Julie's help. "She is confined to a wheelchair," an impatient hospital discharge planner had emphatically stated.

Of course mom can't walk, I thought to myself. She had been in bed the entire time she was hospitalized, without any exercise. The social workers had been immune to my pleas to work with her.

"And, your mother is incapable of making any decisions," she had added, with a hint of sarcasm. It was not only up to me, but there didn't seem to be any option other than a nursing home.

The discharge planner had found a rehabilitation center with an opening, near the hospital. In reality it was a nursing home with a separate wing for short-term stays. I would have checked out the facility on Medicare's "Nursing Home Compare" website but didn't have the opportunity given the abruptness of mom's dismissal from the hospital. Her stay would be brief, a few weeks or so, I had reasoned to myself. Just for rehabilitation. How bad could it be? In any case, the location of the facility was convenient for Julie, who I intended to pay to sit with her every day. At least my mother wouldn't be totally alone.

Dottie remained in the nursing home for nearly a month, from November 7 to December 5, 2012. From the start, it was difficult to get any information about my mother's progress. The facility's telephone system itself was in such disrepair that when I called to obtain updates on her condition, it frequently disconnected me. At times the system didn't work at all, most conspicuously in the mornings. When I finally reached a nurse, I inevitably was told that mom was progressing well. Julie wasn't so sanguine, although unsurprisingly I had difficulty understanding her. And mom's mental abilities had deteriorated so badly that she predominantly rambled, at times mumbling nothing more to me than "hallo, hallo, hallo." I had to get there quickly.

&.

I drove to Hillcrest Nursing and Rehabilitation Center straight from the airport, grateful that my trusty GPS had guided me there without a hitch. It was a one-story facility, with the visitors' entrance at the back. There was only one remaining spot in the gravelly parking lot and it was a tight fit for my rented car. I headed toward the glass doors warily, not knowing what to expect. My research and writings on nursing homes, most of which depicted generally dismal conditions, did not exactly inspire confidence in me. Despite my apprehension, I felt somewhat hopeful. I suppose it would have been too unnerving to imagine my mother residing in a horrific place.

The nursing station was down the hall from the entrance, on the right, but nobody was there. Over the next several days I would find out that it was usually empty, and when the charge nurse was on hand, she made it clear that my questions were interrupting consequential business. Nurse's aides generally bustled around in the back, but they also ignored me.

I wandered down the long corridor in search of mom's room on my own. The number, which I had hastily written down on a scrap of paper and had tucked haphazardly in my pocket, was now so crumpled I couldn't decipher it. I wrinkled my nose. The palpable stench in the air, a mix of stale urine and feces masked by disinfectants and ammonia, was hard to ignore.

Hillcrest Nursing and Rehabilitation Center was a 240-bed for-profit facility with a high occupancy rate. Regardless, it had received a one star ("Much Below Average") overall rating from the Centers for Medicare and Medicaid Services (CMS) and even that low assessment didn't begin to capture the deplorable conditions I encountered. Indeed, the place was a veritable nightmare.

My mother's semi-private room was tiny, with two beds jammed in like cans on a supermarket shelf. Dottie's bed was close to the window, and it was nearly impossible to squeeze her wheelchair around her roommate's bed to leave the room. The wheelchair itself, as with the walker and other paraphernalia, had to be kept in the small, shared bathroom that contained a toilet, sink, and open shower. Luckily for us, the roommate used only a bedpan and was never bathed, at least for the week I was there. Since the end of my mother's bed all but touched the bathroom door, Julie had to jimmy the wheelchair out, and place it in the hallway, when she showered mom.

There was a small dresser adjacent to the bathroom wall that held the few neatly folded T-shirts and socks that Julie had brought from mom's apartment. She didn't trust the nursing home's laundry service and had been washing them herself. Next to the bureau was a tall, narrow closet where Julie had hung shorts, pants, two sweatshirts, and a light jacket. Beneath them were mom's blankets from the apartment, a bedpan, and other odds and ends, shoved in, piled high.

A night table was tucked in between mom's bed and the window. The surface was empty since Julie had refused to bring in any of my mother's personal belongings, especially the small talking clock. "Dey steel it," she said. "No goot here."

In the night table's one drawer, Julie had placed the soap, lotions, powders, and other toiletries that she used to tend to mom each morning. I added some of mom's favorite treats to the cache. On the other side of the bed there was a small stuffed chair that poked at the drab, colorless privacy curtain. Nearby was an adjustable over-bed table that had been dotted with specks of food and sticky smears when I arrived. I washed it after every meal with a wet towel.

The space was so tightly packed that there was no place for a second chair. I gave Julie the week off, with pay. That settled the need for two chairs, but it soon became apparent that the situation would be too problematic without her. I had been paying Julie to sit with mom, be her companion, and advocate on her behalf. Instead, the nursing home aides had relinquished all morning chores to her and now expected the same of me. Lifting mom into the shower by myself was out of the question, as were most of the other tasks Julie had been handling. Her "vacation" was short-lived.

I put a stop to Julie's recruitment as staff for mom's roommate, Sarah, which she was too timid to do for herself. The aides had Julie assisting in Sarah's care too, washing and feeding her or, at times, making her bed when Julie had completed mom's morning ritual. Some of it, of course, was because of Julie's warm heart—Sarah couldn't eat on her own and the food was frequently left on the tray for an hour or so before an aide fed her. The hungry young woman would wail in frustration as she looked longingly at her uneaten meal. For the week that I spent at the nursing home, nobody paid any attention to her at all.

The privacy curtain was almost always pulled between the two beds but you could hear her intermittent howls into empty space whenever she wanted something. The aides seldom responded. I attempted to get help for her but they ignored my requests as well. Sometimes when someone had pulled the curtain open, Sarah would gaze resentfully at Julie and me as we devotedly tended to mom. In due course, she let out a particularly piercing howl. She had no visitors.

It appeared that the aides left Sarah and many other residents in bed for a good portion of the day. Most likely mom would have been too if Julie had not painstakingly maneuvered her in and out of the wheelchair early each morning. However, it shouldn't be Julie's job. After assessing the situation, I marched up to the nursing station and asked for help. An hour later two sullen aides appeared with a mechanical lift to transfer mom to the wheelchair.

Dottie loved the contraption, which I dubbed the "flying machine." It was plain by her grin that she enjoyed souring above us, like a bird who, if only momentarily, had escaped captivity. But why were the aides using a hoist rather than mom's own two feet? Her mobility should not have been that limited. And, it turned out that the nursing home had so few of these hydraulic lifts that we were forced to wait endlessly for one to become available. Beyond that, I had to search out assistance whenever my mother needed to go to the bathroom. No one responded to the call button.

There were other vital matters to attend to, notably the pressure sores on mom's buttocks, elbows, and back of her legs. The aides had haphazardly slapped some ointment and bandages on the fluid-filled blisters. Some of the tape was peeling at the edges. Julie had noticed the pressure sores but everyone had ignored her pleas to turn mom when she wasn't around. Discounted by the staff as "mere help," Julie had not been able to advocate for Dottie in my absence.

"My mother needs to be turned regularly," I told the charge nurse.

She looked up. "What's her name?" I'm sure she knew by now.

"Dorothy Katz, room 116."

"Oh, okay. I'll let the aides know," she said. The nurse turned back to her paperwork.

"She is covered in bed sores," I insisted.

"I said I'll let the aides know," she said, dismissing me.

Mom was in adult diapers. Cheap ones that leaked easily. The linen was somewhat protected by a large, thin pad. There was also a waterproof cover over the mattress. Only Dottie, herself, was vulnerable to the seepage. Julie changed her in the morning, cleaning, powdering and creaming her charge as she had done so lovingly every day over the last several months. It was a tough job that I couldn't do on my own.

Julie had left for the day and mom's diaper was saturated, a sure incubator for another UTI. Mom wouldn't be able to cope with yet another hospitalization, nor I with a further round of her delirium. I walked into the hallway and flagged down an aide.

"My mother needs to be changed," I said.

She smiled pleasantly. "I'll be right there." I didn't see her again.

If wet diapers were an ordeal, bowel movements were even worse. "I have to make a "do-do," mom moaned.

"Can you please put my mother on a bedpan?" I asked an aide who was bringing in the lunch tray. They had refused to walk her to the bathroom, telling me she was too physically disabled.

"It hurts. I need to go." Mom was now whimpering.

The aide set down the tray and disappeared. I was learning the language of this nursing home. "I'll be right there" meant an imminent shift change and the aide would be heading home. If she was already in the room, she'd say, "I'll be right back." That indicated that the aide was going on her break.

❧

Mom had always savored my coffee. She never drank the stuff except when I was in town. The day before my expected arrival at her apartment, Julie would take out the dusty pot and wash it until it glistened. The secret was the vanilla flavoring, mixed with a huge scoopful of coffee mate. Food-conscious Dottie never would have approved of the artificial cream had she known. Why not bring the pot, with all of the trimmings, to the nursing home? For two days a fragrant vanilla aroma pervaded the room as mom sipped contentedly. I had added a bagel and cream cheese for her and Julie, one of their favorite morning treats.

And then the head nurse walked in, bringing in a gust of cold air in her wake. Her steely pale eyes, detached but authoritative demeanor and clipped speech reminded me of Big Nurse Ratched. We were in "One Flew Over the Cuckoo Nest" after all. Her heavily starched, impeccable white lab coat, dark brown, carefully coifed hair, and French-manicured nails let everyone know that she was not a hands-on nurse with messy patients to care for. Her massive lips, painted as bright red as her fingernails, told me in a businesslike tone, "coffee pots are a no-no at Hillcrest." Her large bosom heaved up and down, reminding me again of Big Nurse Ratched.

She eyed the Generlac and Magnesium Citrate bottles, also sitting on the night table. "And no unauthorized medications, none at all," she said. I had brought the offending objects from the apartment to relieve mom's ongoing, painful constipation. Dr. Anna previously had the condition under control through these prescription drugs but neither the hospital nor the nursing home had given mom *anything* for it.

When I had earlier questioned one of the nurses who dispensed my mother's pills, she had stared at me blankly. "I don't know anything about her constipation," she muttered. "You must ask the doctor."

I should have hid the medicine.

Simmering with anger, I looked directly at the Big Nurse Ratched look-alike and said, "I have a list of complaints as well." She tilted her head to avoid my steady gaze. Deciding to limit my grievances to a few vital issues, I settled on mom's increasingly puffy ankles and feet. I had noticed them straightaway and asked one of the aides to elevate them at night. The next morning, mom had one of her two appallingly thin pillows under her legs and was lying flat on the bed, her head only barely supported by the remaining one. "The swelling in my mother's legs is out of control," I told the head nurse. "She needs more pillows under her feet."

"We don't have any extra ones," she said.

"No extra pillows?" I said, my eyes widening in disbelief. "You're kidding, right?"

"I'll look." She returned fifteen minutes later, handing me one of the apparently scarce items.

"You need to do something about mom's eyedrops," I said, quickly ticking off the next item on my list. The head nurse had already pivoted her body toward the door, ready to leave. I was concerned because mom had received only one of her four usual eyedrops this morning. When I questioned one of the LPN's about it, she told me that they only had the one medication on Dorothy Katz's chart and I would have to speak to the doctor about it.

"I'll check into it," the head nurse said. She never came back.

The elusive doctor showed up two days later. Luckily I was there when he entered mom's room. In nursing homes, the physician is sovereign, like a head of state. It was impossible to pinpoint a day, not to mention a time, when he would be available. When I asked one of the nurses when the doctor was coming she looked at me quizzically. "He comes whenever," she sighed. "We never know."

"I need to talk to you about my mother's swollen ankles and feet," I said to the doctor, now that I had him cornered.

He went over to my mother and pressed around the puffed-up areas with his hands. He tapped around her knees. He listened to her heart with his stethoscope, telling her to take deep breaths. Mom complied, unsure of what was going on. He then touched her swollen ankles again, this time more gently.

"It's not too bad," he said. "We'll have her mended in no time." He was trying to soothe me but was obviously in a hurry. "We'll put her on a low-salt diet."

"She's already on a low-salt diet," I said.

"I'll put on her chart that she needs pillows under her feet at night," he responded.

I shrugged my shoulders and he, like the head nurse, was gone.

ℰ

The food at the nursing home was just as unpleasant as the dirty bed table. Since Julie hadn't mentioned any problems about Dottie's meals in our phone conversations, I had tucked the issue of her vegetarianism into the "I'll think about it later" part of my brain. "Later" came soon enough. Despite low expectations, I was nevertheless taken aback by the sorely inadequate diet. They had been giving mom the same meals as everyone else but without the main dish. Because she didn't eat chicken or meat, most of the time she received *no protein at all*. A typical dinner consisted of a portion of dried-up vegetables, an ample helping of mashed potatoes, a small lettuce salad, and a slice of bread. They served her a barely edible full dinner only when fish was on the menu.

Breakfast consisted of hot cereal that looked like mush, two slices of bread, slabs of butter, and an orange or banana. Still no protein. I brought in a bowl from mom's apartment, and her usual morning meal—bran cereal and vanilla soy milk. It became an ordeal to keep the soy milk stored at the nursing home since the refrigerator was located in a locked room and someone at the mostly unmanned nursing station had to retrieve it for me. Sometimes the wait was a half hour.

I was determined to have mom walking again. After all, she had been able to use her walker to toddle around the block before her recent hospital stay. When I had first called my mother's assigned physical therapist, Linda, she had told me that mom wasn't making much headway. "We're doing all we can," she said. "Your mother just doesn't seem up to walking." Unlike the nursing station, the therapy room had been more easily accessible by telephone. I checked in every day from Pennsylvania. "No progress yet," the therapist would say.

I met Linda on the second day of my visit. Visitors weren't allowed to watch the actual therapy sessions because their presence was considered a distraction for the patient and others in the room. I stood in the hall, peeking around the corner, to check on mom's progress. She was using her walker but in fits and starts. She stopped after a few steps, out of breath. Every few minutes someone measured her oxygen level as I anxiously awaited the verdict. If it fell below ninety percent, Linda, or someone else, forced mom to rest for what seemed like forever. The therapist moved on to another patient in the interim. If it happened repeatedly, Linda terminated the day's already short session.

I discovered that Dottie received, at most, an hour of physical therapy a day and for only six days a week. Wasn't rehabilitation the whole point of her being in this place? To get her walking so that she could move back to her apartment?

⧉

Hillcrest didn't offer very much for its residents to do. On the way to rehab, we passed through an activities room. It was so narrow that we had to squeeze mom's wheelchair around its central table to get to the physical therapy building. The activities room had a decent-sized television, hanging high on one wall, that was always blaring some sort of game or talk show—Ellen De Generes, Oprah, Let's Make a Deal, The Hollywood Squares. Usually eight or so wheelchairs were arranged in front of it. A few people appeared attentive but the rest of the faces were glazed over. Books were lined up on shelves, mostly "dime novels," and a number of magazines had been scattered about on the back benches. I never saw any newspapers.

Every so often the activities director—it was a one-person operation— organized a sing-along but only a few individuals participated. At other times a few residents, thick crayons in hand, filled in coloring books or randomly marked construction paper. Half-broken crayons lay everywhere. Some looked as if they had been bitten off.

The nursing home periodically held "events" in the dining hall, especially picture bingo. According to the "Activities Sheet," posted on bulletin boards throughout the facility, that was a foremost entertainment. Twice a week, in fact. There were monthly birthday celebrations as well, where they served cake, cupcakes, and sometimes ice cream. Sporadically, residents had an opportunity to watch a movie or live entertainment. And there were church services every Sunday morning. A chaplain had come by to encourage mom to attend a protestant service. Mom is Jewish.

⧉

Until my appearance mom had no fresh air at all. She sat in her dank, unventilated room nearly all day. At least the aides threw open the curtains

From Bad to Worse | 81

every morning to let in light. Nobody ever took her out, not even Julie. It would have been too challenging because Dottie was tethered to an oxygen supply, attached to the wall. A nasal cannula, which was hooked around the ears and inserted into her nostrils, delivered a mixture of oxygen and air.

I eyed a portable oxygen tank that the therapists used to transport patients, and requested one from the charge nurse, who seemed perceptibly irritated by the inconvenience. The nursing home didn't have too many of them. Every afternoon, I asked for the small tank and waited impatiently for an aide to fetch one for me. A nurse had to connect the device, generating another long delay. Neither the aides nor family members were allowed to do this. Perhaps they thought we'd blow the place up.

I slowly learned how to manipulate the wheelchair, oxygen tank hanging on its rear, through the exit that led to the commons area outside. Since the two glass doors weren't automated, you had to hold them open while simultaneously pushing the wheelchair through. It was tricky but I soon got the knack of it. Every so often an aide, or someone else, helped out. I was always grateful.

We reached the grassy area, the only really pleasant place in the nursing home. It had wooden chairs, round metal tables, and concrete benches strewn intermittently along two short paths. One led to the small therapy building. The other stretched along one side of the main building and then circled around back again. I sat down, watching the sun beam on mom's face. She had her eyes closed, enjoying the warmth. She worshiped the sun. That's why she left for Florida so many years ago.

We periodically strolled along the pathway. I thought the motion would soothe mom, give her the sensation that she wasn't stuck in one place. We went round and round, like a hamster spinning its wheel. More likely I was doing it for myself. It made me feel useful.

&.

Then, out of the blue, I was thrown a curveball. Rosalia, from the social services department, wanted to see me as soon as possible. I walked down the hall and made a right at the nursing station. The door to her office was open.

"Be seated," she said. "I'll be with you shortly." That meant, of course, that it would be a long wait. She made several phone calls, scribbled on some papers, and subsequently looked up.

She gave me a smile that disappeared within seconds. "Your mother is ready to be discharged," she said.

I needed a second or two to take this in. "Discharged?" I said stupidly. "I thought she would be walking before you sent her home."

Rosalia's expression turned quizzical. "Home?" she said. "Your mother is nonambulatory." She stopped and looked at me. "Without full-time services, and I mean twenty-four/seven, she's never going home."

"My mother needs to stay in rehab longer," I said. I had intended for mom to go back to her apartment.

"Therapy has decided that you mother is not progressing," she said. "We must discharge her." I knew what that meant. Medicare would no longer pay for the rehabilitation. Mom had to leave.

Rosalia handed me a card. "Call Daniella," she said. "She can give you a list of assisted-living facilities if you'd like."

All nursing homes and hospitals have discharge planners like Rosalia. In many respects they are the public face of the place, serving as the interface between the client and institution. It seems to me that their main objective is to enhance the firm's bottom line by telling you what you want is not possible, placing obstacles in your way, and searching for other avenues of support that do not include their institution. The preferred outcome is to induce you to go away.

Excerpts from Dorothy Katz's Medical Records at Hillcrest Nursing and Rehabilitation Center

In order to more fully understand my mother's situation at Hillcrest Nursing and Rehabilitation Center, two years later I requested her medical records from the nursing home, which placed not a few obstacles in my way. After persevering for months on end, and at a cost of $63.00, they finally materialized. The 156 pages of paperwork documented countless half-truths, double-talk, and outright lies, as well as slapdash adherence to legalities and procedures. They made a mockery of nursing home regulations and patient rights, however lacking they were to begin with.

There were a considerable number of shoddy entries and misrepresentations that indicated a slapdash approach to patient care. Throughout the pages, starting with the initial evaluation, nobody seemed to notice that Dorothy Katz was legally blind. Social

workers and nurses alike had checked off that her vision was "good" or "adequate," depending on the choices. In one place, the question "Is resident visually challenged?" had been marked with a "no."

The much touted "Care Plan," which enumerated problems, goals, target dates, and approaches/interventions, proved to be nonsense, at least in my mother's case. In the "Impaired Vision Care Plan," for example, the social worker had selected large-print reading material as a primary means of helping her vision problem (Dottie was totally incapable of viewing the pages, no less any print on them). The most useful intervention, assistance with use of radio, CDs, and books on tape, was conspicuously not checked off.

A boilerplate approach to patients and their needs was evident everywhere. A member of the staff claimed to have filled out Dottie's "favorite activities" at her side, nearly all of which were antithetical to her actual interests. In another place it was purported that "Mrs. Katz watched trivia shows/contests and listened to classical music at bedside." Mom couldn't watch any television at that point and she had never appreciated classical music—she was partial to the golden oldies.

The section devoted to my mother's stated preferences regarding "Advance Directives," an issue Dottie had always been fervent about, again showed the facility's perfunctory attention to resident needs. At a much earlier time mom had pressed several signed and notarized papers into my hand, insisting that my sisters and I respect her request to avoid all means of artificial life support. Yet, Hillcrest's intake worker had checked on the form that she preferred "Cardiopulmonary Resuscitation," "Artificial Respiration (including respirator)," and "Artificial means of providing nutrition or hydration." The person also noted that mom had no "Advanced Directive" or "Living Will" (untrue) and nobody with Durable Power of Attorney or Health Care Agent (I had both of these, but no one had asked me). Such misstatements demonstrated a flagrant disregard of Dorothy Katz's deeply held wishes.

Other inconsistent and outrageous details would be hilarious if they weren't so appalling. They apparently had given mom "a full orientation to the facility," including an introduction to her roommate (the same one who was incapable of communicating with anyone except through howls). Various assessments of Dottie's mental and behavioral status ranged from "confused" to "alert and responsive." And then there was the bald-faced lie that contributed to the severe undermining of her health: the weekly nutrition statements asserted that my mother was consuming at least four servings of protein each day. Certainly, neither Julie nor I saw much, if any, protein on her plate. Just as disconcerting, because of my complaints, a nurse "discovered" swelling on mom's extremities for the first time, but reported the "swelling resolved" three days later (this was another shameless falsehood; the life-threatening edema had lasted throughout her stay at Hillcrest).

Nevertheless, the most telling and egregious issue was the blatantly contradictory information about Dottie's inability to regain mobility. Mom had been discharged abruptly, with warnings from the social worker that not only was she not improving but most likely would never regain her ability to walk. Prior to the last hospital stay, in early November, my mother could get out of bed by herself by grabbing the small bar I had placed there. And, she could manage a walker for short distances. I personally had watched mom's progress, however slowly, in Hillcrest's physical therapy room. The ongoing care plan clearly indicated that the nursing home's goal, and mine, was for Dottie to regain her ability to walk so that she could return to her own home.

And her functional ability, according to the initial intake report said, "Needs assistance from one side only" for transferring and getting to the bathroom—is a one-person assist."[1] Contrary to what I had been told by the physical therapist, "Progress Notes" from November 7, 2012 to December 5, 2012—the entire duration of her residency at Hillcrest—stated that "Ms. Katz received therapeutic exercises which improved strength and durability." In another "Summary of Progress," the physical therapist had written, "Patient demonstrates improved capacity to benefit from skilled rehabilitation therapy and goals have been upgraded accordingly." In another place, she noted, "Patient demonstrates good rehab potential for stated goals [getting patient back to her home] as evidenced by prior level of functioning, ability to follow 1-step directions, support system in place, strong family support and resolving medical issues."

So what happened? How and when did my mother become a lost cause? Certainly, she had encountered innumerable roadblocks, including severely restricted amounts of therapy; development of an upper respiratory infection, contracted at the nursing facility itself, along with the accompanying oxygen deficiency that limited rehab sessions; and an unwillingness of the nurses and aides to help her walk. In nearly every daily note that the Hillcrest nurses had recorded, regardless of the time of day, Dorothy Katz was "resting in bed." Languishing would be a more appropriate term.

And because of laziness or sheer incompetence—probably both—they used bedpans instead of taking her to the bathroom with the walker. Indeed, Dottie had been forced to urinate in her diaper a good portion of the time. Her medical records specified that she was never "mentally aware of toileting needs," allowing the aides to disregard her (in reality, my mother had been conscious of her need to go to the bathroom but could rarely find an aide to assist her). It seemed that the nursing home stay itself had been a strong contributing factor in my mother's lack of progress and ultimately in her inability to return home.

8

Through the Looking Glass

They were kicking mom out of Hillcrest. I shifted into "go" mode. Sadness was too much of a luxury right now. As was panic. And indecision. And hopelessness. I was mostly numb, struggling to keep myself and the situation under control. My approach was methodical, like an automaton. I had only three days to pull this together.

I decided to put mom in assisted living here in Florida, at least temporarily. She could stay there until Walden 11 had an opening. It was time for Pennsylvania. Caring for my mother from afar had become too precarious. Since she would have to be placed on the waiting list, the journey most likely wouldn't be for several months, in spring. Probably best, anyway. I was reluctant to subject her to the bitter cold of the Northeast. Never a fan of winter, mom would probably suffer even more in her advanced old age.

I carefully explained the situation to my mother. It's not certain that she fully understood but her head nodded in agreement. She recognized that she couldn't live alone, at least for the time-being, without more help. I didn't tell her that she was never going back to her apartment or about the long-range plan to leave Florida.

I telephoned Daniella, who asked about our price range. She was used to the urgency of the situation, people needing immediate placement. That's her business: abruptly discharged residents. It happened more frequently than not. Within two hours she walked into my mother's room. Click, click. Daniella was wearing stilettos, red ones that matched her elegant red checkered suit. She was gorgeous, statuesque, and had a caressing smile. I felt shabby in my creased T-shirt, shorts, and well-worn sneakers.

She handed me a list of three possibilities, along with brochures. These were to start with, she said. She had several more but didn't want to overwhelm me. I was surprisingly grateful for the limited choices. I dutifully called and made appointments at all three of them, although one was a bit higher priced than my outer limit. The next two days were a mad rush of visiting with mom at the nursing home while also inspecting the three premises. Choosing an assisted-living facility at such short notice was like picking out a casket on the same day that a parent had died.

Periodically I calculated what it would cost to have more care for her at home. Round-the-clock assistance was out of the question. Julie wanted to help. She offered to quit her other client, who she now also worked for off the books. What if I stretched out Julie's hours from six to eight per day? Nine? And we still had the two hours of Medicaid Waiver funded care in the evenings, during the week. Could I leave mom unattended through the night? What about weekends? How much more money could I add? It was just too risky—and costly.

The first two assisted-living facilities were small, independently owned businesses with about twelve to fourteen residents living in semi-private rooms. The proprietors showed me around. The places seemed homey, although at the second one I was a bit unsettled by the line-up of wheelchair-bound elders staring at the TV in the living room. In both facilities, the aides were related to the owners and appeared attentive and friendly. I became less discouraged.

At the third dwelling, the most expensive of the three, Shoshana greeted me. She was both the administrator (she ran two facilities—Miriam's Place, Inc. and Sunshine Place, Inc.—within a mile of each other) and the owner's daughter. The house was spacious and immaculate. Much of the flooring was tiled in white, which sparkled like TV ads for a cleaning product.

The livingroom featured a posh blue rug, spread over most of the tiles. The area was furnished in traditional décor that included a two-person mahogany couch and a matching accent chair, all covered in softly textured light blue and pink fabric. Their curved legs and handles were delicately carved. Two pale blue accent pillows had been placed on both ends of the sofa. Positioned in front of it was a rectangular coffee table, with a large pottery vase filled with dainty synthetic flowers. On each of the two coordinating end tables sat a white, oval ceramic lamp. The long curtains were drawn open and sunlight flooded the area.

All of the rooms were tastefully decorated, achieving a warm, pleasing appearance throughout. Shoshana showed me the bedroom available for my mother, the semi-private one at the back of the house. The door to a single occupancy room was open and I stopped, peered in, and wanted to scream, "Perfect. That's what I want." The monthly price was out of the question. But the airy shared room, with twin beds on each side, seemed lovely too. Just like the rest of the house, it was well-designed, color-coordinated, clean, and tidy.

The outside grounds clinched the deal for me. Large sliding glass doors led to an ample brick patio surrounded by well-tended shrubs, blossoming flower beds in a riot of colors, wicker lounge chairs and rockers with comfortable cushions, two bird baths, a large round wooden table surrounded by four chairs, and several end tables scattered about. There was even a small swimming pool that my mother couldn't possibly use, or see for that matter. I was enveloped in assorted fragrances, chattering birds, and the warmth of the Florida sun.

I estimated total costs: monthly facility fees, retaining Julie for four hours daily in the mornings, miscellaneous expenses. It was way too much. I resolved to do it. If the owners took such good care of the house, I reasoned to myself, they most likely would provide high quality care to mom. Or so I assumed in my delirium with the place. Whatever was I thinking? In the past I had always been guided by my father's axiom: if it seems too good to be true, it *is* too good to be true.

We walked to the dining room, where Shoshana spread out a bunch of forms on the long, rectangular mahogany table, and we began final negotiations. "Mom's a vegetarian," I told her for the third time. You're sure you can accommodate that." Now that I already decided to send my mother to this place, anxiety set in lest something went wrong. I held my breath.

"I'm a vegetarian myself," one of the two aides piped up from the kitchen. She walked into the room. "I'll prepare your mother special meals myself." I released a satisfied sigh.

"And Julie," I said. "She will be with my mother for a few hours every morning. To keep her company." Despite the expense, I just couldn't leave mom totally with strangers, at least initially.

"That's fine," Shoshana said. "But I assure you that your aide won't be necessary. We provide personalized attention to all of our residents." I sighed again.

She answered more questions. The place had a transportation service that would take Dottie to her physician at the Chen Center, even though she assured me that they had a highly competent doctor who routinely made his rounds at the house. He was also on call 24 hours a day. Physical therapists came directly to the facility as well and would work to get mom walking again. Shoshana would arrange for a wheelchair, a hospital bed, medications, and anything else mom needed. Medicare would pay for everything, she informed me.[1]

We went over the residency agreement, including expenses, in detail. There were some upfront charges that I had not anticipated, but by now I was committed. I wrote the check. Besides, I had to leave the day after tomorrow.

That evening I went through a few of mom's personal papers to take back to Pennsylvania with me. Strangely, I found burial arrangements among them. It appeared that a decade ago a door-to-door salesman had talked her into buying a pre-funded funeral for $4,000, paid off in $85 monthly increments over the course of six years. I stared at the document in disbelief, shaking my head. Ouch! Yet another financial worry: when I moved her to Pennsylvania, we would lose the fully-paid contract. More expenses. Ka-ching!

I decided to clean out her apartment at a later date since there was just too much to do before I left. In any case, I was not ready to let go of it—what if my mother miraculously rallied? I would keep paying the rent until then. Ka-ching!

The next day turned out to be a disaster. Rosalia had promised me that she would arrange for a transportation service to take mom and me to Miriam's Place early in the morning. The nursing home aides had Dottie dressed and ready to go at 8:00 a.m., a half hour before the van was supposed to arrive. We waited. "Soon," Rosalia said, two hours later. It was 11:00, then 12:00, 1:00, 2:00, 3:00. Rosalia kept telling us to have patience. Mom was exhausted and confused, while I fumed. Rosalia waved me off. She was always on the phone. At 4:00 p.m. I charged up the hall, yet again, to her office. The door was locked. Rosalia had gone home. When the van finally arrived the next day, Julie and mom had to make their way to Miriam's Place without me.

&.

Julie brought Dottie's belongings over to the assisted-living facility bit-by-bit, but there wasn't enough room for too many things. Soon she was more or less settled in. However, I sensed that something was wrong almost immediately. Whenever I asked mom if she was enjoying the sunshine, she told me that she hadn't gone outside that day.

When I questioned Julie, she said that it was too hard to get the wheel-chair out the door and the aides wouldn't help her. She murmured, "I tink da gartins fuh visitahs only." A few days later Julie reported, "Da fut no goot. Mom don eat."

I gradually learned that the aides weren't helping my mother walk any-where, not even to the bathroom. The place regarded her as an "Assist 2," which meant that mom required two people for support, and Shoshana was unwilling to provide that much assistance. She wasn't receiving any physical therapy either, despite the fact that it was supposed to be continued at the facility. At least that is what I had been told by Rosalia when she discharged mom from the nursing home.

"Place no goot," Julie said after I questioned her about my mother's care. Apparently Julie was giving mom a sponge bath every morning because the aides weren't showering her. Just as serious, Julie found her lying in a dripping wet diaper in the mornings because nobody would help her to the bathroom or even change it during the evening. I had been promised night care. I also gathered, from our phone calls, that mom was languishing all afternoon, when Julie wasn't there. It became evident as well that the assisted-living facility was resisting Julie's attempts to take my mother to her doctor appointments at the Chen Medical Center. Shoshana kept insisting to me that she should use their physician instead.

Two weeks after my mother had moved into Miriam's Place I received a call from Shoshana to let me know that Dottie was in the emergency room. She had been acting strangely, the administrator said, so their aide called 911. Most likely it was a urinary tract infection, although I never managed to obtain a precise diagnosis from anyone. Mom returned to Miriam's Place, with a prescription for antibiotics, before I could fax the hospital my Durable Power of Attorney document. Without it, the ER wouldn't give me any information about her condition. Indeed, they wouldn't even tell me that she was there. Julie, as usual, had stayed with her.

A short while later I received another one of those dreaded phone calls. Dorothy Katz had been sent to the ER for a second time and, after nine hours, was admitted to the hospital. It took an additional five hours to find an available bed. Naturally, Julie was with her the entire time. Nevertheless, it became increasingly obvious that although she was lending a hand willingly, and I always paid her for any extra time, Julie was sustaining too much of the burden. She never complained but sounded exhausted.

Julie attempted to keep me informed but the hospital personnel would not tell her anything, even though I gave them permission to do so. And, predictably, I couldn't get much information either. Whenever I called, her attending nurse was either busy with other patients, had just arrived on the shift, or was ready to depart. My frustration transformed into panic as I pieced together some of the details of my mother's condition. It was clearly more serious than last time. Not only did she have a UTI but they were administering antibiotics intravenously. She was hooked up to other solutions, although nobody would tell me exactly what they were or why she needed them. Mom also was undergoing oxygen therapy again. I learned, too, that she had been seriously dehydrated when she arrived in the ER.

Once more, mom could not communicate with me. She was incoherent but at least this time I knew why. The long-distance situation, even for the short term, clearly had become untenable.

❧

My cell phone rang and I recoiled. What now? I didn't even want to answer but instinctively pushed the button. It was the hospital's social worker, Marilyn, who needed permission from me to discharge Dottie to a rehabilitation facility.

"I don't want her going to a nursing home," I said. "Please send her back to Miriam's Place where she now lives."

"We can't do that," she said. "Your mother requires daily antibiotic injections."

"Why can't a nurse give them to her there? Medicare funds home health services."

"The assisted-living facility is not licensed to do that. And your mother can't walk. She needs physical therapy." I could hear the growing impatience in Marilyn's voice.

I was caught off guard. The last time I had authorized a rehabilitation facility my mother had lashed out at me, enraged. "You'll have to get the approval from my mother, not me," I said at length.

Mom acquiesced, although I was not entirely convinced that she knew what she was agreeing to.

The social worker had already picked out a place, but I was having none of that. I told her firmly that I'd call her back after checking out the "Nursing Home Compare" website. This time my mother was going to a five-star place. Little did I know!

Ultimately, I chose Memorial Manor, the most highly rated facility in the area. Its overall score was "Much Above Average." Pleased with myself, I telephoned Marilyn. She had to check with admissions. Two hours later she told me that the nursing home wouldn't accept my mother. It had something to do with her insurance. The news baffled me because Medicare Advantage had to cover post-acute care. After much persistence I convinced her to let me call one of Memorial Manor's social workers myself. She gave me a name, Janine, and her direct number. But there had been a shift change and a new social worker answered the phone. Someone else also had replaced Marilyn at the hospital. Once more I was drowning in social workers as I struggled to keep all of their names straight.

I wasted the entire next day in phone conversations with Tisha and Nancy, and then Nina and Stacy, in a vain attempt to convince someone that Memorial Manor should admit my mother. I actually pleaded, dispensing with any pride. The facility that the hospital had picked out, Hollywood Hills Rehabilitation Center, had a "Much Below Average" overall rating and I cringed at the thought of mom going there. The assorted social workers at my chosen nursing home, Memorial Manor, remained firm. "Your mother may have to be in a facility for a while," one of them said. "We can't be sure that her insurance will pay for that long." She had checked out my mother's situation. Apparently, a "Much Above Average" facility could pick and choose its customers and Humana Advantage clients were not at the top of their list.

I was warned that time was running out for finding a nursing home placement. Most likely mom had exhausted her allowable Medicare days and, as usual, it was the discharge planner's job to force her out. Marilyn (I think it was her) puts it differently. "Your mother is ready for a more appropriate placement."

After going back to the drawing board and failing to find a "decent" rehab facility that would actually take my mother, I was forced to capitulate. Hollywood Hills did have three stars for staffing and quality measures I reassured myself. And, it would only be for a short time, until she could return to Miriam's Place, in itself a dubious goal.

Two weeks later Shoshana called me again. I could prevent another round of hospitalization to nursing home routine, she told me, if I put my mother in hospice care. Miriam's Place had an approved program and she could arrange everything.

"Is my mother dying?" I asked, my voice quaking.

"No," she said. "But she can be in hospice anyway."

The news both alarmed and perplexed me. "I thought hospice was only for people who are dying."

"We can set it up here," she said again. "We have several residents in hospice." She sounded confident.

Shoshana briefly explained what Miriam's Place could do for my mother as a hospice patient but never clarified how she would qualify for such care without having a terminal illness. The administrator assured me that it would be "better" for mom and more "convenient" for me. Dottie would be safely ensconced in the assisted-living facility, presumably in bed.

"We'll be able to make your mother more comfortable," Shoshana said. "Our doctor can prescribe medicines for any pain. Outside nurses will come in to attend to her needs." She paused for a moment and said, as if clinching the deal, "And you will be less anxious."

I listened, astounded. It sounded as though the major beneficiaries would be Shoshana and her mother (the proprietor), who would not only have an easier time caring for Dottie but also would receive extra income from Medicare. Were they con artists? What had I done?

A Place in Pennsylvania

Dorothy Katz was unceremoniously sent to Hollywood Hills Rehabilitation Center for post-acute care. I tried to keep apprised of her condition but, predictably, they wouldn't tell Julie anything and, for the most part, mom was incommunicative. I only knew that she was getting antibiotic injections for a urinary tract infection. The facility's caseworker wouldn't talk to me without the "Power of Attorney" document.

At various times, I attempted to reach my mother's several nurses at the facility—Raina, Wanda, and others (as usual, I lost track of their names)—anyone who was willing to keep me posted. They threw out incomprehensible terms (at least to me) like septicemia, coagulopathy, congestive heart failure. I asked whoever was at the other end of the line to spell them out so I could look them up. Each disorder sounded serious, even life threatening. Dottie also had a lower than normal amount of potassium in her blood. It was unnerving but nobody would explain what was going on. The nurses were unavailable, preoccupied, or abrupt.

Nonetheless, nurses at the facility telephoned periodically to advise me that my mother had a tear on her arm, a nick on her leg, a scratch on her thigh. These family calls were obligatory—federally required—even though I couldn't gain access to the more vital information about mom's medical issues.

Long-distance caregiving wasn't even vaguely workable. I purchased two airline tickets, this time to take my mother back to Pennsylvania with me. My daughter Alix, seven months pregnant, decided to join me.

❧

An onslaught of emotions collided with practical realities as I slowly grasped the full extent of what a move to Pennsylvania would entail. I experienced alternating waves of fear, uncertainty, and agitation that drained me. Could I really relinquish my mother's apartment? That seemed too final. What if she fully recovered? That, of course, was irrational but the thought lingered anyway. Maybe we should still wait until spring, only four months away. The weather in Pennsylvania was so bitter right now. And Julie? What is my mother going to do without her aide, her best friend, when we left? Earlier concerns flooded back, like an overloaded river during a hurricane. Could I really tear mom away from Dr. Ana and the Chen Center specialists? Then panic set in. What if the Medicare Advantage plan in Florida dropped her before a new insurance policy could be secured? What if she required emergency care in the interim? What about her medications and eyedrops?

Selfish fears emerged, percolating through the anxieties about my mother. What was going to happen to me? Were my days going to be so intertwined with hers that I would have no life of my own? Was my writing career over? Was I going to become a substitute for Julie? I envisioned days on end consumed with caring for mom, punctuated by doctor appointments. My Pollyanna mother, whose cup was always half full, never planned for tomorrow, much less her old age. I railed at her irresponsibility, at weighing me down, knowing perfectly well that none of this was her fault.

꙼

As my to-do list was gradually put together, I became more detached and "Go" mode took over. The question of where mom would live was the top priority. I pulled out my copious stack of "mom" folders and looked again at the residential options in my area. The administrator/owner at the Walden 11 assisted-living facility, my preferred place, had called a while back to let me know that he had a spot for her but we had not been ready then. It was too late now, in any case. One of the facility's main criteria was mobility—residents had to be capable of transferring and moving about the home on their own. At this point Dottie was considered a two-person assist, thereby disqualifying her. She also required too much help with bathing, eating, and other basic needs. I wistfully fingered the brochure.

Given mom's current condition there were only two affordable alternatives and I made an appointment to tour both places. The first was a chain of assisted-living facilities in the region, Alexandria Manor. They had advertised their Bath location, near my home, as having advanced care options that seemed appropriate for mom. The cost, which didn't include adult diapers, personal supplies, and other items, was far more than Dottie's income and even beyond my budgeted supplement but at the moment I was desperate.

I drove up to the building and glanced around. There was no grass, trees, or place to sit outside, except for a small balcony on the second floor. The grounds were covered in concrete, like a shopping center parking lot. I walked in and wrinkled my nose at the same foul-smelling odors that had pervaded the first nursing home in Florida. Although the Alexandria Manor website boasted that "All of our homes are modern, elegant and most important homelike," the facility was rather grungy. Still, having been previously fooled by the glossy environment at Miriam's Place in Florida, I resolved to give it a chance. The tour only reinforced my distaste. There was clearly a dearth of assistance for disabled residents, the food appeared pasty, wheelchairs lined the walls with half-asleep inhabitants, and the overall atmosphere seemed gloomy. I left, disheartened.

Gracedale Nursing Home, the next stop, had been only a back-up, a place to put my mother if all else failed. And now, it seemed, the county facility was my last and possibly only prospect. Apprehensively, I maneuvered my car around the sprawling complex of red brick buildings and parked near the massive main unit that towered over the rest. Since my appointment was not for another half hour, I decided to take my own tour.

The glass doors to the lobby slid open and, much to my relief, there weren't any noxious smells. I randomly rode the elevator to the sixth floor and peeked around the corner. The room was brightly lit, with sunlight streaming in from huge windows covering almost an entire wall. Someone at the nursing station glanced at me and smiled. "Can I help you?"

I was feeling a bit sheepish, unsure of whether they allowed visitors to wander around. "I'm thinking about placing my mother here," I blurted out, adding, "I want to see if it's okay." Despite my sixty-seven years, I sounded like a whimpering child.

The woman's eyes were kind. "It's a good place," she said. "My own mother resided here for several years."

Another nurse had been listening to our conversation. "I'd bring my parents here too," she said. "Many residents are relatives of people who work at Gracedale."

The first nurse took my arm and steered me down the hall. "Let's take a look," she said.

People were bustling around. A congenial-appearing man in a blue T-shirt pushed a tall silver food cart past us, leaving appetizing whiffs of lunch in its wake. Utility carts of varying sizes, carrying adult diapers, bibs, assorted lotions, cups, straws, coffee urns, napkins, boxes, and other miscellaneous items, were scattered about. Two people in yellow were mopping the floor, carefully placing "slippery" signs near the wet spots. A resident in a motorized wheelchair whizzed by. Aides in many-hued scrub shirts and pants were propelling wheelchairs, carrying trays, inputting data on computers, all with a seeming sense of purpose. It was a colorful, vibrant environment that lifted my spirits.

Then, we entered one of the residents' sleeping quarters and my whole body tightened in disappointment. It was a relatively large room but it was curtained off into four small separate areas, as in a hospital. Despite the outsized windows the room was shut off from much of the light by one of the partitions. Two others were partially open, each revealing a hospital bed and basic furniture squeezed tightly together. In the first space, a woman was sitting in her wheelchair half-watching a barely audible TV. There were no showers or toilets in the room. I burst into tears.

❧

As I headed, with hesitant steps, to the social services building for my appointment with Maggie, the admissions officer, I felt even more reluctant to place mom here. My mind churned with visions of Dorothy Katz living with three strangers, feeling demeaned and betrayed. She'd always had an independent, solitary nature, certainly more extreme than most people. As a married adult, she had kept her social world small, surrounding herself mostly with relatives. Mom's only real friends had been her four sisters. She especially savored time spent alone, often impressing on me how much she enjoyed her own company. It was most likely a defense mechanism but, still, could she endure a life with no privacy at all? A cubbyhole surrounded by a curtain for personal space?

Taking a few moments outside the office door, I convinced myself that mom's stay at Gracedale would be temporary, an emergency placement to provide us with more time to assess the situation. Perhaps her abilities would improve with more occupational and physical therapy, services that I intended to secure for her. If she regained her mobility she could move to Walden 11. I made a mental note to call the assisted-living facility and put her back on the waiting list.

My heart felt heavy as I filled out the over thirty pages of screening questions and consent forms in Gracedale's admissions packet. I granted permission to provide vaccines, cut Dottie's hair, administer medical and dental care, repair personal property (at a charge), move mom to another room, if necessary, change her official address, and have the place handle her personal funds. I also agreed to a long list of policies and regulations, most of which I barely read. My mother's monthly Social Security checks were assigned directly to Gracedale. The last signature gave me pause as I could foresee endless, frustrating phone calls to the Social Security Administration when we had to reclaim the benefits for Walden 11. Mom would not be residing at the county nursing home for long.

I signed financial responsibility papers too, unsure as to what that signified. Mom had not yet applied for Medicaid. If they turned her down would I be liable for the fees, which totaled slightly over $8,000 a month, or $98,500 a year? These charges were way higher than I had envisioned for a government-run facility and certainly beyond my ability to pay. Maggie assured me, given Dottie's income, that Medicaid would cover all of the charges.[1]

The admissions officer also told me, much to my relief, that mom would become a resident of Pennsylvania immediately—there was no waiting period. But what if she was deemed ineligible for some other reason? Flickers of doubt tugged at me.

With a smile that lingered as though she meant it, Maggie handed me a thirty-page "Welcome to Gracedale" brochure, and a Medicaid application, both of which I tucked into my briefcase. I promised to fax certain documents to her, along with medical information from Dottie's physician in Florida. The admission's officer informed me that although the facility was currently at full capacity, she expected at least one opening within the next few days. She'd call me.

Next on my list were the arrangements for getting my mother to Pennsylvania and closing up her apartment. My first concern was transportation. How was I going to take her to and from the airports? If she couldn't walk, how would she board the plane? My mother now weighed roughly 190 pounds. As I began the series of phone calls I braced myself for the inevitable frustrating chain of customer agents, transfers, disconnections, holds, irritating Muzak, and inane automatic apologies for keeping me waiting.

At United Airlines, the standard programmed voice urged me to use their website but, as usual, I stubbornly stayed on the line. In due course, an airlines representative answered, and transferred me to their disability desk. A seemingly understanding and knowledgeable woman verified that they had special equipment and assistance for wheelchair-bound customers. She would put a note on my reservation indicating that mom needed help.

Transportation to and from airports was my next challenge. Since it was possible that mom's Medicare Advantage insurance might pay for the Florida segment, I telephoned the appropriate department. The company's agents would only talk to the beneficiary so, frustrated and pressed for time, I pretended to be Dorothy Katz. Even so, there was the usual ritual of "security" questions, answering machines, and holds. After a few days, one of Humana's go-to persons for transportation actually picked up the phone. She promised to check out the situation and call me back. I never heard from her again. Attempts to contact her only resulted in more answering machines and holds.

I next googled "wheelchair accessible taxis," winnowed out what appeared to be credible options and commenced with yet another succession of exasperating phone calls. Apparently these companies weren't allowed to pick up nursing home patients without the authorization of the facility. My approval, despite having Power of Attorney, was not good enough. The reasoning behind this regulation eluded me. Visualizing the maddening struggle that would be entailed in obtaining consent from Hollywood Hills, I kept telephoning places until, eventually, one of them agreed to transport us.

The second half of the journey, the long trip from Newark airport to Gracedale, turned out to be the most troublesome. Nobody at any of the car services in the area seemed to know whether they could take passengers such a long distance or across state lines. They'd get back to me. Yeah, right. With much perseverance, I located a limousine that had a Newark to Nazareth route. Unfortunately, it couldn't accommodate a wheelchair. I almost gave up. Several days later I scored a success and grabbed it, not even asking about the price.

A thought nagged at me. What if my mother couldn't fly at all? Julie had told me that she was connected to an oxygen tank again at the nursing home. Back to the drawing board for fallbacks. I entered "long distance wheelchair transportation" into the search engine and was inundated with responses. More phone calls. More quotes. The 1,250 mile trip From Florida to Nazareth, Pennsylvania, would take from twenty-four to seventy-two hours, depending on the number of drivers, and the price ranged from $4,950 to $6,300. I chose a company and wrote its number down in my spiral notebook, which now contained ten pages of information. Just in case. By now I didn't even pretend to consider the cost of anything.

Then there was the issue of transporting my mother's possessions, and I procured a list of long-distance moving vans from the Internet. None of them would give me an estimate until I completed an online form, with detailed information on what we would be sending. For two nights I fell asleep counting furniture, appliances, dishes, plants, bedding, and boxes. I filled out several questionnaires. What a mistake! I received a flood of e-mails and phone messages on my answering machine. Unlike my earlier experiences, these firms were determined to make contact with prospective clients.

I became obsessed with other particulars, all of which made their way into the spiral notebook. I wrote down locations near my mother's apartment building for buying packing boxes and tape, contacts for businesses that cleared out dwellings (with names like "Got Junk" and "Mr. Trashman"), and cleaning services. For an unknown reason, I didn't want to leave my mother's apartment of nearly thirty-five years grimy.

My to-do list shrank but I still had to sign mom up for a Part D Medicare Prescription Plan and complete the Medicaid application. Timing was of utmost importance. I had touched base with a Humana representative who had warned me about gaps in coverage. As soon as Dottie was insured in Pennsylvania, she would be automatically dropped from the Medicare Advantage plan in Florida. But Medicaid coverage would only begin at the first of the month. My head swam with visions of mom requiring emergency medical care but having no insurance. I decided to continue with the current Florida policy until Medicaid took effect, unsure of whether it would protect her during the interim.

Periodically I recalculated the price tag of home care, second-guessing my decision to place mom in the nursing home. It was a senseless attempt to assuage my conscience, temper the self-reproach. The twenty-four hours of care my mother would need was obviously unaffordable for us. Besides, the complications of bringing her into my house were insurmountable. How would I manage the heavy lifting? At this point, she was dead weight. Mom required too much turning, transferring, and changing of wet diapers. There were also constant medicines and eyedrops to dispense and untold doctor appointments. "It's impossible," I whispered to no one in particular. "It would suck everything out of me. There would be nothing left to love her with." I was now worked up, flustered. "We would end up hating each other."

These hectic weeks of preparation took a toll on me and affected my work and personal life even more than usual. In between the unending phone calls I taught classes, met with students, graded papers, attended assorted committee meetings, and dealt with various other obligations. I performed a few tasks around the house, although George did all of the shopping and cooking. My half-hearted struggle to get to the gym had long been abandoned and, eating insatiably, I put on not a few pounds. I feigned full attention to everyone, including my husband, as my mind focused on my mother's seemingly infinite needs. He knew. I wasn't even able to immerse myself fully in the wonders of my daughter's pregnancy as she forwarded daily updates on my unborn grandson's development. She knew, too.

10

Navigating Our Way Home

Alix and I linked up at the Ft. Lauderdale airport's rental car plaza, both of us weary from our trip. I observed her pregnant figure with a mixture of reverence and concern. Had the plane ride been too taxing for her? Should she have been talked out of coming? My daughter's welcoming smile and affectionate embrace mollified my apprehension. She had a way of doing that.

We headed toward the minivan, chosen in case we had to haul several of Dottie's suitcases back to the airport by ourselves. For a moment I put the impending errands out of my mind and breathed in the balmy air. My reluctance to surrender the last days of the school break to this move had been tempered by the bitter January winds I left behind in Pennsylvania. As with Dottie, my body had been rebelling against the cold ever since my sixty-fifth birthday, three years ago.

It was too late in the evening to visit mom at the Hollywood Hills Rehabilitation Center so we drove straight to her apartment. It appeared the same as always but this time I was more aware of every item that had to be packed, discarded, given away. My nighttime inventories had not done justice to the extent of the job ahead of us. I was revved up and began the sorting; Alix fell asleep.

§

I was guarded as we entered Hollywood Hills Rehabilitation Center, brooding over its low rating on "Nursing Home Compare." My fears were more than justified: the rank odor was worse than the previous nursing home. The smell of sour urine and fecal matter was far stronger as was the attempt to conceal it with disinfectants, ammonia, and chlorine. As we walked down the long hall, the stench coming out of certain rooms was particularly nasty.

Her personal area was slightly larger than that of the previous place—at least you could maneuver the wheelchair into the hall without bumping into objects. Mostly everything else in the room was a mirror image of it, however: a nondescript dresser, nightstand, high but cramped closet (holding mom's T-shirts, shorts, and sweatshirts, along with a wash basin, bedding, and bedpan) and a bed table. There was sufficient space for two folding chairs, a welcome addition. We'd probably need them since Julie would be with mom for her usual hours—no vacation for her this time!

The walls were a faded peach color, with slightly darker—almost salmon—drapes and white aluminum blinds on the windows. The dreary ambience was somewhat ameliorated by the rays of sun flooding the room—Julie kept the dusty blinds pulled up and the dingy curtains drawn back.

Characteristically, cubicle track curtains separated my mother from her roommate, an emaciated woman who looked like a stick figure in the game of hangman. During the six days Alix and I were there Mary mostly lay in bed, curled up on her side in a fetal position. Sometimes she sat in her wheelchair, slouched over. The aides would set down trays of food on her table but I don't remember anyone feeding her, or Mary eating at all for that matter. Nonetheless, the television was always on, blaring. We periodically smiled at her but she avoided any eye contact.

To my dismay, the aides treated mom like an inert object and again relegated her to a bedpan. As she had experienced previously, the charge nurse apparently decided that it was too time-consuming for anybody to walk her to the toilet, a task that Julie could no longer perform on her own. Often they just left her to urinate and defecate in her diaper, letting the discharge spill out onto the bed's protective pads. They didn't shower her either. My mother received a daily sponge bath, but only because Julie was willing to do the job.

The aides, once again, were transferring mom to her wheelchair by a sling and Hoyer Lift. As with the previous facility, they even begrudged this effort to get her out of bed, but we insisted. I suspected that mom had remained in bed for most of the last three weeks. Even though Julie deeply cared about Dottie's well-being, she wasn't very assertive.

The nursing home staff disregarded her, in any case. In fact, everyone at the facility treated Julie badly, almost like a servant. She had been told in no uncertain terms not to park in the visitor's lot and had been trudging several blocks every day, lugging mom's belongings. As usual, she laundered Dottie's clothing, sure that the nursing home would ruin everything. Julie also carried a shopping bag of lotions, powder, and other paraphernalia back and forth, protecting them from what she viewed as "thieving aides." She didn't approve of this place either.

The aides here were as indifferent—and surly—as in Hillcrest nursing home. They chattered to each other, mostly in their native language, above the residents' heads. The patients appeared to be objects to them, people to maintain in stasis rather than to facilitate recovery or ease their discomfort. It was as though they were minding a cemetery rather than tending to breathing human beings. Hollywood Hills was just as understaffed as the previous place and the workers most likely as underpaid, surely exacerbating if not triggering their attitude in the first place.

The evening meal food trays, along with any remains, were frequently left overnight on the bed table, tucked into a corner of the room. One morning we found hordes of fruit flies buzzing around. At another time, an attendant walked into the room chomping on an apple, juices dripping down her fingers. Alix and I exchanged disgusted glances as she periodically licked them while attending to mom. I even observed an aide pushing a man in his wheelchair down the hall as urine steadily dripped onto the floor. None of the staff appeared to notice.

Hollywood Hills earned its Nursing Home Compare "below average" reputation in other ways, including meals. We looked on with incredulity as a dry, unappetizing piece of tilapia arrived on mom's plate for every lunch and dinner meal, three days in a row. It was accompanied with a mound of mashed potatoes and bland, overcooked vegetables that alternated among string beans, peas, and corn. A piece of dry bread, a pat of butter, and a chocolate chip cookie, wrapped in plastic, finished off the tasteless, repetitive menu. At least this facility served protein twice a day.

Breakfast was equally unpalatable, mostly mush with a piece of bread; the only available fresh fruit was bananas. The aides were sulky when we requested fresh cold water for mom; otherwise the same lidded Styrofoam cup, straw protruding, would never have been replenished.

We took my mother outside as best as we could, given that she was again tethered to an oxygen tank. As with the prior nursing home there weren't any automatic switches for the disabled, so it was difficult to get through the glass doors. This time, however, I had my daughter with me. The patio area was relatively small, with worn tables and chairs scattered about. There were ashtrays everywhere, most of them overflowing with butts; the stale smell of tobacco mixed with the humid Florida air. Aides frequently smoked in the alleyway or, at times, adjacent to the "no smoking" signs. Wafts of noxious fumes filled our nostrils.

Sitting on the patio with mom one day, Alix and I watched the activities director present a class on pruning plants to a group of inattentive residents in wheelchairs. The instructor was in her own world as she removed dead leaves and lovingly watered, fertilized, snipped, and cut the vegetation in her care. If only the nursing home would give that much attention to its frail inhabitants.

I thought about my mother's apartment overflowing with greenery. She had always had small plants lining her living room and bedroom window sills, with larger ones sitting on the floor, soaking up the Florida sun. Prior to losing her mobility, she too had watered, fertilized, snipped, and cut. Like my mother, they were now neglected, no longer thriving.

❧

We were mostly concerned, however, with Dottie's physical and mental condition. Why had she remained so seriously disabled? Mom was supposed to be receiving physical and occupational therapy—that's what Medicare was paying for. She wasn't in this place for long-term care. According to Hollywood Hill's website, its "Short-Term Rehabilitation Program uses a comprehensive, interdisciplinary team approach that places the patient and his or her family at the center of the treatment plan. The goal was to return patients to their homes where they can function as independently as possible." Yet, the facility had been keeping mom so sedentary that it was going to be quite challenging, if not impossible, for her to regain her mobility.

We needed answers so I headed for the rehab room. It was dark inside and the door was locked. I asked someone at the nursing station about the missing therapists. "There is no therapy on Saturday and Sunday," I was told. "Everyone is at home."

"Nobody's here?" I said. "My mother's need for therapy doesn't stop because it's a weekend." I could feel my anger rising.

"The staff deserves time for themselves and their families," she said, and turned back to her paperwork.

I couldn't leave it like that. Dottie should be receiving physical therapy on a daily basis. How many rehabilitation facilities close down for holidays and weekends? My mother was languishing in bed most days and received no restorative services at all on Saturday and Sunday. It didn't make sense to me.

Alix joined me and demanded that the nurse at the desk call the person supervising my mother's treatment. At least we could learn more about her condition. But she or nobody else had any idea of who was responsible for Dorothy Katz's therapy. Besides, the nurse informed us, she didn't have any phone numbers for anybody.

"No phone numbers?" I said. "You can never call the director of therapy. Or any of the therapists?"

"No phone numbers," she repeated.

As with the therapy room, the entire nursing home was eerily empty during weekends, beginning Friday afternoon. Other staffing seemed more pared down than usual as well. A limited number of aides scurried around and LPNs still dispensed medicine but everything else was at a standstill. There were no activities at all except for church.

I questioned the nurse about the lack of activities, the shortage of workers. "Weekends are for resting," she said. "The residents like to sleep in on Saturdays and Sundays." Yeah, right.

On Monday, Alix marched into the gym. None of the therapists knew anything about her grandmother and there were no files on her. "Dorothy Katz, Dorothy Katz," someone said, trying to remember my mother or where her records might be.

As they searched, a member of the staff walked up to Alix. "Hi, I'm Wendy," she said. "I worked with your grandmother. But we cut her therapy sessions short. She was not responding to any treatment."

My usually even-tempered daughter was having none of this. "I want my grandmother back in therapy, now," she said.

Wendy shrugged. "I have a full schedule today. You have no idea how many patients I have this week. I'll try to get to her on Wednesday."

Alix put her hands on her hip, defiantly. "You may have lots of patients but I only have one grandmother."

Dottie received another day of exercises before she left the facility for good.

※

Mom's mental condition, which fluctuated without warning, was even more troubling. At times she seemed like someone high on psychedelic drugs, as though she were having an out-of-body experience. She hallucinated. "I love watching those dogs and kittens play together," she told us. "Oh, look, one of the kittens is trying to run outside."

"Dogs and kittens?" I said. "Mom there aren't any animals in here."

She looked at me, her eyes glazed. "Well I can see them."

On another occasion, she started sobbing. "I want my mama. I want my mama." Calming her down was not easy. Indeed, she experienced extreme emotional states and cried a great deal.

She was also confused in other ways. I finally told her that she would be leaving soon for Pennsylvania. "Okay," she said cheerily. It was unclear if she even knew where she was at the moment.

"You're going to have to say goodbye to Julie," I added.

"Okay," she said.

"We'll be taking an airplane."

"Alright."

"We'll see you tomorrow," I said when Alix and I left for the day.

"Okay."

No matter what I told her during these delusionary periods she answered with a monosyllabic pleasantry. And, she never asked about her apartment that we were packing up. She was showing no awareness or even concern that she would soon relinquish the place that she had lived in for nearly thirty-five years, along with a lifetime of pictures and mementos.

Yet, she was lucid for short periods. And these times were just as worrisome. "I'm ready to die," she said. "I can feel my body shutting down."

Alix started to cry. "Grammy," she said. "I don't want you to die."

Her grandmother pleaded with her. "I want to die. Please let me die."

Alix put her arms around her. They were now both weeping. "But I'm not ready for you to die."

Mom seemed like a stranger to me. The optimistic person I had grown up with rarely shed tears. I used to grumble to my friends that I was raised by Pollyanna. She didn't like to have unpleasant thoughts and would gloss over disagreeable events. Dottie's glass had always been half full. Now she wanted to die? Was there a problem with her medications? Too high a dosage of her L-Dopa Parkinson's drug? Perhaps negative drug interactions? Nothing would have surprised me since the LPNs, too, appeared detached from their patients' needs.

Then there was the ongoing constipation that seemed to worsen every time Dottie entered a hospital or nursing home. Given her inadequate water and fiber intake and her sedentary daily life at Hollywood Hills, it wasn't surprising. Nevertheless, her dire abdominal pain distressed us. We were also alarmed by her severely swollen ankles, even though the doctor had prescribed Lasix to control endema. Just as disconcerting, her body was peppered with bed sores again. I needed to get my mother out of this place, fast!

ᡇ

Alix and I decided to take mom to Dr. Ana at the Chen Medical Center for a final checkup. It would also allow them to take leave of each other; my mother and her physician had developed a special connection. And this set off yet another skirmish.

"I'm taking my mother to her doctor?" I said to the charge nurse. "Could you please have her ready by 9 o'clock tomorrow morning?" I had already set a pick-up time with the Chen Center's van service.

"Our doctors can take care of any medical needs here," the nurse said.

"I'd like her prepared to leave at nine," I repeated, with an edge in my voice.

She attempted to discourage me, putting impediments in my way. Was she concerned that Dr. Ana would notice the nursing home's medical neglect? Or perhaps it was because of the additional work for them. Then again, maybe our family had ruffled their feathers too often. But I was adamant and Dottie kept her doctor's appointment. However, at this point mom was too disoriented to say a proper good-bye.

My battle with the charge nurse turned out to be relatively inconsequential compared to the looming full-scale war with the social workers. Three days before we were supposed to depart for Pennsylvania, mom's caseworker informed me that the nursing home was discharging Dottie the next morning. They were sending her back to Miriam's Place.

"She can't go back there," I said. "They don't have the capacity to care for her. Anyway, it'll be too disorienting for her to make so many moves in one week."

"There's nothing we can do," he said. "Her insurance won't pay for any more nursing home days."

My stomach was churning. A move back to the assisted-living facility would not only be hard on mom but would jettison my airport transportation plans.

"It makes no sense to send her back there for two days," I insisted.

"I'm sorry," the social worker said again. He didn't seem regretful at all. For him, it was just business as usual.

My irritation transformed into rage. Just two more days and we'd be gone. There was no question that my mother had to remain at Hollywood Hills for the time being. The social worker told me that the nursing home physician could possibly petition for an extension.

Miraculously, I actually reached the doctor and explained the situation to her. "It's only two more days," I said. "Please let my mother stay." I couldn't believe that I was pleading to let mom remain in this appalling place. We received the approval.

ঌ

The week was hugely stressful and draining. In-between stewing about mom's physical and mental well-being, Alix and I cleared out the apartment. Having been convinced by my cousins back home to unceremoniously toss as much as possible—that's the tack they took with their parents—I had decided against hiring a moving van. As I took stock of what we would have had to pack up and store in Pennsylvania, a sense of relief swept over me, like a caged bird who had suddenly been set free.

There were no heirlooms or valuables to worry about or siblings to take into account. Would Denise, Anne, and I have squabbled over the division of our mother's possessions, despite their lack of monetary value, as so many other families did? Would they have second-guessed every one of my decisions with regard to her belongings? Even though mom had never asked for anything, over the years I actually had bought much of the furniture and other belongings—couch, TV, VCR, DVD, desk, telephone answering machine, bookcases, even the car she had given away to Julie. Denise and Anne never had any money to spare. Regardless, my two sisters sat firmly on my shoulder, questioning my judgment on every detail of the move.

Alix and I worked together synergistically. We tried to be unsentimental in our sorting, to impassively throw away a lifetime of accumulations. Efficiency was the catchword—we had so few days to accomplish the overwhelming task. I had brought four extra-large black suitcases with me that must accommodate everything we carried home with us.

However, it was not that straightforward as I came across a certain piece of clothing here and an article there that reminded me of a special occasion that mom and I had shared together. The bathing suits actually brought tears to my eyes, despite my resolve, as did the bicycle helmet. I lovingly disentangled two large boxes full of senior Olympic medals—gold, silver, and bronze—for bicycling, basketball, and swimming. There were plaques and large trophies as well. These objects represented Dottie's authentic self, the strong, healthy woman who was my mother, Alix's grandmother.

What should we do with the multitude of stuffed animals mom had collected over the years—she had scattered these dusty large, medium, and miniature plush objects all over the place. I'd never quite understood her attachment to them but we picked out a few of her favorites and tucked them into a suitcase. I tied four of the tiniest ones to the luggage, for identification, as mom had always done over the years.

Books and magazines lined one of the bookshelves, long neglected on account of her blindness. They seemed easy to discard until I stumbled upon my own works on elder care that mom had always proudly shown to her every visitor. How much had I really understood about caring for a frail parent until now? Sighing heavily, I made a mental note to re-read them.

Alix's poetry and DVDs, prominently displayed, also couldn't be left behind. Despite the distance, Dorothy Katz had been a part of her granddaughter's successful career as a spoken-word artist. Indeed, mom's picture was spread over the back of one of the DVD jackets. Alix and her friends had always admired Dottie's open-minded view of the world, her strong sense of self.

We ripped down the photo collages covering every wall in the apartment, and dissembled them. Alix then collected the framed photographs strewn about the apartment, as well as the abundant photo albums stacked on another shelf. So many of the faces peering at us, some with grinning faces, others more somber, were now deceased: Mom's eight sisters and brothers, two daughters, husband, her own mother and father. Dottie had countless pictures of Alix and me, my twenty-two or so cousins and their families, and a few other people from the past. My daughter yearned to linger over them, but I sped her up.

I deposited selected snapshots into a suitcase and, with reluctance, tossed the albums out. There were just too many to take home with me. Besides, my mother's eyesight was now so poor she couldn't possibly ever look at them again. However, as soon as I turned my back, Alix surreptitiously retrieved several from the garbage container and sneaked them into a bag. And, just when we thought the job completed, I noticed that the low table we had recently cleaned off was actually a chest. We opened it up and my heart sank: inside were over thirty more photograph albums.

Mom also had boxes of personal papers. Dottie, who like me was not a hoarder, nonetheless had saved every single postcard, letter, and greeting card her children and grandchild ever sent her. There wasn't enough time to read the communications or even sort through them. In this instance I gave into sentimentality and packed everything up for home. I also slipped in a few useless gifts that my sisters and I had given mom over the decades. The four suitcases were now bulging. I groaned, mostly from weariness.

Black garbage bags piled up, ready to be thrown out. We loaded clothing, jewelry, and other items separately, for Goodwill. Furniture, small appliances, television, DVD, bedding—these we labeled for Julie. We told her that she could have anything she would like. She wanted them all.

The plants, badly withering, had to stay. The greenery had always added so much warmth to mom's apartment, to the houses I had grown up in. As adults, my sisters and I had shared exotic varieties with her, with each other. Without the moving van, they couldn't be taken back to Pennsylvania. I watered them anyway. Maybe I should have hired a truck after all.

We took a moment and looked around the now empty apartment. Stripped of nearly everything she owned, Dorothy Katz's existence had been reduced to bare essentials. I'd cleared out my own house on several occasions, relishing the opportunity to divest myself of unwanted odds and ends, duplicate items, outgrown clothing. It had always felt like a cleansing. At those times there was a sense of moving on to a new chapter in life. But this felt different. These were not my belongings. Who was I to decide what to dispose of or what's meaningful or not to someone else, even if it was my mother? And she was not facing new beginnings, only endings.

I still couldn't bear to hand in the keys, to release her home forever. It seemed too final. I unreasonably decided to keep paying the rent for a while.

❧

January 30, 2013. We were finally leaving, venturing forth on my carefully choreographed journey, like dancers keeping to the steps of a delicately arranged ballet. The composition would only work if all of its finely tuned movements were performed precisely. I had served as designer, director, and stage manager but had inadequate control over its final execution. And there were no rehearsals.

The opening act began precariously: Alix and I were so flustered the morning of our departure we got lost in the 6 a.m. darkness on our way to the nursing home. Luckily, our airport transportation waited for us and mom was dressed, ready to go. One of the aides, who was uncharacteristically cheerful, handed me two huge transparent bags filled with various doodad's—toothbrushes, towels, adult diapers, a bed pan, paper cups and the like. She had prepared them for the trip and seemed pleased with herself. Obviously they couldn't be taken on the airplane so I apologetically removed a few useful items and handed the bags back to her.

I embraced Alix good-bye. She was returning the rental car, and then heading straight to her own flight home to Massachusetts. She had not only been a good daughter, but also my lifeline, partner, and friend during this terrible week-long ordeal. "Thanks for everything, for being there for me," I said. My voice cracked with emotion.

She flung her arms around me again. "We were there for each other," she said.

I was now completely on my own. I had stuffed fifty, five dollar bills, in my wallet for tips, knowing that an inordinate amount of help would be required for this undertaking. At the curbside baggage check-in a sky cap grabbed our four huge, crammed suitcases, making a note of their extraordinary weight. I slipped him ten dollars. Another porter fetched mom, who was sitting obliviously in her wheelchair, and headed toward the security checkpoint, assuring me he would take care of everything. I scurried behind him, relieved.

Even though the security inspection went relatively smooth for me, it was a veritable nightmare for mom. A TSA official pushed her to an adjacent area and proceeded to screen her. He painstakingly covered every inch of her wheelchair with his handheld metal detector, attempting to penetrate every nook and cranny. The officer then inspected her entire body, starting at Dottie's head, working his way down to her toes. It went on for what seemed like forever but he eventually cleared her to move on. The United States was now fully protected against a potential granny terrorist.

The porter lived up to his promise and waited patiently throughout the process, periodically setting my mind at ease. He deposited us at our designated gate and, thanking him profusely, I handed him four of the five dollar bills. Act II successfully completed.

I looked up and Julie appeared, with a big grin on her face. However did she slip through security? I didn't ask.

"I say gootbi sweethot," she said, wrapping her arms tightly around my mother. She sat down next to her and held mom's hand. "I miss you dodee."

I bought everyone coffee and bagels. Julie looked as though she were going to cry as she eventually stood up to leave—she had a new client to look after. I slipped her four of the bills for airport parking expenses. We gave each other another round of hugs. As she departed, I felt a lingering sense of sadness in the air.

No more time for sentimentality. I had to concentrate on the next Act of the dance, actually getting mom on board the aircraft. The social workers at the nursing home had insisted that it would be unmanageable; their words suddenly unnerved me. I approached the attendant at the front counter and reminded her, for the second time, that we needed help getting on board. "I know," she said. "Assistance should be here soon." Her casual demeanor suggested that United Airlines had done this before. I flopped back into the seat next to mom's wheelchair.

Just as the boarding announcement for our flight blared over the loud-speakers, two tall, robust guys showed up. They, too, appeared unconcerned as they pushed mom to the gate. She was still passive, seemingly indifferent to the ordeal. After handing over our boarding passes, we headed down the jet way, the only ones embarking at this point. The two men paused for a moment to retrieve a special aisle wheelchair, and nonchalantly lifted mom into it. With another swift movement, they transferred her to the airline seat and buckled her in. Then it was all over, weeks of agonizing melted away, at least for now. It all happened so quickly, almost effortlessly. I gave each of the men six of the five dollar bills, although I was tempted to give them the rest of my bankroll.

Incredibly, despite her seriously weakened physical condition and the absence of an oxygen tank, my mother continued to take everything in stride. She had been compliant and uncomplaining the entire trip, easing the way for me. She didn't challenge any part of this grueling journey or, for that matter, the move to Pennsylvania itself. Was Dottie travelling willingly or was her resistance just worn down? I patted her hand gratefully and settled in for the four-hour flight to Newark. She slept the entire time but with heavily labored breathing. Was I taking her home with me to die?

We were nearing the finale. A sequence of complex steps still lay ahead of us but by now exhaustion had set in. I was on remote control, trusting that the rest of the dance had been choreographed sufficiently well. I depended on the remaining players to complete the performance.

And they did. Subsequent to landing, two sturdy men materialized and boosted mom into another aisle chair, rolled it to her awaiting folded wheel-chair, opened it up, and swept her into it. Twelve more five dollar bills. One of them took us to the baggage area where a porter gathered our luggage and transported it outside. After a few anxiety-ridden phone calls—our driver was lost at the airport—the wheelchair-accessible van arrived, as planned. We were ready to finish the last leg of our trip.

We arrived at Gracedale Nursing Home at 6:00 p.m. My husband George met us in the lobby and stayed with the suitcases while I took mom upstairs to her room. Two beaming aides and a nurse greeted us. "We've been waiting for you, Dorothy," one of them told her. "Let's get you settled in." The door of mom's four-person room already had her name added to the others.

I glanced at my mother, who was totally drained by now. It was unclear whether she was fully aware of the entire venture but she must have experienced such discomfort. She had been jostled, prodded, and swung about. Her adult diaper was soaking wet. Before departing, I asked her if she was alright and she said, "I'm good." We hugged each other hard and I headed home, too tired to hear the audience applause for a dance performance well done.

Excerpts from Dorothy Katz's Medical Records at Hollywood Hills Rehabilitation Center

Dorothy Katz's discharge papers from Hollywood Hills Rehabilitation Center related a story vastly at odds with the reality of her circumstances at the facility. In a nurse's "Brief Summary of Stay," it documented that she had received ongoing OT/PT services. Although Medicare Advantage presumably paid for them, in actual fact she had received hardly any of this desperately needed therapy. Just as disturbing was the "Final Summary of the Resident's Status," in which the therapist recorded that for both bed mobility and transfers, mom was a "Total Assist." The physician's final assessment was even more despairing, stating that "the Resident is "Chronic bed-ridden" (There could not have been any other outcome, given that my mother had received such limited therapy and was kept immobile most of the time at the facility).

As with Hillcrest, the human services personnel apparently had no awareness of mom's status and requirements, despite their reams of paperwork complying with federal regulations. The director wrote that my mother's vision "is adequate" (Huh?); her hearing "is adequate" (Really?); and she "is able to make needs known" (My mother had been in and out of delirium nearly the entire time). According to the activities director, "The resident has met her activity goal while here with us" (What activities? Did they mean her goal was to stay in bed or sit in her chair all day?)

It was also eye-opening to review the long list of medications that mom had been taking during her stay. Beyond her usual drugs for Parkinson's disease, glaucoma, and high blood pressure, the nursing home doctor had prescribed folic acid (for vitamin B9 deficiency); iron sulfate (for iron deficiency); Albuterol (for wheezing); Celexa (for depression); Lasix (for edema); Prilosec (for acid indigestion); Tramadol (for long-term pain); and Colace (for constipation). Except for the latter, Dottie had not experienced any of these disorders prior to entering Hollywood Hills. Were these recently acquired ailments nursing-home induced? Did the doctors at Hollywood Hills automatically prescribe certain medications to every patient because it was assumed that they would contract these conditions? Did the combination of so many carelessly dispensed medications cause adverse drug interactions, thereby contributing to mom's unstable emotional state, including the delusions? I'll never know.

11

Reports of Her Death
Are Greatly Exaggerated

She's in her wheelchair, eyes closed as usual. The tiny, natural white curls surrounding her face have been enhanced by a recent trim. Every six weeks I'm greeted with a fresh hairdo, courtesy of Gracedale's very capable beautician, neither solicited nor paid for by me. My mother looks so lovely, her wrinkled face untroubled. She appears a bit younger than her ninety years.

I briefly savor the moment before allowing reality to kick in. "Mom," I say, leaning in closely (the nurse hasn't yet inserted her hearing aids). "Are you awake?"

"Yes," she says. "I'm awake." She seems so tranquil.

"Then you have to open your eyes," I say, in a gentle but insisting voice. "People are going to think that you're always sleeping. Or, even worse, that you're not 'all there,' merely a vegetable."

Her lifeless, unseeing eyes pop open wide. There are remnants of mom's striking greenish brown irises that are now clouded over, milky-like. She stares uncertainly, almost like a frightened child.

"Hello world!" I say, impersonating her. "I'm really in here."

Instantly relaxing, she chuckles as she always does at these times. She's trying to please me by keeping her drooping eyelids from shutting again but they soon succumb. Mom seems unaware that she has lost the battle.

It's now been fifteen months since I brought her to Gracedale, a stretch of time that has been more like the thud and thump of bumper cars than the stormy, relentless roller coaster ride of earlier years. Nursing home life hasn't always been easy for either of us, to be sure, but by now we have

117

accommodated to its ebbs and flows. Dottie, in particular, has bowed grace-
fully to her new circumstances. In fact, she recently asked me to "take her
home" after a short stint in the cafeteria, where I often wheel her during
our daily visits. Startled, I soon grasped that she meant her room.

Whatever the shortcomings, this place has saved her life. Of that I am
certain. My mother came to Pennsylvania ready to die, organs shutting down,
and now she is not only perky but capable of shuffling down the corridor
for short periods each day. Subcontracted through a private firm, the physical
therapists at Gracedale are unrivaled. Despite the fact that mom had been
wheelchair-bound upon arrival, her first therapist, Amy, was as determined
as I to get her walking. Patient, dedicated, and skillful, Amy believed in
Dotty and her struggle to walk again. When mom was assigned to another
therapist, I initially sought to prevent the transfer but soon discovered that
the entire physical therapy staff is first-rate.

During hour-long sessions, sometimes lengthier, they strengthened her
arm and leg muscles with weights and bicycling until she could actually
get up and grab the walker, with limited help, on her own. I would watch
mom's advances with rapt attention, cooing and shouting encouragements
at her every achievement, no matter how miniscule.

"Faster, mom, faster," I would say, leaning in close to the exercise bike.
"I know you can do better than that." With a wink at the therapist I would
continue, "The race is on and your opponent is going to pass you. Faster,
faster." The needling often worked, sometimes it didn't.

After several months, when mom's progress was at a standstill, they were
forced to cut her off because of Medicare regulations.[1] I suspect Dottie's various therapists fudged the record a bit to keep her with them for as long as
they could. The termination required my signature, not so much of approval
but rather of acknowledgment. A well-dressed social worker with pen and
form in hand, who stopped by mom's room for my signature, was taken aback
by my refusal. "Your mother is no longer eligible for Medicare funding,"
she said through gritted teeth. "She is not making much headway anymore."

Medicare will pay for physical therapy only as long as the recipient is
improving. As a student of the program, I've known about these regulations
but had not realized how misguided and inflexible they were. I was incensed.
For me, maintaining mom's ability to walk seemed like progress enough. My
protest bought mom three more weeks of therapy before I had to capitulate
to the grim-faced social worker, with whom my future dealings have been
mercifully limited.

Nonetheless, Gracedale now provides mom with two restorative aides whose sole job is to take certain residents on daily treks down the hallway for exercise. Mom's main ones are enthusiastic and committed cheerleaders who have prodded Dorothy Katz to maintain her ambulatory abilities, however limited, even when she's hesitant to do so. As with the therapists, these "walkers" are enthusiastic and committed to their work.

People often deteriorate in nursing homes, as mom did in Florida. In contrast, she is physically and mentally thriving here to a large extent. The charge nurse on my mother's floor—Jean—contributes materially to her vastly improved health and well-being. Noticing straightaway that she was suffering from protein deficiency, a devastating condition that no one in Florida had detected, Jean added a life-saving ProSource Protein Supplement to her diet.

The charge nurse also ordered compression stockings, and later a full wrap, to control Dottie's immensely swollen ankles and feet, puffiness that stretched up the legs nearly to her knees. A few months later her limbs were back to normal. At night she sleeps with therapeutic air boots to reduce heel pressure and improve circulation. Aides weigh her every day to catch any signs of fluid retention, at which time they administer diuretics. Jean and the other nurses keep close watch on these developments, as they do with all of the residents' health issues.

Indeed, unlike the previous two nursing homes, everyone takes the care plan required by the federal government seriously. It's not only reviewed every three months but mom and I participate in the assessments. We sit at a large conference table, together with the charge nurse, dietician, social worker, activities director, and other personnel involved in Dottie's case. While these updates are thorough and instructive, it also provides me with an opportunity to question certain aspects of mom's care. I do so with restraint since it soon becomes clear that this should not be considered a medium for complaints.

During the first months at Gracedale, Dorothy Katz's recovery was slow, steady, and wondrous as her mind rallied and body mended. Even though they have oxygen available at her bedside, mom hasn't needed to use it. I can't help thinking about how she was constantly tethered to oxygen machines in the Florida facilities. There also had been the useless skinny pillows that the previous place begrudgingly placed under mom's legs at night. Bedpans are long gone as the aides painstakingly guide mom, using her newly acquired walker, to the bathroom. Gracedale's "Below Average" rating on the Medicare website is incongruous with the top-quality care they actually provide. The county facility has not only nursed my mother back to health but has allowed her to flourish to the best of her capabilities. At least until the first temporary setback.

§⁂

Four months after my mother arrived at Gracedale, on my first day off from visiting her, I'm blindsided by a phone call on the streets of New York City, where I am visiting museums with a long-term friend. My cell phone blasts its "jungle drum" tune, which is loud enough to be heard over honking cars and police sirens. Fully aware that the sound inside my jacket pocket portends trouble, I warily grope for the screeching object. Dottie is in Muhlenberg hospital[2] for a cough, "worsening shortness of breath," and "respiratory distress," possibly pneumonia. It is Wednesday.

That night I arrive at the hospital, uncertain of what to expect. The recently renovated main building is spacious and majestic, with an awe-inspiring entranceway that leads into a long, extended lobby. Sets of comfortable couches and chairs, scattered everywhere, are situated on glossy vinyl flooring. Along the length of the lounge is a fancy gift shop, well-stocked pharmacy, huge information desk and elaborate café with a salad buffet, deli, grilled entrees, pizza, panini, coffee, and exotic beverages. The high ceilings, along with large windows lining the wall on the opposite side, afford a sense of airiness and comfort.

The upstairs, where every patient resides in a single room with floor-to-ceiling windows, is equally commodious. Each of the several floors contains sizable spaces for lounging and reception areas, computers, conferences, and nurses' stations. As I exit the elevator on my mother's level, I encounter workers polishing floors, washing windows, and dusting lovely paintings. The place is spotless.

Yet my mother is drenched in urine. Her hospital gown, sheet, and everything else are sopping wet. Her adult diaper, at least what's left of it, is oozing yellowish liquid and excrement. Her dentures have been placed on the bathroom sink, without the requisite liquid to keep them from warping. Nearby are two large plastic bags, each filled with identical goodies—soap, lotions, shower caps, tooth paste, tooth brush, shampoo, deodorant, and sock slippers. Nothing has been unwrapped. Needless to say, I am taken aback. Apparently, the hospital has relatively few aides to care for patients' non-medical needs, especially older people as frail and dependent as Dorothy Katz.

A few days later, mom is moved to another floor where, the nurse informs me, she will receive more intense personal care. It doesn't turn out that way. Again, it's challenging to find anyone to change her adult diaper, or even clean her. I soon learn that the ratio of attendants to patients is roughly twelve to one. She receives yet another large plastic bag of toiletries; along with the other two, they sit lined up on a shelf.

The food situation is just plain bizarre, as though patients are at a club med. My blind, severely ill mother is supposed to order every meal from an elaborate menu with dizzying choices, ranging from hamburgers and fries to Mexican and Thai cuisine. There is no set meal time—you dial a certain phone number whenever you are hungry. During the few hours that I'm not at her side, mom doesn't receive anything to eat. The bottom line is that there is a dearth of help. When I protest that I can't stay in the hospital for every meal, one of the staff tells me, a bit condescendingly, that it's possible to order from home. I try that once, only to find a cup of melting ice cream sitting by itself on a small table. The actual lunch never arrives.

Nevertheless, I am mostly worried about her precarious health. She is not only mentally confused but her lungs crackle and wheeze as she breathes. Tethered again to an oxygen tank, hanging from the wall, she appears so vulnerable. It pierces me to hear the unremitting, heavy cough as tears roll down her contorted, ashen face. How did she get so sick in only one day?

It turns out that, in addition to pneumonia, mom has another urinary tract infection—at least that is what the first hospitalist reports to me on Thursday.[3] Even worse, a urine culture indicates that the disease is not only resistant to the medicine they have been administering to her, but is resistant to most available antibiotics. The doctor places her on intravenous drugs, although, according to him, the prognosis is uncertain.

There are more than a few questions for the physician swirling in my head, including whether they are treating her for the UTI, pneumonia, or both. There is also the larger issue of why he has so little confidence in the medication mom is now on. Are there alternatives? There is too much vagueness for my taste. By the time my concerns are clearly formulated, the doctor has disappeared.

The following day I meet with a second hospital doctor. It is surreal, and mostly passes in a blur. Without preliminaries, he advises me that because of her advanced age and frailty my mother will not survive what he diagnoses as congenital heart failure and worsening pneumonia. He does not mention the UTI. Dorothy Katz has only a few days to live, a few weeks at most. He proposes that the hospital administer more morphine to ease mom's pain and take her off the intravenous antibiotics, which will only prolong her agony. Shrouded in a smokescreen of ignorance, I approve both recommendations. The doctor also asks whether, if the situation warrants it, he should place a no-resuscitation memo on her chart. Not wanting my mother to suffer needlessly and aware of her views on the subject, I agree to that as well.

Dazed, I mechanically respond to his questions as though I am sleepwalking through someone else's bad dream. Over the last four months, mom's improvement had been so impressive that I am not prepared for the terminally ill diagnosis. It is too abrupt, like an unforeseen downpour on a perfectly clear day.

Without any further explanations, despite my feeble attempts to pry more information from him, the doctor moves on to his next patient. Does he assume that I'm not capable of grasping the complexity of my mother's medical condition? Or, as a hospitalist, does he have more cases than he can effectively cope with?

Now alone, I stagger across the hallway to a windowsill, sit down, and attempt to sort out what has happened. However, as the reality of his words finally register, a deep sadness sweeps over me and I break down sobbing. Not little whimpers but long, hard muffled moans of intense grief. After a short while, thoroughly depleted, I telephone Alix and several cousins, so that they can come to the hospital to say their good-byes to her.

Later on, a hospice professional shows up and provides me with details about end-of-life care for nearly an hour. I mostly remember his soothing words affirming the decisions I had already acceded to. He assures me that my mother will have an untroubled death under the auspices of hospice care and that an interdisciplinary team will focus on her comfort and assiduously manage any pain. Despite his painstaking description of alternative places for the palliative services, I nonetheless insist that she receive them at Gracedale.

On Saturday, Alix and infant Zinn—then only two months old—along with crowds of cousins, descend upon Pennsylvania, both comforting and overwhelming me. Mom is mostly oblivious to the attention, although she clearly appears pleased to put her arms around her great-grandson, the baby that she has anxiously awaited but hasn't met until today. *Now she can die in peace*, I think to myself.

Hospitals project an aura of confidence with their pristine façade and fancy, expensive medical equipment. As these electronic monitoring devices hum, whir, and whoosh, and nurses sit near screens with an impressive array of warning bells, there is a pretense of certitude everywhere. On Monday, I'm sitting next to mom, who is by now mostly sedated on morphine, when a third doctor strides in and, with a wave of her hand, dismisses the notion that Dorothy Katz is dying. "Your mother doesn't have pneumonia or a Urinary Tract Infection," she tells me, avoiding my stunned gaze. "She is recovering just fine." Without missing a beat, the doctor continues, "We're sending her back to the nursing home to continue her usual activities as soon as the hospital can sign her out."

When I question the doctor—about the morphine, antibiotics, and especially the hospice recommendation—she firmly states that my mother doesn't require any of the medications. And, she is not terminally ill. Mom is sent back to Gracedale the next day, leaving me and my family relieved but utterly perplexed.

Excerpts from Dorothy Katz's Medical Records at Lehigh Valley Hospital—Muhlenberg

Months later, still unsure of what occurred during my mother's hospital stay, I request the records. There is a $1.00 per page fee because Pennsylvania law allows the provider to charge for information that, in my view, rightly belongs to the patient. I pay, albeit grudgingly.

According to the documents, Dorothy Katz arrived at the ER on Wednesday, May 22, 2013, with "shortness of breath, "expiratory wheezes," and "trace upper airway sounds." However, she was in "no acute distress." Chest X-rays the next day indicated "no acute disease, despite the pneumonia. Her shortness of breath was described as "mild," with "no respiratory distress."

To be sure, there is nothing in the information I receive to show that my mother had any medical condition suggesting a terminal illness except for a consultation report from a nurse practitioner, whose specialty turns out to be in hospice work. And, he is the same hospice worker that I had talked to. His written comments signified that Dorothy Katz had "respiratory failure," a "UTI," and "Urosepsis" (a UTI infection that has spread into the bloodstream), and "multidrug resistant E. Coli in her urine." (I look this up and discovered that it's possible to carry E. Coli bacteria and the enzymes they produce and not be sick!). In his remarks, the nurse practitioner added, "In the context of functional decline, recurrent urinary tract infections and associated admissions it is recognized by the daughter and myself that the patient is nearing

death . . . *Prognosis appears poor, likely measured in terms of days to weeks. . . .*"
My mother's impending death doesn't seem to have a single verification except for his comments.

Just as shocking, he wrote, "Antibiotic use was discussed by the daughter as being a component that potentially prolongs the process of dying, and therefore is also prolonging and contributing to suffering in that manner. She would like to stop antibiotics in the coming 24 hours following visitation of the patient's great-grandson age 5 weeks whom she has not yet met." Not only did he assume that discontinuing the antibiotics could, and should, hasten mom's death (wrongly, it seems, given the evidence), but that I was actually the one who put the idea forward (wrong, again). He then recommended that Dorothy Katz's morphine be increased from every four hours to every two hours, presumably to ease her dying (which is obviously a bit premature!).

Is the nurse practitioner a quack? Given his specialty, does he have a predisposition toward premature hospice care, especially for the frail elderly? Why do the first two hospital doctors provide me with misinformation and such a dire prognosis? Were they reviewing someone else's medical record by mistake? As far as I can establish from the hospital records sent to me, there is a clear disjunction between what I was told and mom's actual medical condition. Indeed, her discharge papers specified that both her chest X-ray and urine analysis were negative and she should "Resume Normal Activity with Help."

There are other disturbing curiosities related to the reliability of the hospital and its doctors. For example, the ER notes read: "the patient has major depressive disorder." How had they possibly established such a serious mental condition on the first day of her arrival? There was no mention of a psychiatric evaluation.

In another instance, a nurse's clinical report suggested that my mother had an "ongoing problem of being bed-ridden" (wrong!); "wears glasses—this visual impairment is an ongoing problem" (mom is legally blind); and suffers from "cognitive impairment-senile dementia" (mom experiences lapses in memory but has never been diagnosed with senile dementia). Rather than "cognitive impairment-senile dementia," could my mother's disorientation and confusion have been hospital-acquired delirium, an affliction that affects roughly one-third of U.S. hospital patients over the age of seventy. It can be triggered by a variety of sources, including certain drugs, overmedication, infection, dehydration, poor nutrition, an imbalance of electrolytes, interrupted sleep, or a combination of these. There is no indication in the documentation that Dorothy Katz was assessed for that possibility, a treatable disorder.

Why I was led to believe that my mother was dying and required hospice care remains inexplicable. Certainly, her entire week-long stay at Lehigh Valley Hospital–Muhlenberg had been fraught with an amalgam of misdiagnoses, poor personal care, and inaccuracies.

A Good Enough Place

Because mom had been hospitalized for over three days, she is now entitled to Medicare-funded post-acute rehab services again at Gracedale, at least for the short term. It's the only beneficial outcome of the grim hospital experience and, since Dottie was bed-ridden the entire week, she needs the physical therapy sessions desperately. Once more, she progresses under the supervision of the facility's dedicated staff. Before long, she's able to shuffle, with the assistance of an aide and her walker, down the hall and to the bathroom.

We are both more at ease now that mom is safely ensconced in her living quarters at the nursing home. Since arriving at the place, she has remained in the original room, consisting of four occupants, due to my wariness of sabotaging what turned out to be a workable, if not ideal situation. In particular, the charge nurse sets high standards for patient care that possibly isn't duplicated on other units. She also sets an example for the LPNs and aides by participating in hands-on work herself, usually eschewed by RNs. It is not uncommon to observe Jean handing out lunch trays, or cleaning up afterwards, when she could have secluded herself behind locked glass doors at the nursing station.

My largely solitary mother, who can't actually see her three roommates, appears to appreciate the hustle and bustle of aides coming in and out, chatting idly to the residents and to each other. It provides her with a tad of stimulation in an otherwise monotonous daily existence. She has actually hinted as much, in her own enigmatic way.

While the other three inhabitants are not blind, they act, for the most part, as though there are invisible walls separating them. They rarely talk together and, indeed, hardly ever look at each other. Yet, the four roommates are all cognitively alert, to a large extent. I suppose their self-protective instincts have kicked in, the need to shield themselves from the reality of involuntary cohabitation with strangers.

Although it's a large room, each person has limited personal space that includes two small multi-colored dressers—bright green, red, yellow. On one of them sits my mother's nineteen-inch TV, the only size allowed, which is regularly turned on to her favorite 1950s music channel. On top of the other is an audio tape recorder (ordered by someone else and never used), her cell phone (which she can't reach or operate), and various odds and ends the aides throw on it. I diligently tidy up every day even though Dottie can't see the clutter. Two of the drawers are filled with assorted chocolate candies, along with face and hand creams and other personal items that I have brought in for her.

Given mom's size, the hospital-type beds are narrow, but serviceable. Instead of using bed rails to protect residents from falling, the aides lower the mattresses to the floor at night. Removable foam mats, placed around the sides, serve as a further safeguard. And, in case that isn't sufficient, for certain disoriented individuals there is an alarm bell that goes off if they attempt to get up on their own. During the first year, my mother benefited from this warning system, or so I was told. For me the bell was a nuisance since I inadvertently triggered it, and the connected call light, several times each morning. After the first few mishaps, one of the aides taught me how to turn it off. Much to my relief, her bed was eventually disconnected from the annoying alert but the beep-beep still emanates from other places in the room.

❧

Dottie's allotted area is adjacent to a row of five undersized closets, only large enough to accommodate two weeks' worth of clothing. Since I take mom's dirty garments home with me, something few relatives do, there is a big sign taped on hers that states in bold letters: "FAMILY DOES LAUNDRY." Whenever I catch sight of the notice, my lips curl into a smug smile. In my mind it announces that this daughter cares, truly cares, assuaging some lingering guilt about placing her in an institution. The fact of the matter is that the facility's laundry service does a respectable job, even if a few items are lost now and then.

As in other nursing homes, the room is equipped with hospital-style privacy curtains that are clipped to ceiling-mounted tracks. Each of the four look-alike polyester dividers, pinstriped in thin pale colors with white mesh on top, falls to a foot above the floor. When dressing residents, or tending to their other bodily needs, the aides diligently pull them around the bed, thereby providing at least a semblance of privacy. At times, especially during the night when mostly everyone's curtains are drawn and all of the blinds are down, the room has an eerie feel to it, like a creaky old haunted house.

At Gracedale, pictures of relatives tend to be more ubiquitous than actual visitors. Photographs are tacked on cork boards that hang on the wall over every person's dresser. On some they are crammed together, as though the family is desperately seeking to compensate for its absence. This seems to be the case with Betty, one of my mother's roommates, who even has a digital picture frame that repeatedly flashes at least one-hundred different snapshots of husband, children, and grandchildren at various stages of their lives. I've only seen her son and daughter visit twice, the former expressing surprise that his mother is confined to a wheelchair.

She is a sweet, gentle woman who never fails to thank the aides for bringing the food tray or anything else they do for her. Roughly eighty-five years old and extremely hard of hearing—even with hearing aids—Betty sits all day distractedly watching TV. Twice she has beckoned me over, wagging her index finger in a slow, deliberate way. "I watch you," she says, with an engaging smile. "You are so good to your mother." There is no trace of envy.

Betty weeps periodically, with soft whimpering sounds that carry across the room. Every so often I put my arms around her and whisper comforting inanities, but mostly I respect her personal space, which she seems to prefer. On one occasion, a social worker asks her why she cries so often. Betty looks up at her and says, "Because I'm here." Touché.[1]

In contrast, Margaret, the cranky eighty-year-old whose bed is closest to moms', never stops complaining. Demanding and bitter, she stays in bed until nearly noon, either working on puzzles or dozing. Marge can be downright nasty—abusive at times—to the aides, even ill-treating the most considerate of them. The only resident in the room requiring a Hoyer Lift, she often flails her arms, screaming obscenities, as they transfer her into the wheelchair. At breakfast, I've heard her shriek "bitch, you're a bitch," to whoever is attempting to adjust the bed to prevent her from choking on the food. From time to time, the aides retaliate in kind. In one instance, when Marge knocks over a large Styrofoam cup, spilling icy water all over the bed, her screeches are met with stony disregard. I understand.

Marge insists on keeping the blinds down over the three enormous picture windows that take up an entire wall. My yearning for mom's area to be bathed in light has triggered a tug-of-war between us. It's obviously more for my gratification since Dottie doesn't seem to know the difference. I've had to settle for two half-uncovered windows and a relatively dusky ambiance as a result. All the same, residents have control over the florescent lights over their bed and I always pull moms' to the highest intensity.

For the most part, I try to keep a distance from Marge, who consistently attempts to lure me into doing tasks for her. Once they are accomplished, she always has more chores for me. Not wanting to be callous, I remind myself that my mother is my main obligation, and her needs are overwhelming enough. Marge always responds to whatever I do for her with "God Bless." Despite her offensive behavior to everyone, she thinks of herself as a highly religious person, with crosses and pictures of Christ tacked all over her bulletin board. She often whispers prayers under her breath but, in spite of the regular Sunday and special holiday services held in the nursing home chapel, she never attends.

Occasionally, however, she displays small acts of kindness. When her daughter visits—which she does most Sundays for an hour or so—Marge offers mom pieces of whatever goodies she brings for her. Dottie, who has little relationship with her roommate, never refuses anything. And, Marge routinely announces to me, "You have such a good mother-daughter relationship." In this case there is envy in her voice.

I know the least about Terrie, especially her age (which appears to be no more than fifty), or why she is institutionalized. Guarding her privacy by wrapping the curtain around her bed whenever she can manage it from a seated position, she spends long stretches sleeping during the day. At other times, she scoots around the nursing home in her wheelchair, propelling it with her feet. In the spring, we often encounter her outside, cigarette in hand, and we exchange pleasantries. Unlike us, she avoids the out-of-doors in cold weather, lighting up instead in the smoking area on our floor. Her space in my mother's room has a lingering stale odor, like a dirty ashtray. I've seen an aide or two wrinkle their nose in distaste while making her bed.

Terrie has no visitors and, except for holiday handouts crafted by volunteers, she hasn't tacked anything on her bulletin board. Often garish and in bright colors, I, too, find uninvited Christmas bows, crayon drawings of pumpkins, hearts, leprechauns, bunnies, and even pictures of crosses and other Christian symbols pinned to moms'. Passover, Chanukah, Rosh Hashanah— these celebrations are unacknowledged. I keep meaning to cover mom's display board with pictures of her granddaughter and great-grandson but I'm neglectful.

❧

What makes Gracedale such a decent place for its frail residents, including my mother, is its overworked, underpaid but committed staff. Not everyone is dedicated and caring but, in my experience at the facility, even the most burned-out aides tend to their charges with steadfast professionalism. There are lapses, for sure, since it's exhausting, backbreaking work. The staff is immersed in a frenetic pace of washing, grooming, dressing, and toileting sometimes immobile bodies, hoisting them into wheelchairs (either mechanically or manually), fetching trays, and attending to insistent call buttons (aides must respond to them within fifteen minutes).

These same caregivers prepare beds (which can be soaked in urine), gather dirty clothing, hang up laundered garments, and take people to facility-based doctor appointments and activities. They are also expected to detect and report every rash, nick, sign of discomfort, or incipient malady (physically and emotionally) in each of their many charges for the day.

It is notable that most of them are even accommodating to demanding, rude, and insulting residents, though periodically I've witnessed some under-the-breath muttering. Sweet smiling old ladies in wheelchairs are not always what they seem. One in particular shares pleasantries with me but harasses the staff nonstop.

When the facility is especially short-staffed, it's up to the aides and LPNs to take up the slack. Their greater burdens at times include twelve-hour shifts. It's been an eye-opening experience to realize the extent of their obligation just to show up, regardless of weather conditions or personal troubles. Since residents can't take a day or two off from having their essential needs met, the staff must contend with heavy snowfalls, icy roads, and torrential rain. Sudden school closings or late openings and illness leave many workers scurrying to obtain care for their young children. And they are required to alternate holidays and weekends, irrespective of family commitments.

Even the best-intentioned among them, and I have met quite a few, are often undercut by the stark efficiency requirements of the facility. Since there are never sufficient aides on a floor, though the situation is seemingly better than in most other nursing homes, they are forced to adhere to a strict regimen. One morning, my mother, more radiant than usual, almost dancing in her wheelchair, informs me that she had the best shower ever. Usually, when asked about her regular Thursday morning bath, she says, "Oh, they just sprinkled me. I wish so much I could get a good scrub."

Showers have always been essential to Dottie's contentment so I am especially appreciative of the aide's extra effort and seek out her name. When I compliment the newly hired caregiver to the charge nurse, she sighs heavily. "Yeah, it took her so long that everybody else had to do the rest of her job. We can't allow that, sorry."

Although my role is to defend my mother, ensure that she is cared for properly, my endeavors are not always successful. I ask, at the regular family conference, if I could shower my mother myself. "Absolutely not," the social worker, charge nurse, and others in attendance at the meeting say, almost in unison. "Insurance rules." Mom is stuck with the quickie showers, though one of the aides still steals a bit more time with her, whenever possible.

Indeed, there is always some incident that affects Dottie's fragile well-being. At times they tumble out one after another. Early on, my attempts to safeguard her against every mishap proved ineffective at best, counterproductive at worst. With a forced smile I would knock at the charge nurse's open door and say, "Can I please speak to you for a moment."

Jean would look up from her paperwork. "What can I do for you?" Her eyes were often narrowed with weariness from her own unremitting load.

Words of some grievance or other would gush from my lips as I shifted back and forth on my feet. "Mom's favorite blanket is gone." "She can't eat because her dental bridge is cracked." "One of her hearing aids seems to be missing." "Her toenails may be infected." "Nobody is brushing her teeth." "What happened to one of her eye medications?" "Did anyone see a blue fleece jacket (that I forgot to send for labelling)?" I did my best to be non-confrontational but it became obvious that I was being viewed less as a devoted daughter than as a thorn in her side.

In subsequent months I learn to stick to the urgent issues and, later on, to let some of these slide. Missing articles are a fact of institutional life, and I've found that they can mysteriously reappear. Other concerns can also be shrugged off and, on occasion, laughed at—even when they're not particularly funny.

Not being able to shield mom from every problematic situation, I must defend her from the most serious ones. Pick and choose my fights and focus on one concern at a time. Such a tack is not easy since it's the accumulation of "little things" that often rattle me. But it's essential to be pushy only about vital issues.

And a urinary tract infection falls into that category. These days I am attuned to mom, and can sense when something is awry. There is a barely perceptible change in her responses and gestures that suggests the likely recurrence of the disorder. It reappears periodically and, despite the misgivings of nurse and doctor, at these times I risk being viewed as a pest. Every so often lab results confirm the infection, and, within a few days of antibiotics, her cognitive capacities are progressively restored.

I'm not always able to differentiate between inconsequential and essential matters, given that my mother's priorities differ from mine. For her, going to the bathroom, on demand, ranks in the uppermost category. At ill-chosen moments, face scrunched into a pained expression, she blurts out: "I gotta go. I gotta go." Or, "Oh, oh, oh, a doodie is coming." Sometimes a simple cry, "Bathroom!"

The urgency in her voice is often met by a roll of my eyes. It could be during mealtime, when the attendants are especially busy, just after we arrive outside the building, or in the middle of an elevator ride. Anywhere, any time. Back on her floor, I look around us. The place is humming with activity. Aides are never simply waiting around, at the ready, for mom's sudden "need to go." It's an awkward situation and I approach them sheepishly. Other times I squeeze mom's bell and wait for someone to appear. My stance toward her toileting needs alternates between tender concern and irrational fury.

And her toileting requires two people, an even more difficult prospect for on the spot assistance. Dottie, who has quite long legs, requires extra help in getting on and off the toilet only because it is so low to the ground. Since the nursing home will not allow me to bring in a raised portable seat—it's one of those requests that I grudgingly abandon—mom and the aides have to live with the pointless struggle several times a day.

Mom's attitude toward the role of men engaged in these intimate tasks has been another "Aha!" moment for me. Gracedale has floating male aides who are available for patient care that entails heavy lifting. I have long viewed exposing a female resident's naked body to them as an indignity, a violation of their basic human rights. And yet my mother not only doesn't feel awkward about it but actually prefers the men. "Their hands are so strong and steady," she says. She is more concerned that they make her feel safe than with issues of modesty.

Have I been projecting my own concerns onto residents? Are others residing at the facility actually humiliated by the male presence? In any case, Dottie's attitude, perhaps typical of her generation, is not entirely justifiable because a significant percentage of the female aides transfer and guide her with sturdiness and vigor. And, at great risk to themselves. According to the U.S. Department of Labor, nurse's aides, orderlies, and attendants are among the top ten occupations subject to work-related stress and injury to their bodies.

❧

I have a decent relationship with the direct-care staff but there aren't too many occasions for idle chatter. Besides, they are rightly wary of outsiders like me. But slowly, bit by bit, a few of them have let me into their private world, although such conversations are frowned upon by management. I've mostly learned that many of them lead complex, exacting lives as they juggle second jobs, single-motherhood, disabled children, and care of their own elderly parents. Their travails pull my attention away from any self-pity when I have a particularly distressing day with mom.

My inclination is to share a sense of mom's prior life with them, but I don't. They are too bogged down with wiping her bottom to hear about her athletic achievements or quirky, endearing lifelong traits. They have too many bodies to look after. Yes, I want the "real" Dorothy Katz to be special, but the staff only knows the person she has become. And, that is the way it must be.

Several of the aides and nurses have met mom's granddaughter and great-grandson. For her ninetieth birthday, the four of us celebrated with a chocolate cake, champagne—and plates and glasses for the staff as well. A few of them even took out a moment to sip some of the bubbly and greet two-month-old Zinn. Having been dispatched to the beautician for the special occasion, my mother looked particularly fetching that day. I suspect it was also the joy of holding her great-grandchild, so evident in her adoring, flushed face and squeals of delight.

While she was still in Florida, my mother once told me that she was keeping death at bay only until she could embrace her yet unborn great-grandchild. What's keeping her motivated nowadays? She rarely mentions the subject of dying at all. Nevertheless, during one of her rare "bad" days, brows knit together in a pained expression, she says, "I'm ready to die. You must let me go." It takes me aback because her pain is so palpable. She is not afraid to die, only that I won't accept it. My mother is worried about me. I let her know that it's okay, and she seems satisfied. The topic vanishes as abruptly as it materialized but is always there, under the surface.

ﾎ

A cheery aide brings mom's breakfast tray and sets it on her small table. At 9:00 a.m. or so, every day, it arrives in a mobile holding cabinet, containing nearly forty other similar plates. A robust worker propels these heavy, massive carts, two at a time, from the kitchen on the floor below. Today's egg quiche, set on an individual warming plate, is hot and delicious, as is most of the food served at Gracedale. It's a hearty breakfast that, for mom, also includes a large glass of orange juice, bowl of cold cereal, a bagel with cream cheese, hot chocolate, and an orange. Everyone else in the room has sausages or bacon but the food services staff, much to my relief, readily accommodates mom's fastidious eating habits. Indeed, when the dietician learns that I am bringing in a bagel every morning, she offers to add it to mom's regular breakfast menu. Contrary to my expectations, there are relatively attractive food choices for everyone that the resident, or an aide, picks out on a weekly basis. That is one of my tasks, which occasionally can be taxing. I not only have to guess at ingredients, such as whether the stuffed peppers, panini, and wraps are meatless, but also juggle the limited vegetarian alternatives.

There is no communal dining in my mother's building except for holidays or other special occasions. During these times, the cafeteria is fully decorated in festive motifs, which for the most part are garish but afford the residents pleasurable visual stimulation. Mom's favorite is the monthly ice cream social where she indulges in an enormous banana split, as do most of the other residents. Surrounded by balloons, streamers and other glitzy décor, they spoon the gooey treat with relish. Although it drips all over their face, hands, and bib, no one seems to notice.

The activities overall tend to be relatively unsophisticated, yet provide an essential diversion for incapacitated people who are holed up in an institution and otherwise alone all day. In the past, I've viewed such events as demeaning, treating the elderly as though they were living in "glorified playpens," so labeled by Gray Panther founder Maggie Kuhn. However, as I gaze at the wheelchairs crowded together, their occupants' usually vacant eyes lighted up and hands clapping, the sing-alongs no longer seem silly to me. Even mom's body moves with the rhythm while she taps her feet on the wheelchair's two footplates.

Other previously assumed notions about age-appropriate pursuits and entertainments come unraveled. The occupants of Gracedale would decline more rapidly without the elementary and often childish arts and crafts projects, concerts, cooking groups, birthday parties, word games, wheelchair exercise classes, and card games. My only regret is that my mother's loss of vision prevents her from participating in so many of them.

The shortage of aides and their hectic schedule preclude the kind of all-encompassing care many of the residents require. For mom that means that her teeth are rarely brushed unless I take over. Now that she has almost completely lost her eyesight and has only limited hand coordination, she can't do very much for herself. When I am away, an aide sometimes places Dottie's toothbrush, toothpaste, and spit bowl on the nearby table but the process is just too frustrating for her to accomplish on her own. Sometimes they hand her a disposable oral swab instead.

A mutually satisfactory rhythm has been set between mom and me and, despite the challenge of daily visits, for the most part I have accepted my part-time role as nursing home daughter. I arrive nearly every morning and immediately take care of her teeth, which tends to lift her spirits. "My mouth feels so yucky," she says, waiting for me to begin. I use only organic products even though at this point she doesn't really seem to notice, or care.

Gargle and spit, gargle and spit—as the mouthwash gushes into the kidney-shaped dish, dribbling all over her chin, I avert my eyes not so much in revulsion as in some peculiar inner impulse to provide her with a modicum of privacy.

Perhaps Dottie's helplessness at these times reminds me of an earlier version of my mother, someone who fanatically devoted hours to her teeth several times a day—water pic, dental floss, polishing and more. It's difficult to conjure up the sense of irritation her long periods in the bathroom previously provoked in me. After all, I was not responsible for her welfare then.

Since breakfast is her favorite meal, she prefers that I come early, in time to feed her. As I slowly spoon the food, her mouth is gaped like a baby robin awaiting worms. Mom is mostly silent as she savors the small feast. Until recently, she was predominantly on her own for lunch and dinner and the food most likely landed everywhere but through her lips. These days, she is helped by an aide if one is available. According to my mother, who can still come up with the occasional guilt trip, no one does it as well as me.

At breakfast, she handles the bagel by herself, along with the steaming coffee I brew at home and prepare precisely to her taste. Every once in a while I forget the thermos and come in empty-handed. She purses her lips together and, in a quiet voice says, "I'll miss having the coffee today." It seems less an accusation than an appreciation of my specially prepared blend.

As part of our morning ritual, I wash mom's face and hands, put on lotion and brush her hair briskly, the way she prefers. Her eyes shut, chin tilted upward with pleasure, she clearly enjoys these attentions. Although many of the aides take pride in the appearance of their charges, they sometimes overlook certain basic tasks. It's not uncommon for a resident to have "bed head," a matted down look from uncombed hair. Unlike some others, my mother is always well-coiffed.

During winter months, the frigid temperature often prevents us from venturing outdoors. Instead, we head to the cafeteria and try to catch a sunbeam from one of its outsized windows that cover an entire side of the spacious room. Mom sits there, bathed in sunlight, radiant and relaxed. "I could sit here like this forever," she murmurs. But I must leave, get back to my own life.

When winter turns to spring we take in the fresh air, mostly sitting in one of the several patio areas. Regardless of the weather, the entire area surrounding the building tends to be uninhabited except for a few staff members stealing time out to smoke. Mom would stay there all day, soaking in the sun, if she could. Many of the other residents never venture outside at all; it's not part of Gracedale's standard schedule.

When there's a bit more time, I wheel her to the lovely gardens. As we traverse the maze of pathways, I point out the various blossoming plants and bushes that she invariably can't make out, a riot of red, yellow, pink, white, purple, orange, and green. Scattered around the carefully landscaped grounds are benches, gazebos, and several mini waterways. Few people, employees and patients alike, take advantage of this charming setting, a pity given the huge investment in time, money, and space.

❧

Whether outside, in the cafeteria, or sitting on a folding chair near her bed, the unhurried moments when we simply sit together, without chores, are precious. I hold her hand, softly stroking it, while watching her untroubled face. It usually seems as though she is asleep but she responds to my questions, reacts to my touch. Periodically I remind her to "open her peepers," and am rewarded with the flutter of eyelids and a brief blank stare.

Mom rarely initiates conversation and seems content just to have me nearby. What's on her mind during our idle times together? It's hard to say because she shares so little of her inner world. Never has. Dottie was not only a loner but also a most private person. My father, too, never revealed himself to anyone, including his family. Their mutual emotional barriers must have precluded any real sense of personal intimacy between them.

Her expressions rarely betray her either. Growing up, my two sisters and I could never actually "read" our mother, who always had a prototypical poker face. Only the anomalous tear-like drip from a tiny open pore just below her neck gave us any inkling that she was in distress. Sometimes it oozed, like a leaky faucet. Anne was most disturbed by it but she rarely received a satisfactory accounting. Now that the telltale discharge has disappeared, there are few visible signs of any innermost turmoil.

Sporadically, when she is most quiet, seemingly deep in thought, I'll say, "Mom, what are you thinking right now?"

She delays her answer, as though giving it thorough consideration. "Chocolate," she says. "I'd like a chocolate." Or at another time, "The hair on my chin. It needs to be plucked." Am I hoping for something profound?

On the other hand, at times she is unpredictably aware and perceptive. One morning, while wiping her mouth, I jokingly tell her that she looks undignified with egg all over her face. She immediately counters, in a soft but not self-pitying voice, "Dignity? I've lost that long ago."

Throwing my arms around her, I say, "Never, mom. You'll never lose that." She smiles with pleasure.

I broach her past, but she is reluctant to talk about it. She rebuffs any bid on my part to learn more about her childhood and kin with "I don't

136　|　Elder Care Journey

remember." Parents and grandparents? "I don't remember." Her eight siblings? "I don't remember." Her marriage? "I don't remember." She becomes peevish if I persist.

For me, my mother's "I don't remember" is merely indicative of her long-standing lack of curiosity about people generally, including our large Zager clan. She always blocked any conversation about the extended family by saying, "You ask too many questions." I suspect her attitude toward bygone eras, "They're over, move on," is more about her embarrassment at having never been interested enough to learn about them in the first place.

These days it's only when conversations about *my* memories are brought up—and they must be upbeat and affirming—is she willing to reminisce. And, more and more these remembrances are expressed in terms of the happy childhood only she believes that I had.

That she never asks about the Florida apartment or her possessions mitigates any qualms about disposing years of accumulations so unceremoniously. Yet it unnerves me that she can wipe clean such a large piece of her life. Mom doesn't recall the lovely bushes she planted near her high-rise, and how they thrived over the years. Or the building itself. Or her bedroom, bursting with greenery and family pictures. The collages and photo albums surprise me the most because of the great care she took in creating them. Now they are gone, without as much as a comment. Could she really have blotted out decades of her previous life? Yet, if I promise to bring her chocolate, sure enough, the first thing she says the following morning is, "Where's my chocolate?"

At times she is confused, occasionally blending past and present. In the midst of what appears to me as a reasonable conversation, she will ask me to pick up a few items at Whole Foods, the supermarket in Florida. On another occasion, in a matter-of-fact voice she tells me that she's going to do a laundry later in the afternoon. Or, after I brush her teeth, she'll stare at the cup of mouthwash in her hand and ask, "What am I supposed to do with this?" A few times she's even called me "mama." These "out of the blue" comments always take me aback.

It's the enigmatic statements that are the most disconcerting. "The baby was crying all day," she'll announce. What baby? Or, "John took me for a ride yesterday." Who is John? It's not clear what she's alluding to and it can't be wheedled out of her.

She often blanks out on certain words or names, which is humiliating for her. That mom feels so embarrassed by these minor memory lapses surprises me since she has always been somewhat absent-minded, especially when it comes to people. If we are both stumped by a particular aide's name, which occurs regularly, mom grins broadly and whoops with glee, "See! See! Your memory is as bad as mine."

In earlier years, that would have been one of her toxic darts, stinging deeply. Even after years of therapy I remained vulnerable to my mother's caustic remarks, particularly when they were well-aimed—and they usually were. But now, contemplating the satisfaction lingering on her face, I say, "Yes. My memory is not so great either." We both smile, as though in collusion.

To be sure, her memory is patchy and, it seems to me, a bit selective. She consistently recollects what is essential to her daily existence in the nursing home, such as treats, rude treatment, and any variations in my visitation schedule. When winter descends again, I warn her that I may have to skip a day if I am snowed in or the roads are too icy. When a blizzard strikes, and I apologize, she brushes me off with, "I didn't expect you. There was a storm."

My mother's cognitive impairment, like so many people at an advanced age, is uneven, unpredictable, and focused on her immediate needs. As it ebbs and flows, catching me unawares, I've had to adjust to the person she has become. It's not always easy.

13

A Nursing Home Daughter

The thick, ominous envelope sits on my table unopened. There's definitely been less bureaucratic busywork over the last several months so the unwelcome correspondence from the PA Department of Welfare unnerves me. I unseal it warily, certain it portends more form-filling. Sure enough, it is an eleven-page annual renewal document for mom's Medical Assistance eligibility. Nothing has changed in my mother's financial situation, of course, but it has to be completed anyway. Do they think a ninety-year-old blind woman with Parkinson's disease in a nursing home is suddenly earning too much money for Medicaid? My first impulse is to send it back, address unknown, or forward it to Gracedale, and make it someone else's problem.

But I fill it out instead, painstakingly answering the identical questions as the original application. For her income sources, I write down the meagre Social Security and VA benefits. The SS check now flows directly to the nursing home so I have to call to find out what she received last year as an annual raise; it's under $20. The monthly VA check is still deposited in my mother's bank account, which I dutifully transfer to Gracedale.

The lengthiest part of the Medicaid recertification form pertains to financial resources. I write "none" for real estate holdings, mobile home, burial arrangements, life insurance, automobiles, recreational vehicles, trucks, motorcycles, IRA, savings accounts, stocks, bonds, trusts, mutual funds, and cash on hand. Because Dottie is in a nursing home, Medicaid pays most of the bill.[1] However, since she has no assets, she doesn't have to "spend down" resources to attain eligibility.[2] Mom's zero net worth also means that the nursing home is not whittling down any inheritance either. Shaking my head in amusement, I realize that this is the first time I have appreciated my mother's total lack of funds. For decades I supplemented her scanty retirement income so that she could meet expenses and even have a "little extra." Those days are now over, along with any residual resentment over her limited means.

Although mom is receiving Medicaid, she doesn't have any spare money beyond the $45 monthly personal allowance. Since the whole of her SS and VA pensions is allocated for nursing home care, any additional expenses fall on me. Not begrudging her anything, I gladly purchase winter clothing, fleece sweaters, cozy pants and shirts, organic oral care products, special lotions, treats, and any other extras that she may be in the mood for or need. I don't want to deny her anything.

All the same, it is reprehensible that the U.S. Department of Veterans Affairs (VA) has withheld the $90 monthly Aid and Attendance allowance that my mother is entitled to.[3] That the appropriate form was signed and mailed to the agency well over a year ago seems to be of no significance to anyone I've contacted. They also have failed to re-route her widow's pension from her checking account to the nursing home. The Social Security Administration accomplished that not-so-challenging task within two months of mom's arrival at the facility.

Dealing with the VA counterbalances, by far, the lighter bureaucratic load in other areas. Its help line, a misnomer given the lack of any assistance whatsoever, is a timewasting amalgam of automated choices and meaningless chatter. Persistence—my usual forte—is ineffectual since after pressing dizzying button after button you rarely reach the prize, a real person. Most days, despite phoning at varying hours, I am greeted with a not-so-sorry robotic voice that intones, "Your call is important to us," followed by "Due to heavy call volume during this period our benefit counsellors are currently assisting other customers and are unable to assist you at this time." The mechanical system then attempts to redirect beleaguered callers to its website, advises them to try again later, and unceremoniously hangs up. Intermittently I hit pay dirt, allowing me to hold on for a representative, usually for twenty-five minutes or more.

If the agency is so damn busy with customers why don't they just hire more assistants? Stressed veterans, just back from their second or third tour in Iraq, inevitably discover that their government is too busy to deal with their issues, problems, or needs. The VA certainly is not interested in dealing with a WWII soldier's frail ninety-year-old widow. The system seems carefully designed so that you reach a dead end.

Their customer service representatives are neither friendly nor helpful on the infrequent occasions I reach one. And, in my experience, they're woefully uninformed, lacking knowledge about the most basic information. I've been told, depending on the particular agent, either that they're still working on Dorothy Katz's request or that they never received it. One representative is unaware of the Aid and Attendance Allowance altogether. At best, they read from notes left from the last person you spoke to or, in rare instances, who actually worked on the case. But they always repeatedly, and perfunctorily, thank you for the veteran's service.

In 2012, the backlog at the Veterans Benefit Administration's Philadelphia office is roughly a year. As a result, my mother forfeits well over $1,000 in Aid and Attendance benefits that she is entitled to. At my instigation, our district's congressman requests that the agency look into the matter for Dottie and eventually she receives the allowance but not the back payments. There are dozens of vulnerable older people at the nursing home, and most likely thousands more across the nation, in a similar situation as my mother.

The VA also finally gets around to paying the money directly to Gracedale. Soon after, I close down mom's checking account, which now has a zero balance; I had kept it open only for receipt of the VA checks. Unfortunately, when I fill out my mother's Medicaid recertification form seven months later, a huffy administrator at the PA Department of Welfare insists that I send her mom's final bank statements. Is she afraid that I absconded with her riches? Indeed, last year's form showed no assets whatsoever. When I protest that it will be too difficult for me to obtain them at this point, she snidely tells me that my mother is at risk of losing her Medicaid benefits and therefore her nursing home care. I drive the two-hour round trip to the nearest Chase bank to obtain them.

At least my fears over health insurance have become a non-issue, to some degree. Now that mom is in Pennsylvania and in a nursing home she is income-eligible for all of the Medicaid benefits offered in the state, including dental care and eye examinations. As a fully "dual eligible" beneficiary, she is entitled to original Medicare as her primary coverage, with Medicaid subsidizing the premiums, deductibles, and coinsurance.[4] As a bonus, Medicare's

"Extra Help" program picks up the tab for the entire Part D prescription drug coverage.[5]

At Gracedale, a full range of specialists are on-site, including ophthalmologists, rheumatologists, dentists, audiologists, urologists, psychologists, podiatrists, opticians, orthopedics, otolaryngologists (ENTs), and proctologists. Dottie takes advantage of more than a few of these doctors, and although the quality of services is uneven, their ongoing assessments of her health has alleviated many of my medical concerns.[6]

Regardless, there are sufficient problems to keep me occupied, especially since they tend to fall into the "urgent/serious/vital" category. A cracked dental partial that takes far too long to replace, despite my repeated urgings, substantially impairs mom's ability to chew her food. The low-grade substitution proves to be both uncomfortable and difficult to handle, though I eventually talk the insurance company into paying for an upgrade. Damaged or lost hearing aids, another consequence of institutional life, must be awaited with more patience than I generally possess. At one point my blind mother suffers from both absent teeth and the loss of sound, a situation that is difficult for her (and me) to endure.

Prior to mom's arrival in Pennsylvania I spent hours on the Medicare Part D selection process to secure an insurance company that would cover her specific medications. That done, I envisioned the task as finalized. Ten months later we receive notification that Azopt, the steeply priced but vital eyedrops, is being dropped from the firm's formulary.[7] Gritting my teeth, I glance over the time-consuming appeals process, determined to keep mom from sliding into total darkness. It requires information that I don't have access to. Although the charge nurse agrees to take it on, she only manages to attain a generic substitute. Jean assures me that it will suffice and, despite my misgivings, I shrug in resignation. Several months later, the insurance company notifies mom that it is discontinuing the entire plan and she—and that means me—has to sign up for a new one.

Other paperwork streams into my mailbox, some of which is just too ludicrous to waste any time on. One correspondence from the Part D insurance firm is a lengthy form inquiring about various aspects of my mother's employment prospects. For that, I scribble on the top, *"She's 90, blind and in a nursing home."* I never hear from them again on that matter.

And, despite the fact that I am at the facility every day, I still regularly receive the federally required phone calls about mom's run-of-the-mill nicks and scratches; her ninety-year-old skin is thin and fragile. On the other hand, there are no more gloom-and-doom messages from 1,200 miles away, which affords me a sense of relief.

ᕬ

Overall, my form-filling duties, financial burdens, and other obligations have been lightened considerably. Accordingly, my relationship with mom has shifted to a more loving one. Her affectionate attitude toward me is most likely in response to my newly acquired tenderness toward her. After bringing her to the nursing home, a choice mostly thrust upon us, I determined to be gentler with her and she responded in kind.

We have begun to know each other for the first time. The greatest revelation is Dottie's sense of humor, a piece of her personality I was not fully aware of. She can be really funny, and at the oddest moments. One morning, as I was pacing nervously around her wheelchair waiting for the cold water to turn hot, she says, "You could never be a doctor. You wouldn't have any patients."

At another time, I park her in the hall for a moment. "Now don't let anybody steal you," I joke. "There are plenty of people looking for a mom."

"Oh, they won't," she assures me. "This one is too much work."

She teases me so affectionately it nearly breaks my heart. And I tease her back with the same light touch. Had she always been this way, or did I just fail to notice?

During the harsh winter days, I take her briefly outdoors, bundled up in a wool hat, earmuffs, scarf, down coat, and mittens. During one such outing we are sitting together, chatting, surrounded by mounds of snow. Gazing at her raw face peeking out of the headgear I say, "You must really long for Florida right now."

She slowly shakes her head from side to side. "No, I'm glad I came to Pennsylvania. To be near you."

And, she regularly informs the aides—and everyone else for that matter—what a wonderful daughter I am. Grateful words spill out to me as well. "I don't know what I would do without you," she says. Or, "I'm so lucky to have you." Or, "Thanks for being there for me." Mom's deep appreciation is nourishing, the food that propels me to go on with these endless hours at the nursing home.

She always viewed me as the serious, hard-working daughter who couldn't—wouldn't—take time out to "smell the roses." I once asked her,

A Nursing Home Daughter | 143

many years ago, which daughter she most enjoyed being with. "Anne," she said, without hesitation. "She's the most fun." I didn't actually expect her to choose.

Now I say, playfully, "Who is your favorite daughter?" Her lips curl into a sly smile. "You are," she says. "You're the best." There is an ache in my chest.

Mom's lifelong optimism, her incapacity to keep adverse events in mind, always rankled and bemused me. It was as though her brain were a sieve that could filter out unpleasantries at will. Sometimes it seemed like she were sleepwalking through life, rousing only to pick and choose her own reality.

It afforded her, I suspect, less empathy for the struggles of others, especially her daughters. During some of my deepest crises over the years, even my devastating divorce from my first husband in the early 1980s, my mother's unhelpful response was "Get over it. Move on," words I can still hear buzzing in my ears. That had been her way of dealing with adverse situations. Dottie skirted over so many incidents, large and small, even my father's demoralizing job loss, Anne's alcoholism, Denise's multiple sclerosis, my stomach cancer. She had an uncanny confidence that, no matter what the challenges, she and her family would surmount them. Mom never clung to an outside power, such as religion, for support. No, it was sheer personal will that would get her—us—through any difficulties.

It is this enduring sureness and buoyancy that keeps despair mostly at bay during her stay at Gracedale. There has always been a childlike joy in everyday experiences that she now brings to her new home. The aides seem to marvel at her intermittent bursts of song when they wash her, recognizable tunes with mostly improvised words. She can hum for hours along with the songs on her TVs *Golden Oldies* station. These days we often sing together as I push her through the long halls, both of us ad-libbing lyrics.

My prior antipathy toward my mother's odd optimism, the bane of my young life, has become a lifeline instead. We both grab on to it as she loses control over nearly every aspect of her daily existence and is forced to accept the rhythms and routines of institutional needs over her own. That it's in Dorothy Katz's character to go along with the flow—that she has willed herself to brave this next phase of her life in good spirits—is her gift to me.

In doing so, there is a tacit pact that her steadfast daughter, the not-so-fun-loving but reliable offspring, will be her advocate, protect her. Mom was always my Rock of Gibraltar as a child, now I am hers. At times, the role reversal leaves me uneasy, as though it were unnatural. Do lion cubs, kittens, fawns, ducklings ever have to take charge of their mothers?

❧

Nearly every day I take the ten-minute convoluted route to mom's room: from parking lot, through automatic sliding doors, up the elevator to the second floor, down a lengthy atrium, and up another elevator to a different building's second floor. It's an attractive walkway, surrounded by continuous windows that flood the area with light when the mini-blinds are pulled open. There are usually visitors and residents seated on comfortable chairs, arranged just below the panes; wheelchairs are scattered nearby.

My purposeful stride is slowed down periodically by quick waves of the hand, fleeting smiles, and "good mornings." Most of the greetings are pro forma but others represent a genuine regard on my part for certain individuals who have been part of my mother's care. There is steady traffic across the passageway: staff, loaded carts, volunteers pushing wheelchairs, residents driving motorized vehicles. If one were to stay there all day, every employee probably would pass by at some point.

And then there are the visitors, some of them ever-present fixtures, ensconced in the atrium with their wheelchair-bound family members. I am particularly struck by an old man of roughly ninety, using a walker himself, who sits dutifully by his ailing wife's side nearly every day. At first we exchange nods of recognition, which progresses to short chats. His endearing, toothless grin, rounded face, slits of pale blue eyes, and bald head with wisps of white hair become a familiar sight to me over time. One day, eleven months after I first noticed him, he is no longer there. His wife had died.

There is also a parade of colors everywhere. There is an egalitarian feel to the caring staffs' uniforms. RNs, LPNs, and aides alike are clad in nursing scrubs of all shades and designs. Except for her authoritative demeanor, the charge nurse blends in with the others. On Fridays, everyone is allowed to sport jeans but there is a one dollar charge, contributed to various charities, for the privilege. Given their inadequate wages, even such a token payment seems unfair to me.

A few positions at Gracedale's are color-coded, with T-shirts designating their roles. Yellow indicates maintenance, the employees who clean and polish. With their tiny pails and large hallways, it often seems like these hard working people are simply pushing dirt around. But the place is certainly clean enough. And, there are no noxious odors.

Then there are navy blue tops for food service employees and short dark blue lab coats for the ubiquitous volunteers, many of whom appear as though they are only one step away from institutionalization themselves. Then again, so am I.

Amidst the bustle of multihued outfits are social workers, secretarial and administrative personnel, activities department employees, medical suppliers, dieticians, and other health care professionals who stand out in their business casual garb. They scurry every which way, many with clipboards in hand, always appearing as though they're in a hurry. There are also carpenters, gardeners, painters, electricians and other technicians, laundry workers, and therapists. Assorted ministers in suit and tie, and priests dressed in black, pass through on their way to the chapel. An occasional doctor roams about as well, identifiable by his or her white coat.

Every so often there is a dog or two hanging around, held loosely on leashes by their owners. Animal companionship often has a therapeutic effect on institutionalized elders and they have been brought in to cheer up family members. These calm, gentle canines remind me of my mother's fondness for animals. Indeed, my childhood home was teeming with creatures of all sorts. In our tiny three-bedroom apartment in the Bronx, at various times the Katz family included a standard poodle, cats, large fish tanks, a duck (who lived in our bathtub until he was dropped off at the children's zoo), an assortment of frogs, lizards, and salamanders, a succession of parakeets, gerbils, and hamsters, and possibly other pets that have faded from memory. Dottie especially adored cats and, at one point after her children were all on their own, had eight or so running around her house.

Inspired, I decide to certify my English Setter so that he could visit mom with me. Surely, he would soothe her, evoke fond memories from the past. Instead, he jumps on her lap, digging his untrimmed nails into her thighs. "Ouch!" mom says, recoiling. With a pained look on her face she demands that I take him away.

&

As I head, once again, to my mother's room I'm struck afresh by the interminable days ahead of me at this place. When I first transported mom here, she was so ill that I expected her stay to last a few months, six at most. My initial decision to visit daily was not an open-ended commitment to forever. Gazing around at the overly familiar spaces at Gracedale, and the enormity of my future obligations, I wonder how long this will stretch out. Is this how I am going to spend my "golden years"?

It's tiresome to wrap my day-to-day schedule around mom and balance that with other family obligations, work, and personal pursuits. I'm inundated with conflicting sentiments, a desperate desire to run away, and shame for yearning my freedom. Yes, a chapter of my life ended and a new one has commenced as I settle into Dottie's institutional existence. Sustaining the tedious routine and relinquishing such a huge chunk of time to my mother has exposed an unfamiliar side of me. Having tenaciously fought my entire adult life to keep anyone from wresting control over my schedule, no matter how negligible, I am now at her beck and call.

Some days I don't know how I feel. Mechanical motions allow me to perform mom's morning tasks, sit for a while, and then move on to other matters. It's my ability to remain detached now and then that allows me to manage the tug of war among the many pieces of my life. Although the volatile Florida days are long gone, the fact remains that there are still multiple concerns to take into account. I have fewer hours for writing, one of my main passions. My relationship with George can't be ignored, nor can my classes or other responsibilities at the university. Then there is Alix, and grandson Zinn, whom I yearn to hold and spend more time with in Massachusetts; he is growing up without me. Skype mostly has to do for now. Friends are fit in ad hoc, as are the hodgepodge of other people and things that demand my attention. It is an everyday juggling act.

I've picked up the art of compartmentalizing by giving myself permission not to think about my mother after I leave the nursing home. I also have summoned the strength to leave early, when necessary, or to skip a day once in a while. It's been more difficult to reject bringing her to my house for holidays but after the first Thanksgiving and Christmas fiascos it had to be done. It was just too hard on everyone. In fact, these holiday experiences—and the overwhelming complications—have allowed me to forgive myself for placing her in a nursing home.

Some days the full weight of my permanent responsibility for Dorothy Katz bears down on me. As the sole survivor of three daughters, this obligation is mine alone. So many adult children bemoan sibling rivalry, the fierce and sometimes escalating disagreements about the care of their disabled elderly parents. Surely, that would have been the case in my family where Denise and Anne were as dogmatic and strong-minded as I. With their deaths I escaped tempestuous decision-making regarding mom, but at what price? Flashes of our childhood together whirl through my head like an old homemade movie. There are scenes of harmony, friendship, and mutual support intermingled with those of rancor and antipathy. A knot forms in my stomach as discordant sensations wash over me. How could they have left me to deal with our mother by myself? Oh, how often have I ached for my sisters' help?

This is especially true when, eleven months after mom's arrival in Pennsylvania, George and I decide to take a vacation. Fearing her reaction, I broach the topic cautiously. Drawing close, my fingers lightly touching hers, I begin, "Mom, I'm going on a trip."

"For how long?" she says, somewhat apprehensively.

"For two weeks or so."

We sit for a while in uncertain silence. "I'll be fine," she says. "You need to have a break."

My friend Betty offers to visit during my time away, allowing me to deflect the gnawing guilt. Yet, despite her kind attentions and Dottie's uncharacteristic affinity toward her, it's clear that mom suffers during my absences.

My role as nursing home daughter is burdensome. And yet, I conjure up my mother's gently wrinkled face, lips curved slightly upwards with tiny whimsical lines forming near the eyes, her easygoing disposition full of optimism, and the oft-stated appreciation of me and our time together. Our random conversations. In the garden, I read dad's ten-page 1944 proposal letter to her, discovered amidst her papers. It stirs flickers of buried memories, of her young self, that she unaccustomedly shares with me. I eagerly hang on to every word, soaking up nuances in expression, whether real or imagined.

The other day, when she is in an atypical funk, she tells me, in a tiny little voice, "I'm scared." I hold mom close to me, softly caressing her. I regularly throw my arms around her, and with gentle kisses let her know that I don't feel burdened. "You're kisses are so sweet," she assures me back. So helpless and vulnerable, alone really, except for me. Flashes of affection, tenderness, and love infuse my whole being. She needs me for sure, but I also need her.

Peeling the Onion

A Glimpse into Long-Term Care Provider Ownership

Health policies and programs for the elderly and disabled absorb a considerable percentage of federal and state budgets. At the national level, Medicare funded fully $466 billion for their needs in 2012, or 12.3 percent of the federal budget.[1] Medicaid paid another $165 billion, or 4.4 percent of the total.[2] States, too, contribute significant funding of their own, amounting to another $121 billion that year, or nearly two-thirds of their overall Medicaid spending.[3]

Long-term supports and services (LTSS) alone is among the costliest government expenditures. Out of the nation's overall LTSS bill ($208 billion), public sector payments amounted to over $137 billion, or 66 percent of the total, mostly from Medicaid.[4] In addition, through the Older Americans Act, the federal government contributed another $1.4 billion for home and community-based services (HCBS), caregiver assistance, preventive health, and nutrition.[5]

Such astronomical outlays ostensibly suggest that the United States has committed undue resources for the LTSS needs of its older and disabled populations. Nevertheless, a closer look at the beneficiaries of these dollars paints quite a different picture. In essence, Medicare and Medicaid are "big business," and their budgets support and enrich entire industries. To varying extents, hospitals, pharmaceutical firms, nursing homes, home care agencies, insurance companies (including managed care organizations), and durable medical equipment manufacturers depend on these programs for a steady flow of revenues and siphon off a sizeable percentage of public funds in profits, high executive salaries, bonuses and stock options, advertising, and other expenses unrelated to concrete services.

In 2012, these two programs accounted for 80 percent of total U.S. home health care revenues ($78 billion) and over one-fifth of drug company earnings.[6] Medicaid fully supports slightly over one-third of people entering nursing homes and at least some of the expenses for 60 percent of all residents. Along with Medicare reimbursements for post-acute care,[7] these costs represent nearly half of all nursing home income.

During our elder care journey, my mother and I encountered various service providers in the long-term care, medical, and insurance industries, most of them proprietary companies. The next section attempts to unravel their ownership structure, when feasible, and assess whether U.S. taxpayers are getting their money's worth.

Nursing Homes

The profit-making approach to nursing home care has been particularly insidious and antithetical to decent care. Although widespread since the 1930s, the percentage of propriety facilities grew rapidly in the 1960s. By 1980, the vast majority of institutions were owned privately, increasingly by publicly traded multi-facility corporate chains. Over the next several decades, nursing homes became not only larger but ever more concentrated through merger and acquisition activities.[8] In 2012, of the 15,643 Medicare and Medicaid certified facilities, roughly 69 percent of the total were for-profit establishments (mostly chains), followed by nonprofit (25 percent) and government-owned (5.9 percent) entities.[9]

There is an even more disturbing trend toward Private Equity (PE) consortium ownership, especially since the turn of the twenty-first century. PE firms solicit large pools of capital from wealthy people and large institutional funds, promising them higher than average rates of return. The money is then used to purchase a portfolio of operating companies that is controlled by one or more of the PE firm associates (General Partners—GPs). The health services sector is particularly attractive because of its potential for continuous growth, along with a steady flow of revenues from Medicare and Medicaid. Since 2000, PE firms have invested roughly $3.4 trillion in 18,300 companies; nearly 11 percent of the total is in health care-related establishments.[10]

Unlike publicly traded corporations, PE firms buy companies by using extremely high levels of debt that is then loaded onto the newly acquired enterprise; the PE firm itself is not responsible for repaying it.[11] The GPs thereafter manage the business, making all of the decisions related to its operations. The goal is to make as much quick money as possible for the GPs, who garner millions through lucrative "advisory fees," "management fees," "transaction fees," and "monitoring fees." The PE firms, which most often acquire healthy, relatively high-performing establishments, also generally utilize various financial engineering maneuvers to strip the newly purchased corporation's assets, especially its real estate holdings, and pay out high dividends and dividend recapitalizations to themselves and the other investors.[12] Their intention is to sell the entity within five years at a higher price, although it is sometimes driven into bankruptcy. As Applebaum and Batt put it, the PE financial business model is one in which "companies are viewed as assets to be bought and sold for the sole purpose of maximizing profit."[13] The outsized earnings generally accrue to the GPs and, to a lesser extent, the limited partners.

For the most part, there is little concern for the long-term viability of the establishment, its customers, or employees. Indeed, because of high levels of debt from heavily leveraged buyouts, and subsequent dividend recapitalizations, the exorbitant interest payments force the GPs to cut operating costs, sometimes drastically.[14] In the case of nursing homes, these include reductions in staff, with a callous disregard for the adverse effects on the quality of patient care or the well-being of the already underpaid and overworked nurses and aides.

Similar to many publicly traded nursing home chains, the PE firms protect themselves against legal liability for substandard care and financial fraud. In the most extreme cases of patient negligence and abuse, for example, they potentially could face exclusion from the Medicare and Medicaid programs, a nursing home's main sources of funding. Government overpayments, violations of the federal False Claims Act and its whistleblower provisions, or malpractice verdicts would put them at risk for monetary penalties.[15]

Consequently, the PE firm incorporates each facility in its newly acquired nursing home chain as a separate limited liability company (LLC). It also splits every home into legally distinct nursing home operations and real-estate investment entities.[16] Such restructuring shelters the entire enterprise in the case of a judgment against any one facility in the chain. Just as important, even if the operating company of a particular nursing home is found guilty of misconduct, it has few resources to satisfy any patient or government claims against it.[17]

Unlike publicly traded companies, however, PE firms are generally not subject to disclosure and other U.S. Securities and Exchange Commission (SEC) requirements and regulations, including openly reporting their income, profits, assets, and ownership.[18] As Applebaum and Batt note, there is no complete information on the financial activities of PE firms: ". . . private equity's lack of transparency makes independent analyses of its data all but impossible."[19]

Overall, organizational structure seems to have a considerable impact on the quality of nursing home care. The evidence suggests that for-profit ownership, especially chain affiliation, reduces the delivery of decent services. In fact, the worst facilities have the largest Medicaid populations because "better" nursing homes are more interested in the higher per diem fees of private-pay or Medicare customers.[20]

In a national study comparing both access and quality among three ownership structures, researchers found that for-profit nursing homes have a significantly lower quality of care as compared to public and nonprofit facilities. The largest proprietary providers grant the greatest access to Medicaid recipients but offer the lowest performance outcomes.[21] Similarly, in an analysis of nursing home survey results for 1999, another group of investigators determined that investor-owned facilities had far more deficiencies than did nonprofit or public facilities; again, chains were associated with the worst quality of care. They note: "Rates of severe deficiencies in investor-owned facilities were 40.5 percent higher than at nonprofit homes and 35.8 percent higher than at public homes."[22]

To be sure, inferior care is linked to lower staffing levels. Since personnel costs tend to be the most significant operating expenses in a nursing home, high profit extraction causes owners to skimp on direct-care employees. Such cost-cutting strategies clearly compromise resident care. For example, O'Neill, Harrington, Kitchener, and Saliba show that proprietary facilities with the most extreme levels of profit-taking had not only more total deficiencies but also the most severe ones.[23]

On the other hand, many nonprofit organizations, which often have higher quality of care, tend to limit access to Medicaid patients.[24] Serving a more lucrative market, they rely extensively on private-pay clients. One study argues that although their profit levels can be similar to proprietary nursing homes, they tend to reinvest earnings in greater staffing and other improvements for their "elite" clientele.[25] As Amirkhanyan, Kim, and Lambright aptly put it: "one sector shuns Medicaid clients and the other sector profiteers from them using public dollars."[26]

Finally, there are a small and decreasing number of public facilities that serve a large proportion of Medicaid residents and provide relatively high-quality care. In fact, government nursing homes, which are mostly county run, appear to maximize both access and quality.[27] Places with such a significant percentage of low-paying Medicaid patients, of course, experience fiscal problems, forcing many counties to subsidize their facilities to a greater or lesser extent. At the same time, since the vast majority of government-run homes are unionized, wages and benefits tend to be more than in voluntary and for-profit institutions.[28] In addition, many public nursing homes operate in old buildings that can result in regulatory violations requiring costly renovations.[29]

As a result, there has been a steady divestiture of county-owned nursing homes. Between March 2000 and December 2003, roughly 10 percent of all such facilities changed to nonprofit or proprietary status; a number of them were simply closed down.[30] Given the willingness to provide decent care to at least a small percentage of impoverished frail elders, county nursing homes have proven essential to many communities.

Our neediest older citizens, however, are mostly shunted into for-profit facilities with the lowest level of care. In fact, fully one-third of all certified nursing homes in the United States receive an overall rating of one or two stars (much below average and below average, respectively) by the Centers for Medicare and Medicaid Services (CMS).[31] Most of these places have high levels of deficiencies that jeopardize their residents' health and safety. Even facilities with the worst records receive a steady stream of revenue from the Medicare and Medicaid programs.

&.

Dorothy Katz's first nursing home, Hillcrest Nursing and Rehabilitation Center, LLC,[32] is typical of the industry in that it has been repeatedly bought and sold with the main goal of profit maximization for its various stockholders and private equity investors. Likewise, as one home in a multi-facility chain, it has a convoluted history of ownership that I couldn't fully unravel.[33]

From what I have been able to identify, Hillcrest most likely began as part of Centennial Health Care, a publicly traded company. In 2000, an affiliate of the PE firm Warburg Pincus, LLC[34] bought Centennial's outstanding stock for $65 million. The new Warburg Pincus Centennial Health Care, which included 100 nursing home operations and the separate real estate holdings of sixty-six of them, was now a private corporation.[35]

The following year (2001) Warburg Pincus, along with several Centennial executives, launched Florida Health Care Properties to acquire the operations of more nursing homes. In addition, Pincus soon obtained an indirect ownership in the nursing home operations of Seacrest Health Care Management, LLC and other such businesses, all of which eventually became subsidiaries of the combined Pincus-led chain LaVie Care Centers.[36]

Operating 122 nursing homes and earning $1 billion in revenues in 2010, LaVie was sold to the PE firm, Formation Capital Investment Group, at the end of the following year.[37] Subsequently, in the fall of 2012, La Vie/ Formation Capital purchased the equity interests of Consulate Health Care, LLC and took on its corporate name for the combined enterprise.[38] With more than 200 facilities and over 30,000 employees in 22 states, Formation's portfolio company LaVie/Consulate Health Care is now the largest nursing home management corporation in Florida and the sixth largest in the nation. In 2013, its total revenues were in excess of $1.6 billion.[39]

The nursing homes' real estate seems to have had a different but related trajectory. According to the Government Accountability Office, in 2004 Formation Capital acquired whatever land and buildings the Warburg Pincus/ Centennial nursing homes owned and leased them (and other nursing home properties) to Florida Health Care Properties/La Vie, thereby becoming their landlord.[40] In 2006, those properties—along with additional Formation Capital nursing home land and buildings master-leased by Centennial and other enterprises (186 properties in total)—were bought by GE Capital, Healthcare Financial Services–real estate, another PE firm, for $1.4 billion.[41] Since then, Formation has continued to purchase and sell nursing home real estate, leasing them to various operating companies, including a growing number of Consulate Health Care affiliates.[42]

As suggested earlier, PE firms such as Formation Capital, with their complex financial, management, and operational structures, have been increasingly gobbling up and spitting out nursing homes with the sole goal of financial gain. By spreading ownership over a number of related firms, especially separate real estate and operating companies, they isolate themselves from financial risk, complicate ownership, obscure relationships among their associated firms, and enhance profits.

At the time of my mother's stay, Hillcrest Nursing and Rehabilitation Center, LLC had received the lowest rating by Medicare.gov Nursing Home Compare—one star or "much below average"—which it maintained in the ensuing two years. In the 2012 and 2013 federal nursing home inspection reports, many of the egregious conditions that mom and I encountered were carefully noted as affecting a few or many patients but nonchalantly written off as causing only "minimal harm or potential for actual harm." For instance, the assessors wrote, "Based on observation, interview and record review, the facility failed to provide and prepare food that is nutritional, appetizing, tasty, attractive, well-cooked, and at the right temperature." From my personal experience, this lack of proper nourishment had a *serious adverse effect* on my mother's health and well-being.

How negligible an impact is the report's finding that Hillcrest "[i]gnored patients that had to go to the bathroom, encouraging them to wear diapers instead?" For Dorothy Katz it meant that it stymied her progress in regaining mobility, despite the fact she was placed in the facility for that very purpose. Instead of going home, she ended up in an assisted-living facility. *Sounds to me like serious harm.*

Much of the other "deficiencies" uncovered by the surveyors[43] resulted in far greater damage to my mother and others than merely "minimal harm or potential for actual harm." These include the facility's failure: "to protect in an environment that promotes dignity for residents; to provide housekeeping maintenance services necessary to maintain a sanitary, orderly environment; to ensure that its staff members perform their duties under sanitary conditions; to make sure services provided meet professional standards of quality; and to conduct initial and periodic assessments of each resident's functional capacity."

Such harmful practices have been observed by inspectors year after year without any real consequences for the perpetrators: Hillcrest didn't receive any Medicare or Medicaid payment denials and has been fined only $4,300 in penalties since 2010. Nor were the parent company, Consulate Health Care, Inc., or the PE investors held accountable for the severely deficient care of the residents.[44] Meanwhile, taxpayers continue to foot the bill.

Hollywood Hills Rehabilitation Center, LLC, my mother's second short-stay, post-acute care nursing home in Florida, also has a sustained one star, "much below average" overall rating history. From my family's experience, not only is the extremely low assessment well deserved but the conditions in the facility are so atrocious that it should be shut down entirely, or at least have its Medicare and Medicaid certifications revoked. After eighteen days in the nursing home, Dorothy Katz's physical and mental health had seriously deteriorated. Despite the generally dismal care, Hollywood Hills didn't receive any fines or payment denials from the government over the last several years.

To the contrary, as with Hillcrest and other extremely low-rated nursing homes, the for-profit company collected significant taxpayer dollars. During 2010, this relatively small family-owned facility (152 certified beds) derived fully 64 percent of its $13.5 million in revenues from public sources (Medicaid, 43 percent or $5.8 million; and Medicare, 21 percent or $2.8 million). Its CEO, Karen Kallen-Zury, and at least one other officer, Tanir Zury, both of whom are related to the home's owner, Lenore Kallen, earned an additional $560,000 and $200,000, respectively, in salary.[45]

In 2007, as part of a government offensive on deceptive financial practices, aimed at nine cities, the U.S. Department of Justice established the Medicare Fraud Strike Force. Six years later, it targeted Karen Kallen-Zury and four other people. They were subsequently convicted of a fraud and bribery scheme that bilked Medicare out of $39 million in payments to the fifty-bed Hollywood Pavilion Mental Center, a facility associated with Hollywood Hills and also owned by the Kallen family. Karen was sentenced to twenty-five years for swindling the government. Notably, the focus of the government's lawsuit was to protect Medicare funds; nobody has ever been held accountable for the appalling treatment of residents in the nursing home, including my mother.

Despite my efforts to find a higher rated facility, we had been stuck with Hollywood Hills. Obviously other individuals, especially Medicaid recipients, have limited choices as well since the nursing home's occupancy rate is 84 percent, just under Florida's average of 87.6 percent.[46] Hillcrest's occupancy rate is even higher, 95 percent in 2014 (out of 240 beds). There apparently is very little competitive pressure to improve the conditions at these exceedingly deficient places.

In my view, official inspections, along with the Nursing Home Compare scores, are not reliable indicators of nursing home conditions and services in any case.[47] There are vital details you just can't capture on a standard government survey or observe during sporadic official visits, many of which are prepared for ahead of time by nursing home administrators. These federal and state assessments tend to be undependable, both overestimating and underestimating the actual situation. And, they do not and cannot capture the complex, multifaceted aspects of nursing home life. This became apparent to me after personally witnessing everyday events at Gracedale, which has consistently received only a two star, "below average" rating over the years. The county-owned institution offers far better care than either of the two proprietary nursing homes in Florida.

Known as Gnadenthal (Dale of Grace) in 1745, a farm owned by the Moravians, it was purchased by Northampton County to serve as a poorhouse in 1837. Later, officials constructed a small three-story stone building, transforming the property into an old age home, Gracedale. [48] In 1975 a huge tower structure was added, allowing for a capacity of 688 beds at the facility.

While most of the rooms have as many as four occupants, there are spacious and relatively attractive accommodations for private family gatherings and resident activities, including several reading rooms with ample books, newspapers, magazines. and computers. The common areas in the nine tower floors all have enormous windows overlooking vast, lovely gardens. In addition to staff physicians, various specialists are regularly available on-site. The therapists, subcontracted to a commercial vendor, are outstanding. And the food is not only first-rate but the nursing home caters to individual tastes. Furthermore, the managers do not seem to stint on residents' basic needs. Unlike the for-profit institutions, nearly every dollar of taxpayer money is used for patient care, including a higher than average staffing level.[49]

For most of its history as a nursing home, Gracedale earned a profit but later started losing money, costing Northampton County taxpayers $4.6 million in 2009. The following year, the County Council voted to privatize the facility, put out bids, and selected a buyer. However, nine months later the Coalition for Alzheimer's families, along with other supporters, forced the proposed sale to a referendum. Seventy-two percent of the county residents voted to withdraw the deal; in May 2011 the facility was given a five-year grace period.[50]

Afterwards, the County Council outsourced the administration of Gracedale to a consulting and management firm—Premiere Healthcare Resources, LLC, located in King of Prussia, Pennsylvania. The nursing home is currently operated by a team of individuals from the company, including the facility's administrator, Millard D. Freeman. He has initiated a number of cost reductions and other policy changes[51] over the past three years and most likely will now concentrate on employee give-backs, at least for the newly hired, since salaries and benefits are the largest category of expenses. Although most of the aides and nurses are unionized, and their salary and fringe benefits tend to be more generous than in commercial nursing homes, they still struggle financially. It is unclear whether Gracedale will be able to continue recruiting and retaining its generally well-trained, hard-working and caring direct-care staff if their earnings are lowered to a great extent. After all, it is such employees who are mainly responsible for the residents' well-being.[52]

In my estimation, much of Gracedale's negative ratings stem from the fact that the buildings are old, thereby generating certain "regulatory compliance issues."[53] For example, the place was almost shut down during my mother's stay because of a malfunctioning boiler. At least one of the several ancient and creaky elevators is generally out of commission. Regardless, these infractions do not seem to infringe on the health of residents and their overall quality of life. Yes, Gracedale is timeworn, but the care of its frail inhabitants is decidedly underrated by Medicare's Nursing Home Compare website.

Home Care Agencies

Along with the aging of the U.S. population, and a trend toward home care for the chronically disabled, the in-home services and supports (IHSS) industry has been proliferating over the last several decades. Consisting of dual but overlapping sectors, home care agencies (HCAs) supply skilled health services, personal assistance, and sometimes both. Medicare spending on medically oriented home services has swelled as the federal government attempts to keep Medicare beneficiaries out of hospitals and nursing homes. By 2010, there were roughly 8,500 freestanding Medicare-certified HCAs. Seventy percent of them are for-profit companies, up from 7 percent in 1980; about one-third is part of a chain.[54] These home health agencies receive a significant percentage of their income from Medicare.[55]

At the same time, there has been an expansion of personal care companies serving the frail, dependent elderly population and persons with disabilities. Initially dominated by small, privately-owned mom-and-pop businesses, a growing number of them are now for-profit franchise chains. Today, roughly

62 percent of the total is proprietary companies.[56] They are highly lucrative entities, with total revenues of $28.9 billion in 2009.[57] Because Medicare does not pay for long-term personal care services, most of their income comes from Medicaid or directly out of pocket. In 2011, Medicaid HCBS programs supported at least partial personal and custodial assistance for 3.2 million people across the nation, at an approximate cost of $55.4 billion.[58]

As with other forms of elder care, the vast majority of HCAs concentrate on their earnings; the needs of their elderly clients are secondary at best. In addition, the spiraling growth of for-profit companies, whether for medically oriented services subsidized through Medicare or personal assistance covered under Medicaid, has rendered it difficult to monitor unnecessary care, overpayments, other types of financial fraud, and the standard of services.[59]

In the case of Medicaid-supported services, states are responsible for licensing the agencies as well as any educational and training standards for nurse's aides; nineteen states have no certification requirements and in other jurisdictions they can be quite modest.[60] Investigators at *The Columbus Dispatch* observe that not even certification by Medicaid or Medicare provides sufficient protection: they found more than a few low-quality businesses in Ohio that are run by unscrupulous proprietors. As in other states, the overworked, underpaid aides receive inadequate training; there are high turnover rates as well.[61]

Moreover, consumers do not have reliable means for evaluating HCAs. The recently established "Medicare.gov Home Health Compare" website would not have proved very useful to me since only one of the companies providing services to my mother is listed and the data on that agency is far too incomplete to be worthwhile.[62] Yet, HCAs are highly profitable companies that feed at the government trough and, similar to nursing homes, have complicated organizational structures that often obscure accountability. They have increasingly become targets for PE firms, as well.

༄

Similar to other low-income elders, my mother received only limited Medicaid-supported at-home care, and could not afford sufficient additional help on her own; she could manage only ten hours per week of private-pay services, which she obtained through ResCare, Inc.

As with many other HCAs, ResCare has a complex history of ownership. After an initial public offering (IPO) in 1992, the company began trading on the NASDAQ exchange. Subsequently, in 2004 and 2010, respectively, two Canadian Onex Partner Funds (both private equity investment firms), together with Onex, Inc. (the parent management and investment firm),[63] purchased 98 percent of ResCare's outstanding common stock for a total of $452.4 million; ResCare is now a wholly owned subsidiary of Onex ResCare Holdings Corporation, which in turn is owned by the Onex investors.[64] The PE firm operates in a wide variety of industries in addition to home care.[65] In 2013, its President, CEO, and Chairman of the Board, Gerald Schwartz, received $85.3 million in salary, bonuses, and stock options.[66] He owns 19 percent of Onex (after selling a million shares in November 2013); his overall net worth is $2 billion.[67]

Since its takeover by Onex, ResCare has steadily acquired numerous other firms, including a large number of HCAs throughout the United States. Home care is one of ResCare's four main business segments, which in 2013 accounted for slightly over 22 percent of its total revenues, or $365.9 million.[68] That year, the company earned $1.6 billion, with a total net profit of $49.9 million.[69] Its top five executives alone received $3.3 million in salary, bonuses, stock options, and non-equity incentive cash awards.[70]

It is noteworthy that Medicaid and, to a lesser extent Medicare, comprise a substantial portion of ResCare's income, primarily through its residential and home care subdivisions. In its 2013 SEC report, the company clearly noted its financial dependence on American health and LTC programs.[71] Thus, the steep executive salaries and benefit packages are largely paid for by U.S. taxpayers.

In contrast, my mother could secure only limited in-home care because of ResCare's high charges, $16.50 an hour, plus mileage. Yet, as suggested earlier, her aide earned only $9.00 an hour (and some small undisclosed amount for gasoline); although Julie was covered under Social Security, she received no health care insurance or other benefits and relied on Medicaid for her three children. In essence, Rescare siphoned off for itself a considerable percentage of the money mom paid for her personal services.

The sizable disparity between Rescare's billing rate to customers and the wages the firm pays to its workers is typical of how the industry treats the caring labor force as a whole. In 2008, the national average cost of personal assistance services was $19.82, but the mean starting salary for the aides was $9.69 ($20,000 per year for full-time employees).[72]

Despite the grueling nature of the work, which is one of the most physically demanding jobs in the nation, roughly 40 percent of home health aides rely on Medicaid and other forms of public assistance for themselves or their families. Moreover, there are generally few or no benefits.[73] The vast majority of these caregivers are women (90 percent), most of whom are minorities (53 percent); nearly one-third are immigrants (28 percent). Currently, there are nearly 2.5 million personal care assistants in the United States and the number is expected to grow dramatically over the next several decades.

❧

In addition to ongoing help with the basic tasks of daily living, my mother also obtained Medicare-funded post-acute care from home health agencies subsequent to several falls and two hospitalizations. In one of these instances, three separate organizations had their hands in the till, which not only complicated accountability and raised costs but also fostered a detrimental lag between mom's discharge from the hospital and the delivery of desperately needed restorative therapy. The convoluted process was initiated by Univita Health, Inc., a case management company, which assessed and certified mom's need for services; she languished for two days in her apartment before the evaluation was made.

Following the appraisal, Univita informed Primary Medical Staffing, Inc., a home health agency, what services she was eligible for. That company, in turn, authorized Affordable Rehab Services, Inc., one of its subcontractors, to send out a physical therapist. After another two-day wait, as discussed earlier in these pages, my mother's actual therapy consisted of spinning her legs around a puny portable pedal bike for fifteen minutes, twice a week, for a month.

Univita was formed in 2008 by a PE firm, Genstar Capital, LLC, which invests in the health care, software, financial services, and industrial technology industries.[74] According to its website, "Genstar Capital partners with leading industry executives [in the case of Univita with Ben and Hugh Lytle] to accelerate growth and profitability at our portfolio companies." Genstar currently has $4 billion of committed capital under management by its several GPs, whose only goal is to enhance their financial position.

Providing 450,000 in-home assessments throughout the United States during 2013, Univita Health has poised itself to take advantage of the lucrative Medicare-funded post-acute care market. According to a profile by Hoovers, Inc., the firm had $47.5 million in revenues during 2012.[75] Recently, it has been acquiring its competitors, including Enurgi (2009); Atenda Healthcare

Solutions and its affiliated companies (2010); and All-Med Services of Florida, Inc. and its subsidiaries (2012).[76]

The second agency involved in Dorothy Katz's post-acute care, Primary Medical Staffing, Inc., has been a Medicare certified for-profit home care firm since 2007. Serving Florida's Dade and Broward counties, it is co-owned by Prinston Jean-Glaude (president) and Edwige Jen-Glaude (vice president). Its annual revenues in 2013 were roughly $250,000.[77] Since 2011, they have incorporated three more health/medical agencies, including Primary Medical Center and Urgent Care Clinic, Inc. (2011); Primary Doctor at Home, Inc. (2011); and Primary Medical Rehab Center, Inc. (2013). The small establishment that actually sent out the therapist, Affordable Rehab Services, Inc., is co-owned by a physical therapist and a nurse, both of whom also own two home health agencies. Founded in 1997, Affordable Rehab Services' revenues were just under $500,000 in 2013.[78]

Medicare Advantage Plans: The Case of Humana Health Plans, Inc.

Medicare has become increasingly privatized since 2003 through its Part C Medicare Advantage (MA) managed care alternative, thereby handing over more taxpayer dollars to proprietary firms. Buttressed through generous payments to the insurers (some analysts report that the compensation is at least 13 percent higher than for the traditional government-run program)[79] and enticing auxiliary benefits for customers, these managed care organizations have grown steadily and now cover nearly 30 percent of the eligible elderly and persons with disabilities.[80] Costing roughly $115 billion in 2012, or 25 percent of total Medicare outlays, profits soared at public expense.[81]

It is not only the supplementary benefits, however, that have lured individuals into MA plans. Certain segments of the noninstitutionalized low-income population, like my mother during her Florida years, have income that is too high to qualify for Medicaid in their state; they simply cannot afford to pay for the huge "gaps" in original Medicare coverage.[82] Nor can they afford the expensive supplemental policies. Although Dottie received a number of "add-ons" through her Humana Medicare Advantage plan, such as drug coverage, she was short-changed in many essential ways.

For instance, within Humana's limited network it was difficult to find a decent primary care doctor—or at least one who would take the time to figure out what was wrong with her. If any of her initial physicians had truly listened to mom, observed her and read through the records carefully, the Parkinson's disease could have and should have been diagnosed years earlier. Suitable specialists were even scarcer. She also needed more serious attention to her out-of-control glaucoma, which eventually led to blindness. And, her eyedrops were so micro-managed by Humana that at times she had to do without one of the essential, more expensive medications.

The evidence suggests, as mom and I later found out, that Medicare Advantage tends to be more satisfactory for the healthiest segments of the sixty-five and over population than for those with continuous, expensive medical needs. Judith Stein, Executive Director of the Center for Medicare Advocacy, argues:

> Private Medicare Advantage plans work for people when they are relatively well, but fall short of traditional Medicare when they are sick or disabled . . . This is particularly true for our clients with long-term and chronic conditions, many of whom also have low incomes. They are often denied coverage for necessary skilled care, or it is terminated before it should be, while the same coverage would be available in traditional Medicare.[83]

Covering 17 percent of Advantage plan clients (or 2.4 million people), Humana, Inc., is the second largest managed care company serving the elderly.[84] Fully 66 percent of its total revenues and 58 percent of its profits accrue from Medicare dollars.[85] Its net profit in FY 2013 was $1.2 billion, and its share price gained 16 percent over the following year.[86] Concomitantly, according to 2013 Security Exchange Commission records, its top executives earned a total of $24.5 million in base salary, bonuses, stocks, option awards, and other benefits.[87] Critically, these firms are only intermediaries between the national government (which pays them) and the providers (who deliver the services); they do not provide any direct services to their elderly and disabled enrollees.[88]

Assisted-Living Facilities

In addition to home care services, other alternatives to nursing homes are proliferating, especially assisted-living facilities (ALFs).[89] Fully 82 percent are for-profit, the highest proportion among long-term care provider types. Over two-thirds are relatively small places, ranging from four to twenty-five beds. Nevertheless, the larger facilities serve 81 percent of all residents and a significant portion of the homes is chain affiliated.[90] Although Medicaid funding for AFL services is increasing in some states, the vast majority of such care is paid for privately, out-of-pocket.[91]

There are no national standards or guidelines for residential homes; licensing, the extent of regulations, staff training requirements and the type of enforcement measures, if any, vary considerably among the states. In any case, their rapid growth and in most instances relatively small size have rendered it difficult to monitor them effectively. Conditions vary considerably; places with first-rate accommodations can be quite pricey, way beyond the resources of low-income households. The better ALFs eschew Medicaid beneficiaries even where state subsidies are available. At present, there is relatively limited data on ALFs, despite mounting concern about their quality of care.[92] And since there is no government rating system, it is challenging to select a residential care home. I certainly did not fare very well.

My mother's brief stay in one of Florida's small-scale ALFs had been a disquieting experience, to say the least. Even though I personally checked the place out, its glossy appearance unfortunately appealed to me; I was a daughter desperate for decent care. As suggested earlier in these pages, mom had been treated like a commodity on a production line, her services organized to maximize revenue for its sole proprietor. It has not been possible for me to uncover financial information about the owner's two enterprises (Miriam's Place, Inc. and Sunshine Place, Inc.) or even the extent of public funding for the residents.

Some Final Observations

Whether in nursing homes, assisted-living facilities or at home, the aged tend to be at the mercy of proprietary companies, including publicly traded chains and increasingly PE firms, where the health and well-being of clients is secondary, at best, to financial considerations. Care work is also shaped by providers to conform to business practices, which has adverse effects on the way services are delivered.

Elderly long-term care users are in no position to fight back against any neglect, deficient care, or even abusive conditions. About 30 percent of home health patients, nearly 50 percent of nursing home occupants, and 40 percent of assisted-living residents experience Alzheimer's disease or other types of dementia.[93] Their beleaguered families, too, are no match for these corporations. In my experience, they have little power over the type, extent, or quality of care provided.

The placement of government-subsidized services in the hands of impersonal markets and the sanction of the profit motive over the needs of elderly and disabled people have led to an abdication of social responsibility for our most vulnerable citizens as well as a lack of accountability for public money. The evidence clearly suggests that the current private/public partnership model feeds the U.S. medical and LTSS industrial complex but does not foster widespread access to quality care.

15

Conclusion

The Future of Long-Term Care

I have been a nursing home daughter for over three years, still engaging in certain hands-on care and, periodically, pointless paperwork largely for income verification purposes. Even at Gracedale, which has served mom well, there is an ongoing need for me to advocate for her since so much can go wrong at an institution. Partial dentures and hearing aids are intermittently crushed underfoot, items go missing, ingrown toenails reoccur and personal hygiene occasionally falls short. Still, my onerous long-distance caring duties have ended, together with the financial burdens, and I can now center my attention on giving my mother the emotional support and affection she so desperately craves and deserves.

My elder care journey with my mother, mostly unbidden, can—and does—happen to millions of adult daughters and increasingly sons. Yet, they are mostly on their own, without sufficient public long-term supports and services (LTSS) to ease the way. In most states, home-based assistance for elderly individuals through Medicaid is sparse relative to need, and the economically disadvantaged are shunted into low-quality nursing homes unless unpaid relatives assume primary responsibility for hands-on care. There are few first-rate private accommodations that accept the poor, and government facilities like Gracedale are relatively scarce. Middle-class households must impoverish themselves in order to qualify for Medicaid and they, too, often wind up in an institution unless the family steps in.

Abdication of social responsibility for our care-dependent older population has led to emotionally, physically, and economically beleaguered adult children who, like me, may be seniors themselves. Untrained and inexperienced, they contend with a confounding array of complex illnesses and multiple functional and cognitive disabling conditions, including Alzheimer's disease and related dementias. Long-term care (LTC) services in the United States consume a large percentage of the national and state budgets (one-third of Medicaid) but fail to effectively serve our disabled aged or their overwhelmed family caregivers.

The Affordable Care Act: Long-Term Supports and Services

The Patient Protection and Affordable Care Act (ACA), which President Obama signed into law in March 2010, set out to achieve universal health insurance for medical care. The few and scattered programs inserted into the law for LTC, despite the dire need for far-reaching action, occurred as an afterthought. Besides, the White House was committed to pricing ACA at under $900 billion and the sizeable estimated cost of LTSS precluded a more comprehensive approach. Nevertheless, ACA contains several provisions aimed at expanding access to home and community-based services (HCBS); improving nursing home quality; developing the direct-care workforce; and enhancing the financing of care for dually eligible Medicare and Medicaid recipients.[1]

The legislation offers several voluntary opportunities for states to rebalance LTC away from nursing homes and toward HCBS, with various federal matching rates. These include the Balancing Incentive Payments Program (BIP)[2] and new or expanded alternatives for amending standard Medicaid plans, such as the Community First Choice Option (CFC). BIP provides enhanced federal dollars to states that are currently spending less than 50 percent of their LTC budgets on HCBS. It requires participating jurisdictions to render organizational revisions, such as a "no wrong door-single entry point system," and to standardize their eligibility assessment instruments. Under CFC, states are permitted to add attendant services to their Medicaid plans for people who otherwise would require institutional care. Another endeavor directed at alternatives to nursing homes amends the Deficit Reduction Act of 2005 by raising allowable eligibility levels for Section 1915 (i) at-home benefits and lets states pinpoint specific groups for assistance.[3]

The impact of these approaches most likely will be quite limited because they depend on voluntary state action and furnish insufficient financial incentives relative to the costs of increasing HCBS. In the case of CFC, the financial burdens could be substantial since states cannot target services to specific groups or geographic areas and waiting lists are prohibited. Moreover, BIP is a time-limited demonstration, with a national budget cap. It also requires costly structural changes and has extensive reporting requirements that most likely will deter budget-conscious state leaders.[4]

An additional area of concern for ACA was the ongoing unsatisfactory care in a large portion of nursing homes. Notwithstanding the extensive dependence of LTC firms on Medicare, Medicaid, and other public programs for revenues, government regulations are weak as is their enforcement.[5] The Nursing Home Reform Act of 1987, for instance, has categorically failed to upgrade conditions in institutions despite its requirement that residents achieve or maintain their "highest practicable physical, mental, and psychosocial well-being." The survey and complaint processes, in conjunction with a dearth of severe sanctions imposed on poorly performing institutions, have proven inadequate to meet these goals. Since the law's enactment, the prevalence of abuse, neglect, and substandard care has continued unabated.[6]

According to one research group, any attempts since the passage of that act to advance more rigorous regulations had failed, primarily because of opposition from the powerful nursing home lobby.[7] Supporters of legislation that had been thwarted in 2009—the Elder Justice Act (EJA) and the Nursing Home Transparency and Improvement Act—subsequently slipped the main provisions into ACA. These center on four tactics: greater transparency on facility ownership and staffing levels in conjunction with an enhanced Nursing Home Compare Website; culture change within facilities via internal compliance and ethics programs; development and implementation of a standardized complaint form and an improved resolution process; and better training of aides.[8]

As suggested in this narrative, these new measures will not even begin to address the structural and financial aspects of deficient care in so many U.S. nursing homes. For example, the proprietorship information that ACA requires, though beneficial, does not allow the government or consumers to untangle the complicated operational configurations or render individual facilities, their larger chain owners, and PI firms accountable for substandard care. Not only can they still hide behind legal protections but the industry defeated an imposition of severe penalties (including facility closure) for ongoing offenders.[9] Likewise, the directive for culture modification through self-directed mechanisms is wildly out of sync with the reality of the situation: the economic goals of the mostly for-profit companies aim to take as much value out of the facilities as feasible, regardless of the impact on residents.

ACA also seeks to improve the recruitment, retention, and training of direct-care nursing aides. According to Robyn Stone and Natasha Bryant, this is the first congressional focus on LTC workforce issues, particularly frontline staff.[10] All the same, the emphasis is on greater training opportunities; more precise data on facility and agency staffing levels, turnover rates[11] and benefits;[12] and encouragement of national criminal checks. The law does not tackle, however, the more fundamental barriers to hiring and retaining workers: meager salaries that are substantially below those of other U.S. workers; few benefits; backbreaking work; and a paucity of career advancement opportunities. Further, while accurate staffing data may increase transparency, it would have been far more valuable to mandate higher staffing levels and an increase in the minimum federally required training hours.[13]

Another ostensible objective of the reform bill is to lower the cost of caring for dual eligibles while also upgrading their access to and quality of services. These nine million adults who are entitled to both Medicare and Medicaid, like my mother, are a medically complex and expensive group.[14] ACA offers states grants for demonstration projects to test payment and service delivery methods that integrate the two programs. Notwithstanding, David Graboski argues that such financial alignment models may in fact enhance services for recipients but they do not typically save money. He concludes that if we want to better serve our economically disadvantaged elders and people with disabilities, we most likely will have to pay more, not less.[15]

The enormity of the LTC challenge is plainly dwarfed by the several ACA initiatives. They offer states a hodgepodge of alternatives that foster marginal changes, at best. What remains, in the end, is the same LTSS system and its inherent systemic problems. Individuals in need of personal assistance must still rely on a needs-tested program that demeans indigent people and impoverishes the middle class. They and their family caregivers will continue to endure burdening paperwork and bureaucratic hurdles not encountered by participants in other social programs such as Social Security. Similarly, the aged poor have not gained access to better-quality nursing homes or assisted-living facilities. It's unlikely that any of the more recent policies would have changed Dorothy Katz's adverse experiences as a low-income elder.

Although ACA broadens state Medicaid HCBS options relative to institutional care, a rebalancing that appeals to beneficiaries and LTC policy analysts alike, it does not allocate sufficient national funds for low-income people to remain in their homes without substantial family help.[16] State budgets are already under pressure to control Medicaid outlays, not to enlarge them. My mother would not have gained extra caregiving hours in Florida, or at least not enough to have kept her at home.

Lastly, geographic location will persist in determining the amount, scope, and duration of services for the chronically ill population and not the extent of their physical or cognitive disabilities. Perhaps mom would have fared better had she lived in a more generous state. As Andrea Campbell tells us in her poignant memoir about her suddenly disabled sister-in-law, "Nowhere else can your fate differ so much from one locale to another within the same country."[17]

A Better Future?

Due to advances in medicine and population aging, federal and state LTSS outlays are expected to swell over the next several decades. By 2030 the number of people age sixty-five and over should reach 75 million or 20 percent of the U.S. total, compared to 13 percent today. The oldest of the old, individuals most in need of personal assistance in performing activities of daily living, will climb from 5.5 million in 2010 to 19 million by 2050 as the last of the baby boomers turn eighty-five.[18] Fully 70 percent of them are expected to use some form of LTC services.[19]

One of the more promising ACA initiatives, the Community Living Assistance Services and Supports (CLASS) Act, was repealed before implementation.[20] It was a voluntary, contributory LTC insurance program, run by the federal government, available to nearly all workers regardless of their medical or physical situation. Still, because it relied exclusively on individual premiums and precluded adverse selection, the program was financially unsustainable over the seventy-five years of solvency mandated by the law.[21] What is more, the cash benefit would have covered only a fraction of an individual's daily LTSS expenses.[22]

The evidence indicates that private long-term care insurance is not a viable solution either. Premiums tend to be prohibitively expensive for moderate- and low-income families, and recently have been skyrocketing for people who already own policies.[23] Plans typically pay far less than the actual cost of care, cap the number of benefit years, impose elimination periods (generally ninety days), and usually are not indexed to inflation. Collecting on contracts can be challenging as well since qualifying conditions for claiming benefits tend to be stringent.[24] Just as critical, insurance companies cherry-pick the healthiest clients, refusing to enroll people even at risk for disabling disorders.

In my view, in order to meet the current and future needs of care-dependent individuals, the United States must implement a mandatory, government-run LTSS social insurance program. It would broaden the risk pool and ensure sustainable per capita financing. At the same time, a universal single-payer system would de-stigmatize the receipt of benefits; eliminate the pauperization of middle-class households; drastically reduce income verification requirements, recertification, and other burdensome procedures; and save money through lower administrative costs.

It would also equalize access and benefits, irrespective of household income or where one resides. Older people not only would be eligible for the same services in each state, but they could move to another locale more easily and expeditiously. It definitely would have simplified my mother's relocation from Florida to Pennsylvania as it would for other needy elders who want to be closer to their adult children and grandchildren. Moreover, in an all-embracing public program the choice between entering a nursing home or obtaining HCBS would be the same everywhere in the nation and the quality of services would no longer depend on one's ability to pay.

In order to recruit a sufficient, committed, and professional labor force, such a publicly financed LTC program must be accompanied by higher wages and benefits, advancement opportunities and workplace improvements for direct-care workers. As in other industrialized nations, the social insurance system could be funded through a mix of payroll taxes, premium payments, and general revenues.[25]

Finally, we need to reevaluate the structure of the service delivery system. The current private/public "partnerships" for LTSS extract extreme value from our nation's resources for the for-profit sector to the detriment of frail seniors and disabled younger adults. They have contributed to the unacceptably high private and public costs for services as well.

Complicated legal arrangements for nursing homes and home health agencies have allowed several layers of companies and related entities to pocket large portions of the Medicare and Medicaid pie while sheltering the businesses from consumer lawsuits and government sanctions for deficient and sometimes harmful care. Concurrently, PI firms rake in millions of government dollars but are not accountable to their customers or the public for the standard of services provided. If we strive for high-quality LTC, policymakers must break up the multi-facility nursing home chains, outlaw the takeover of home health agencies and nursing homes by PI firms, establish tough regulations for the industries, and impose harsh penalties for violating them.

Pharmaceutical corporations and their elevated profits, too, must be reined in. We are the only nation in the industrialized world where drug prices are not controlled. Despite its potentially huge financial bargaining power, even Medicare has been prohibited by Congress from negotiating fees. Any future LTSS social insurance must cap payments for prescription medicines.

In addition, a government-run system would have no need for insurance companies as intermediaries. While ACA caps the medical loss ratio (MLR) of Medicare Advantage companies at 85 percent, original Medicare operates at a 97 percent MLR.[26] With an elimination of the two commercial segments of Medicare—Part C (Medicare Advantage) and Part D (prescription drugs)—taxpayer dollars that have been used for non-medical purposes could be diverted instead to direct beneficiary services and benefits.

Overall, the health care system, specifically the long-term care sector, is ill-suited for market strategies and the concomitant pressures of profit maximization. As with many other economically advanced nations, the United States would benefit from a restructuring of the nursing home and home care delivery systems from commercial to predominantly public and nonprofit providers. Such a shift would not only eliminate the perverse incentives that currently prioritize financial gains over people, but it could foster a less costly and more humane means of serving our vulnerable citizens.

Clearly, even though the U.S. public sector spends billions of dollars for long-term care services, the needs of frail older people and their caregivers are for the most part not being met. This elder care journey with my mother made me appreciate more fully numerous issues I had earlier discerned through research and it acquainted me with new ones, along with their complications, that could only have been discovered firsthand. My immediate intention in sharing these insights is to let other caregivers know that they are not alone in their struggles, clarify some of the policy and implementation dilemmas, and perhaps assist people in figuring out solutions. A larger goal, however, has been to shed light on the underlying systemic problems deeply rooted in the American LTSS system and how these have affected such vital concerns as high costs, inequitable access to services, and low quality care. It is also to inform readers about the essential need for alternative approaches. Unless our elected officials advance fundamental structural changes, the long-term care industries that have positioned themselves to feed at the public trough will continue to thrive at the expense of the chronically ill aged, younger disabled individuals, and their struggling paid and informal caregivers.

Notes

Prologue

1. Laura Katz Olson, *The Politics of Medicaid* (New York: Columbia University Press, 2010).

2. A limited amount of needs-based public LTSS are available through Medicaid, a joint federal-state program for the low-income population. Since its enactment in 1965, millions of individuals age eighty-five and over, those predominantly in need of assistance with the activities of daily living, have relied fully or partially on the program, mainly for institutional care. In recent years, the bias in favor of nursing homes has shifted steadily toward HCBS that are offered either under a state's regular Medicaid plan or, increasingly, through Section 1915 (c) waivers. Using several waiver types that must be approved by the Federal Department of Health and Human Services, states are allowed to disregard certain aspects of national Medicaid regulations. In this case, the waiver is a Section 1915 (c) home and community-based services program that provides in-home services in lieu of nursing home care.

The percentage of Medicaid LTSS funding devoted to home and community-based services (HCBS) expanded from 20 percent in 1995 to 45 percent by 2012, reaching a total of $55.4 billion; the waiver programs alone cost $38.9 billion. The number of people served increased by an average of four percent annually; by 2011 over 3.2 million people received Medicaid home-based assistance, including 1.5 million through waivers. Terrence Ng, Charlene Harrington, Mary Beth Musumeci, and Erica C. Reaves, *Medicaid and Community-Based Services Programs: 2011 Data Update,* Menlo Park, CA: Henry J. Kaiser Family Foundation, Kaiser Commission on Medicaid and the Uninsured, December 14 2014, http://kff.org/report-section/medicaid-home-and-community-based-services-programs-2011-data-update-medicaid-hcbs-participants-and-expenditures/.

3. The actual number of service hours provided is tightly controlled and falls considerably short of need. Forty-two states control costs in their waiver programs either through total expenditure limits or hourly per person caps. Nationally, during 2011 the total annual per person expenditure on HCBS waivers for the aged averaged between $11,000 and $12,000. The corresponding figure for Florida was

roughly $9,000. Even in the more generous states, the total amount of allowable services is not sufficient without family help. Ibid.

4. There tend to be long waiting lists for receipt of services in a large proportion of states and these have steadily grown over the last decade. The average national waiting time is fully 29 months. In 2013, forty states had waiting lists for Section 1915 (c) waiver services. Since 2003, the percentage of frail, needy people waiting for LTSS grew by an average of 12 percent annually. Ibid.

5. The national, state, and local Area Agencies on Aging are authorized under the Older Americans Act (OAA) of 1965. For more information, see http://www.aoa.gov/AoA_programs/OAA/.

6. In 2012, the median annual charge for a nursing home stay (in a semi-private room) was $73,000. For an ALF, the corresponding figure was $39,600. Home health and personal services averaged $43,472 ($19 an hour) and $41,184 ($18 an hour), respectively, for forty-four hours of care per week or six hours a day. The Scan Foundation, *Who Pays for Long-Term Care in the U.S.?*, Fact Sheet, January 2013, available at www.TheSCANFoundation.org.

In contrast, the median income of the sixty-five and over population was $28,056; slightly over one-third had earnings under $20,000. The median net worth of such households, excluding equity in a home, was $27,300. U.S. Social Security Administration, Office of Research and Disability Policy, Office of Research, Evaluation and Statistics, *Income of the Aged Chart book, 2012*, April 2014, SSA publication no, 13-11727; U.S. Census Bureau, Table 1, "Median Value of Assets for Households, by Type of Asset Owned and Selected Characteristic: 2011," www.census.gov/people/wealth/data/dtables.html.

7. Loraine A. West, Samantha Cole, Daniel Goodkind, and Wan He, *65+ in the United States: 2010*, Current Population Reports, U.S. Department of Health and Human Services, U.S. Department of Commerce, U.S. Census Bureau (June 2014).

8. The median annual benefit for couples age sixty-five and over in 2011 was $47, 494, as compared to $18,000 for elders living alone, most of whom are female. Social Security Administration, Fast *Facts and Figures About Social Security, 2013*, Office of Retirement and Disability Policy, Office of Research, Evaluation, and Statistics, Washington, DC, SSA Publication No. 13-11785, August 2013. Available at www.ssa.gov.

Nearly half of older women depend on Social Security for 90 percent or more of their income. U.S. Social Security Administration, *Income of the Aged Chartbook*, 2014.

9. Poverty thresholds in 2011 were $10,788 and $13,596, respectively, for a single person and couple age sixty-five and over. www,census.gov/hhes/www/poverty/data/threshld/.

10. In 2010, women comprised 67 percent of people age eighty-five and over; nearly half of them live alone. They represent 63 percent of home health care users, 68 percent of nursing home residents, and 72 percent of assisted living dwellers. U.S.

Department of Health and Human Services (HHS), Administration on Aging, Administration for Community Living, *A Profile of Older* Americans (2012), www.aoa.gov/Aging_statistics/Profile/2012/docs/2012profile.pdf; Lauren Harris-Kojetin, Manisha Sengupta, Eunice Park-Lee, and Roberto Valverde, *Long-term Care Services in the United States: 2013 overview.* Hyattsville, MD: National Center for Health Statistics, 2013.

11. Roughly 66 percent of the aged with functional limitations receive all of their care solely from family members; another 26 percent rely on both kin and paid help. According to AARP researchers, since the mid-1990s families have been increasingly bearing the full responsibility alone. Lynn Feinberg, Susan Reinhard, Ari Houser, and Rita Choula. *Valuing the Invaluable: 2011 Update, The Growing Contributions and Costs of Family Caregivers,* AARP Public Policy Institute, Washington, DC, 2011. Available at http://assets.aarp.org/rgcenter/ppi/ltc/isl-caregiving.pdf.

12. Lynn Feinberg, "Now's the Time for a National Strategy to Support Family Caregivers," AARP Public Policy Institute, Blog posted July 15, 2013, http.//blog.aarp.org/author/lynn-feinberg/.

13. Metlife Mature Market Institute, *Miles Away: The Metlife Study of Long-Distance Caregiving: Findings from a National Study by the National Alliance for Caregiving International,* Westport, CT (July 2014), www.caregiving.org/data/milesaway.pdf; A. V. Chari, John Engberg, Kristin Ray, and Ateev Mehrotra, "The Opportunity Costs of Informal Elder-Care in the United States," Rand Corporation, October 27, 2014, www.rand.org/pubs/external_publications/EP66196.html; The Scan Foundation, "Who Pays for Long-Term Care in the U.S.?," 2013.

14. A recent survey of long-distance caregivers found that half of them visit their frail older kin at least a few times a month. Seventy-five percent spend twenty-two hours a month providing direct assistance and 50 percent devote almost a full day each week to managing services. Nearly 10 percent of survey respondents pay for at least some of the formal assistance for their care-dependent family member. Moreover, eighty percent of the survey respondents providing long-distance care work full time or part time. Metlife Mature Market Institute, *Miles Away,* 2014.

15. In an attempt to keep elderly patients out of hospitals or to shorten their stay, Medicare offers generous post-acute benefits for skilled nursing, therapy, and medical social work services, either in one's own house or in an institution. For each period of a covered hospital stay of at least three days, Medicare pays for up to one-hundred days of post-acute care for beneficiaries requiring skilled nursing or rehabilitation services; both the nursing facilities and HCAs must be Medicare-certified. There are up to twenty days of allowable care in nursing homes without charge to patients; the institutions are paid per day of service. There is no limit on the number of allowable episodes for home health services as long as they are medically necessary and the physician reauthorizes them.

Funding for post-acute care has grown dramatically over the last decade and by 2013 represented eight percent of total Medicare spending, or $46.7 billion. Home health services accounted for 3 percent ($17.5 billion) and skilled nursing homes for another 5 percent ($29.2 billion). Henry J. Kaiser Family Foundation, Kaiser Commission on Medicaid and the Uninsured, *Medicare Advantage Fact Sheet*, Menlo Park, CA: Henry J. Kaiser Family Foundation, Kaiser Commission on Medicaid and the Uninsured, February 25, 2010, *Medicare Advantage Fact Sheet*, May 1, 2014, http://kff.org/Medicare/fact-sheet/medicare-advantage-fact-sheet/.

16. One of the main objectives of HIPAA is to protect the confidentiality and security of a patient's health information. Yet, it often serves as an obstacle for family caregivers when they need to acquire sometimes essential information about their frail elderly relatives or obtain benefits for them. Despite several urgent situations, for example, hospital emergency room personnel would not talk to me, citing HIPAA as the reason. Moreover, although the legislation requires institutions such as hospitals and nursing homes to provide full records to patients at reasonable, cost-based fees, when requested, these charges can be somewhat prohibitive for low-income families.

17. A Durable Power of Attorney (POA) is a legal document that authorizes a designated person to make legal and financial decisions on your behalf, including if and when you become mentally incapacitated.

18. As will be discussed later in the book, mom received ten hours of in-home personal care through the Channeling Project Waiver for people age sixty-five and over. It is one of Florida's several Section 1915 (c) waivers. In 2012, it provided limited home care hours to 1,265 people in two counties. Florida Agency for Health Care Administration, Department of Elder Affairs, *Medicaid Long-Term Care in Florida, Conference on Aging: New Game, New Rules*, August 20, 2012, http//ahca.myFlorida.com/Medicaid/recent_presentations_Medicaid_Long_Term_Care_in_Florida_FCOA_082012.pdf.

19. SSA's automated help line has only one number for its over 55 million beneficiaries; it does not provide the phone numbers of local offices.

20. Medicare's "Nursing Home Compare" website was established by the Centers for Medicare and Medicaid Services (CMS) in 2008. It rates nursing homes from one to five stars on four broad categories, with the higher stars indicating better quality: (1) overall rating; (2) health inspections; (3) staffing; and (4) quality measures.

21. Bradford H. Gray, ed., *For-Profit Enterprise in Health Care*, Institute on Medicine (U.S.) Committee on Implications of For-Profit Enterprise in Health Care (Washington, DC: National Academies Press, 1986).

22. Stephanie Coontz, *The Way We Never Were: American Families and the Nostalgia Trap* (New York: Basic Books, 2000), 6.

23. In 2012, there were 12,200 HCAs (serving 3.9 million elderly), 15,700 nursing homes (serving 1.2 million residents) and 22,200 ALFs (serving 665,000 residents). Nearly 79 percent of HCAs, 68 percent of nursing homes, and 78 percent of ALFs are for-profit companies. Only 6 percent, 7 percent, and 1 percent, respectively, are government-run. Harris-Kojetin, Sengupta, Park-Lee, and Valverde, *Long-term Care Services in the United States*, 2013.

24. Chen Medical Centers, a family-owned business, has eleven locations in Florida. It provides an integrated approach to medical services for elders that fosters the coordination of treatments for sometimes complicated and interconnected disorders: there are in-house primary care physicians, various types of specialists and a pharmacy. They also offer complimentary wheelchair accessible van service for doctor appointments.

25. See, for example, Molly Best Tinsley, *Entering the Blue Stone* (Ashland, OR: Fuze Publishing LLC, 2012); Jane Gross, *A Bittersweet Season: Caring for Our Aging Parents—And Ourselves* (New York: Vintage Books, 2012); John Thorndike, *The Last of His Mind* (Athens, OH: Swallow Press/Ohio University Press, 2009); Carol O'Dell, *Mothering Mother: A Daughter's Humorous and Heartbreaking Memoir* (Largo, FL: Kunati Inc. Book Publishers, 2007).

Chapter 2

1. Despite its extensive coverage of the sixty-five and over population, traditional Medicare contains considerable out-of-pocket expenses for premiums, deductibles, copays, and an array of essential but uncovered health services. Altogether, the program only pays for roughly half of a beneficiary's medical costs. Therefore, older people who can afford to do so purchase a Medigap policy to protect them against many of these charges. Bought from commercial insurance companies, these supplemental plans, averaging just under $200 per month in 2014, pay for many of the costs not covered by original Medicare.

Others, including my mother, purchase a Medicare Advantage plan: it is the successor to Medicare private-sector experiments with health maintenance organizations in the 1970s and later Medicare + Choice that was promoted through the Balanced Budget Act of 1997. Introduced under the Medicare Modernization Act of 2003, Medicare Advantage Part C privatized health insurance for a growing percentage of the sixty-five-and-over population; by 2014, nearly 30 percent of recipients were enrolled, mostly in commercial HMOs. These companies, while covering standard Medicare Parts A, B, and D benefits, control many aspects of the services they provide.

2. Denise, mom's second daughter, had died in 1985.

Chapter 3

1. At the lowest end of the income scale, there are nearly nine million Medicare beneficiaries who are designated as "dual eligibles." Depending on their state's income threshold, a large segment meets the criteria for full Medicaid coverage as well as financial assistance with Medicare premiums, deductibles, and co-insurance. Certain households, such as my mother, qualify for more limited financial aid through

the Medicare Savings Program, which grants various levels of help with Medicare's cost-sharing obligations. There are three separate levels of assistance, each based on a household's income as a percentage of the FPL. States pay for: (1) Medicare Parts A and B premiums and all of Medicare's deductibles, coinsurance, and copayments for people with monthly income limits of 100 percent of the FPL (Qualified Medicare Beneficiary or QMB); (2) the part B premium for people with monthly income up to 120 percent of the FPL (Specified Low-Income Medicare Beneficiary or SLMB); and (3) the Part B premium for people with monthly income limits of 135 percent of the FPL (Qualifying Individual or QI). However, QI funding is capped and not every eligible person receives the benefit. Mom was only eligible for QI.

2. There are stringent income tests for Medicaid eligibility that vary by state. It is often tied to the federal Supplemental Security Income (SSI) program ($674 per month in 2009 for an individual and $1, 011 for a couple): in 24 states, qualification for noninstitutionalized elderly and persons with disabilities was at or below SSI levels (or 75 percent of the Federal Poverty Level (FPL)); in 9 states, it was from 76 percent to 99 percent of the FPL; and in 17 states the threshold was 100 percent of the FPL or higher. In Florida, where my mother resided, the threshold was 75 percent of the FPL or $674.00; her monthly income that year was just under $1,000, rendering her ineligible. She would not have qualified in Pennsylvania either; the state's threshold was 100 percent of the FPL or $898 per month for a single person.

The maximum allowable assets are generally$2,000, though it could be higher in states such as Pennsylvania where it is up to $8,000.

3. Nursing homes and home health agencies are required to draw up a care plan for each patient that includes: an assessment of the patient's medical needs; what services she requires; her health and personal goals; and the means for potentially achieving these. For long-term care these objectives may embrace an optimal quality of life, comfort, and dignity. As will be shown in later chapters, these were not taken seriously by the nursing homes in Florida where my mother stayed for post-acute rehabilitative services. Their boiler-plate approach to her needs indicated a slapdash compliance with federal regulations. In contrast, Gracedale, her nursing home in Pennsylvania, took advantage of the care plan to enhance my mother's health and well-being.

Chapter 4

1. Although blindness can occur from Glaucoma, it is relatively rare if caught early and properly treated. According to one source, two-thirds of the people who eventually become blind from the condition either has serious vision loss at the time of diagnosis or do not participate fully in their treatment recommendations. At the same time, a small percentage of individuals with the disease develops an aggressive

form that requires more vigorous treatment. Online: www.glaucoma.org/treatment/understand-your-glaucoma-diagnosis.php; www.hopkinsmedicine.org; www.littlerockeye.com/glaucoma/.

Dorothy Katz's Glaucoma was identified in a timely manner because she regularly went to the eye doctor for annual check-ups and followed the care instructions after she was diagnosed. I'll never know if my mother's subsequent loss of sight was caused by her first ophthalmologist's medical neglect or whether she is just one of those unusual individuals whose glaucoma cannot be controlled.

Chapter 5

1. Eligibility for U.S. needs-based social welfare programs is merciless: they penalize people whose family assists them financially. Therefore, I couldn't officially declare the extent of my monetary help that, in fact, my mother could not do without.

2. A significant number of home health agencies label their aides and nurses as "independent contractors," thereby permitting the circumvention of certain benefits, overtime pay, and other labor protections under the Fair Labor Standards Act of 1938 and its amendments. According to the U.S. Department of Labor, however, most of these home health workers should be considered as employees instead, so it is unclear to me why the companies are still allowed to deny them their rights under the act. Online: www.dol.gov/whd/homecare/faq.htm#g8.

Chapter 7

1. There are different levels of support for patients requiring assistance in standing, moving, and transferring (i.e., to and from a bed, wheelchair, walker, toilet, and so on). For example, a care plan may document the need for only one helper (a "one-person assist") or mandate an additional aide (a "two-person assist"). A person who is unable to safely initiate and perform any part of the actions on his or her own is labeled a "total assist."

Chapter 8

1. As long as a doctor submits a written order, Medicare Part B will pay for outpatient Durable Medical Equipment, including hospital beds; blood sugar monitors; arm, leg and neck braces; canes; commode chairs; crutches; oxygen therapy; patient lifts; suction pumps; walkers; wheelchairs and power mobility devices; and the like.

Chapter 9

1. Guidelines for Medicaid-funded long-term services and supports tend to be more flexible than those for medical services per se, thereby allowing enrollment by individuals with higher household income but insufficient resources to pay for nursing home care. A majority of states allow Medicaid payments to nursing homes for individuals with income up to 300 percent of the FPL. Dottie qualifies for institutional care at Gracedale through Pennsylvania's medically needy standard which, in 2015, was $425 per month; the asset limit is $8,000. She must pay all of her income (Social Security and VA benefits) directly to the nursing home toward her care; this amount is deducted from Medicaid's contribution, except for a small monthly personal needs allowance of $45.

Although mom also is income-eligible for Medicaid waiver home-based services, she would only receive up to nine hours a week, obviously insufficient for her needs.

Chapter 11

1. Prior to 2013, Medicare used only an "Improvement Standard" as its authorization criteria for therapy services: the patient had to show the likelihood of recovery or actual progress toward that end. In *Jimmo v. Sebelius* (January 24, 2013), however, a U.S. Federal District Court determined that providers must also consider whether skilled therapy services are necessary to prevent further deterioration or preserve current capabilities.

2. Lehigh Valley Hospital–Muhlenberg, in Bethlehem, Pennsylvania, is a short-term nonprofit acute care hospital with 195 beds. It is part of the Lehigh Valley Network that includes several other hospitals in Allentown and Hazleton, along with specialized health services for children and a few outpatient facilities. In 2014, the hospital served 5,278 Medicare inpatients, at an average cost of $56,033 each; they represented roughly 25 percent of its total patient revenues. The hospital's net income that year was $21.2 million.

Muhlenberg's Total Performance Score (TPS) on quality measures was 34.36/100, or below the 37/100 median for U.S. hospitals (Effective October 2012, Centers for Medicare and Medicaid Services established a Value-Based Purchasing (VBP) program; each hospital's payments for Medicare patients are adjusted according to the TPS quality score. Online: www.ahd.com/free_profile.php.

3. The term hospitalist was first coined in 1996 and since then the number of such providers has surged. Dedicated primarily to inpatient hospital care, they are supposedly more attuned to the unique needs of acutely ill institutionalized patients, and more available to them than other types of health care professionals. Needless to say, I was not impressed with their accessibility or competency, especially after

learning about the terminally ill misdiagnosis. Hospitalists can also include Advance Practice Clinicians (APCs) who may be nurse practitioners or physicians' assistants.

Chapter 12

1. Betty has since died. Within several hours of her demise, every trace of her existence had been eradicated from the room. It was disconcerting. Almost immediately, she was replaced by Gabrielle, a wheelchair-bound woman whose attentive husband visits daily. His "FAMILY DOES LAUNDRY" sign competes with mine.

Chapter 13

1. Dottie qualifies for institutional care at Gracedale through Pennsylvania's medically needy standard which, in 2015, is $425 per month; the asset limit is $8,000. She pays all of her income (Social Security and VA benefits) directly to the nursing home toward the care; this amount is deducted from Medicaid's contribution. Although mom also is income-eligible for Medicaid waiver home-based services, she would only receive up to nine hours a week, obviously insufficient for her needs.

2. Middle-class families must first spend down nearly all of their assets to enable program eligibility. Seniors with modest savings, for example, pay for their own in-home custodial care directly out-of-pocket; after a short while many of them outlive their resources and are forced onto Medicaid. Paradoxically, because of the skimpy at-home assistance obtainable under the program, they are then stuck; either they must depend on their relatives to fill in the service "gaps" or are otherwise forced into an institution. Similarly, individuals paying privately for nursing homes often exhaust their assets and they too must rely on Medicaid for their future care. There are strict "look-back" rules: the government does not allow any transfer of assets in the five years prior to applying for Medicaid.

3. Eventually the allowance will be deposited each month into her personal account, thereby allowing mom to purchase more "extras" on her own.

4. Dorothy Katz—whose $946 monthly income was above Florida's Medicaid threshold—had received a small QI benefit that paid for the Medicare Part B premium; to retain it, she had to undergo a laborious annual recertification process. She also contended with a narrow network of providers and other restrictions associated with her Medicare Advantage plan, and faced some uncovered expenses. Yet, with the same income, as a nursing home resident in Pennsylvania she now qualifies as a full "dually eligible" beneficiary: she is entitled to original Medicare as her primary insurance, with no out-of-pocket outlays; she also obtains additional optional benefits through Pennsylvania's Medicaid plan.

5. Authorized under the Medicare Modernization Act of 2003, Medicare beneficiaries must purchase, annually, a separate commercial Medicare Part D prescription drug plan unless they enroll in a Medicare Advantage plan offering that benefit. However, the "Extra Help Program" subsidizes all of mom's out-of-pocket prescription drug costs.

6. These specialists are available to all nursing home patients, mostly paid for through Medicare. However, several of the services, such as the on-site dental and audiology clinics, require a monthly premium; Pennsylvania's Medical Assistance plan is picking up the tab for mom and other dually eligible beneficiaries.

7. For people with multiple, expensive medications the choice of plans can be quite narrow and, as I discovered, a firm is allowed to drop a drug, even within the year, with only a sixty-day notification.

Chapter 14

1. Medicare expenditures include Medicare Advantage (25 percent); hospital in-patient care (24 percent); physician payments (12 percent); outpatient prescription drugs (11 percent); hospital out-patient services (6 percent); skilled nursing homes (5 percent); home health services (3 percent); and other (14 percent). Henry J. Kaiser Family Foundation, Kaiser Commission on Medicaid and the Uninsured, *The Facts on Medicare Spending and* Financing, Menlo Park, CA: Henry J. Kaiser Family Foundation, Kaiser Commission on Medicaid and the Uninsured, July 28, 2014, http://kff.org/medicare/fact-sheet/Medicare-spending-and-financing-fact-sheet/.

2. Total federal Medicaid spending in 2012 was $248 billion. The McArthur and Pew Foundations, *State Health Spending on Medicaid: a 50-State Study of Trends and Drivers of Cost*, a report from the Pew Charitable Trusts and the McArthur Foundation, July 1014, www.pewtrusts.org/~/media/Datavisualizations/Interactives/2014/Medicaid/downloadables/state_health_care_spending_on_Medicaid.pdf.

3. Ibid.; The Center on Budget and Policy Priorities, *Policy Basics: An Introduction to Medicaid*, Washington, DC, May 8, 2013, htpp:cbpp/files/policybasics-medicaid.pdf.

4. The Medicaid portion is fully $123 billion, which represented nearly one-third of the low-income health program's total federal and state outlays in 2012; Medicare and other government programs accounted for another $8 billion or 4 percent. The rest is paid directly out-of-pocket ($46 billion or 22 percent) and through other private sources, such as medical or LTC insurance ($25 billion or 12 percent). The Scan Foundation, *Who Pays for Long-Term Care in the U.S.?*(updated), Fact Sheet, Long Beach, CA: The Scan Foundation, January 2013, www.thescanfoundation.org/sites/thescanfoundation.org/files/who_pays_for_ltc_us_jan_2013.fs.pdf.

Others have estimated the total LTC bill at between $211 billion and $306 billion annually. Lauren Harris-Kojetin, Manisha Sengupta, Eunice Park-Lee, and

Roberto Valverde, *Long-Term Care Services in the United States:2013 Overview* (Hyattsville, MD: National Center for Health Statistics, 2013).

5. This amount represents 71 percent of the total $1.9 billion in funding allocated under the Older Americans Act in 2012. Angela Napili and Kristen J. Colello, *Funding for the Older Americans Act and Other Aging Services Programs*, Congressional Research Service, CRS Report for Congress, February 22, 2013, http://fas.org/sgp/crs/misc/RL33880.pdf.

6. Drugs represented nearly $54 billion or 10 percent of Medicare outlays in 2012. Henry J. Kaiser Family Foundation, Kaiser Commission on Medicaid and the Uninsured, *Medicare Benefit Payments by Type of Service*, Menlo Park, CA: Henry J. Kaiser Family Foundation, Kaiser Commission on Medicaid and the Uninsured, July 15, 2013, http://kff.org/?attachment_id=64757.

7. Short-term, post-acute care costs in skilled nursing facilities amounted to $27 billion in 2012 or 5 percent of total Medicare outlays. Ibid.

8. Bradford H. Gray, ed., *For Profit Enterprise in Health Care*, Institute on Medicine Committee on Implications of for-profit Enterprise in Health Care, (Washington, DC: National Academy Press, 1986). National Academy Press, 1986.

9. There is variation in ownership structure across the states. In Florida, for example, 72 percent of nursing homes are proprietary, 26 percent are nonprofit and 2 percent are publicly owned, as compared to 51 percent, 44 percent, and 5 percent, respectively in Pennsylvania. U.S. Department of Health and Human Services (HHS), Center for Medicare and Medicaid Services (CMS), *Nursing Home Data Compendium 2013 Edition*, Washington, DC, 2013, www.cms.gov/Medicare/Provider-Enrollment-and-Certification/CertificationandComplianc/downloads/nursinghomedatacompendium_598.pdf.

10. The following discussion on PE firms relies heavily on Eileen Appelbaum and Rosemary Batt, *Private Equity at Work* (New York: Russell Sage Foundation, 2014).

11. Applebaum and Batt tell us that about 70 percent of the purchase price, sometimes as high as 90 percent, is funded through debt. In contrast, debt levels for publicly-traded companies are typically only 30 percent. Ibid.

12. This occurs when the PE firm takes on additional debt in order to pay themselves and their Limited Partners extra dividends.

13. Applebaum and Batt, *Private Equity at Work*, 6.

14. For further discussion see David G. Stevenson and David C. Grabowski, "Private Equity Investment and Nursing Home Care: Is it a Big Deal?" *Health Affairs*, 27, no. 5 (September 2008):1399–1408.

15. Joseph E. Casson and Julia McMillen, "Protecting Nursing Home Companies: Limiting Liability Through Corporate Restructuring," *Journal of Law Health*, Fall 2003: 577–613.

16. The operating establishment is then required to lease the property it formerly owned, often at inflated rents.

17. Casson and McMillen, "Protecting Nursing Home Companies"; Applebaum and Batt, *Private Equity at Work.*

18. The Dodd-Frank Act of 2010 now requires some limited reporting by certain PE firms but not the incomes of high level PE executives, which companies they have acquired, or any detailed financial information about them. Moreover, unlike publicly-traded companies these financial statements are confidential. Ibid.

19. Applebaum and Batt, *Private Equity at Work*, 161.

20. Vincent Mor, Jacqueline Zinn, Joseph Angelelli, Joan Teno, and Susan Miller, "Driven to Tiers: Socioeconoic and Racial Disparities in the Quality of Nursing Home Care," *Milbank Quarterly* 82 (2), 2004: 227–56.

21. Anna A. Amirkhanyan, Hyun Joon Kim, and Kristina T. Lambright, "Does the Public Sector Outperform the Nonprofit and For-Profit Sectors? Evidence from a National Panel Study on Nursing Home Quality and Access," *Journal of Policy Analysis and Management*, 27, no. 2, 2008: 326–53.

22. Charlene Harrington, Steffie Woolhandler, Joseph Mullen, and David U. Himmelstein, "Does Investor Ownership of Nursing Homes Compromise the Quality of Care?" *American Journal of Public Health*, 91, no. 9, September 2001: 1453.

23. The investigation focused on state survey deficiencies in California nursing homes during 1998. Ciaran O'Neill, Charlene Harrington, Martin Kitchener, and Debra Saliba, "Quality of Care in Nursing homes: An Analysis of Relationships Among Profit, Quality and Ownership" *Medical Care*, 41, no., 12, 2003:1318–30.

24. Amirkhanyan, Kim, and Lambright, "Does the Public Sector Outperform the Nonprofit and For-Profit Sectors?

25. O'Neill, Harrington, Kitchener, and Saliba, "Quality of Care in Nursing Homes."

26. Amirkhanyan, Kim, and Lambright, "Does the Public Sector Outperform the Nonprofit and For-Profit Sectors?," 348.

27. Ibid.

28. One researcher found that they were 21 percent and 57 percent more in voluntary and for-profit facilities, respectively. Anna A. Amirkhanyan, "The Smart-Seller Challenge: Exploring the Determinants of Privatizing Public Nursing Homes," *Journal of Public Administration Research and Theory*, 17, no. 3, July 2007: 501–27.

29. Ibid.

30. Ibid.

31. Monies, "As Nursing Home Care Improves."

32. It was incorporated as Washington Manor Health Care Associates, LLC in 2001 but on May 25, 2012 its legal name was changed to 4200 Washington Street Operations LLC. The facility is doing business as Hillcrest Nursing and Rehabilitation Center.

33. According to Medicare.gov/Nursing Home Compare, the following are owners and managers of Hillcrest Nursing and Rehabilitation Center in 2014: Troy

Antonik, Director/Officer; Joseph D. Conte, Director/Officer; Christina Firth, Director/Officer; Steven Fishman, Director/Officer; Robert Hartman, Director/Officer, owns 5 percent or more; Jeff Jefferson, Director/Officer; Isaac Neuberger, Director/Officer, owns 5 percent or more; David Reis, Director/Officer; Harold Sussman, Director/Officer; Carmen Telot, Director/Officer, Managing Employee; ZVI Tress. Director/Officer; Sea Crest Health Care, Operations/Managerial Control; Asher Low, Director/Officer and owns 5 percent or more; ALG Lavie, LLC, owns 5 percent or more; Columbia Pacific Opportunity Fund, L.P., owns 5 or more; David Reis Sub S Trust, owns 5 percent or more; Epsilon Health Care Properties, LLC, owns 5 percent or more; FC Investors XX1, LLC, owns 5 percent or more; Florida Health Care Properties, LLC, owns 5 percent or more; General Electric Capital Corporation; Genoa Healthcare Group, LLC, owns 5 percent or more; Lavie Care Centers, LLC, owns 5 percent or more; LV Investment, LLC, owns 5 percent or more; LV Operations 1, LLC, owns 5 percent or more; LV Operations 11, LLC, owns 5 percent or more; MCP Lavie, LLC, owns 5 percent or more; SAY La Vie, LLC, owns 5 percent or more; Senior Care Lavie, LLC, owns 5 percent or more; The 1995 David Reis Family Trust, owns 5 percent or more.

34. Established in 1966 by Lionel Pincus, Warburg Pincus is now a major global private equity firm with more than $39 billion in assets, invested in 144 diverse companies, under its management.

By the end of 2011, its health care sector had $7.9 billion in investments. Appelbaum and Batt, *Private Equity at Work.*

35. General Accountability Office (GAO), *Nursing Home Complexity of Private Purchases Demonstrates Need for CMS to Improve the Usability and Completeness of Ownership Data* (Washington, DC: U.S. Government Printing Office, September 2010).

36. Sea Crest Health Care Management and its skilled nursing home affiliates operated 51 nursing homes in Florida at the time. The parent company is Sea Crest Health Care Investment, LLC. Another LA Vie subsidiary includes Genoa Healthcare Group, LLC.

37. Formation Capital has been heavily involved in a number of large nursing home investments since 1999, financing over $5 billion in nursing homes and other senior housing. For example, it purchased and sold three of the largest nursing home chains at sizable profits: Beverly Enterprises (2002), Genesis Health Care (2003), and Mariner Health Care's Florida homes (2003).

38. The company was co-founded by Joseph D. Conte as Tandem health services in 1997 and incorporated as Consulate Health Care nine years later. In 2012, the firm and its affiliates, Consulate Facilities Leasing LLC and Consulate Management Company LLC, were operating 70 facilities; fifty-seven percent of its residents were funded through Medicaid.

39. www.seniorcaredevelopment.com/investments_lavie_care_centers.php.

In 2011, Brian Beckwith became CEO of Formation Capital. He previously served as managing director of GE Capital, Healthcare Financial Services-Real Estate, a PE firm that invests in various health care sectors. In addition, a recently hired vice-president at the investment firm, Stephanie Hammer, also previously worked at GE Capital, Healthcare Financial Services. Revolving doors are common among such companies.

40. GAO, *Nursing Home Complexity of Private Purchases.*

These could be the original sixty-six nursing homes, acquired by Warburg Pincus, LLC in 2000, that retained its real estate.

41. With this purchase, GE Capital owned half of the nursing home real estate in Florida. GE Capital also financed five of the top ten nursing home operators and five of the top ten assisted-living companies in the nation. "GE Healthcare Financial to Buy 186 Nursing Homes," *McKnight's*, June 27, 2006, www.mcknights.com.

42. "Investing Through Alignment of Interests," See the Formation Capital website, www.formationcapital.com.

43. According to the surveyors, these are based on observations, record reviews, and interviews.

44. In 2014, the following people were officers/directors/owners of Consulate Health Care as well as officers/directors of Hillcrest: Joseph D. Conte, President and CEO (in 2014 earned $463.9 million in salary and bonuses); Jeff Jefferson, Exec V.P. and COO; Troy Antonik Senior VP and CFO; Christina Firth, Director/Officer; Steven Fishman, Director Officer; Robert Hartman, Director/Officer, owns 5 percent or more; Asher Low, Director/Officer, owns 5 or more; Isaac Neuberger, Director/Officer, owns 5 percent or more. www.consulatehealthcare.com.; www.hoovers.com.

45. www.MYHealthSource.com; Dun and Bradstreet company reports, www.dnbi.com, accessed May 29, 2014.

The nursing home company was started by Herbert and Lenore Kallen who each held fifty percent of the stock. In 2005 it was registered as an LLC. The proprietors own both the real estate and the operation of the nursing home, along with a nearby psychiatric and substance abuse hospital (Hollywood Pavillion Mental hospital). In 2010, the firm's net worth was $3.1 million ($4.6 million in assets and $1.5 million in liabilities). www.dnbi.com, accessed May 29, 2014.

46. Henry J. Kaiser Family Foundation, Kaiser Commission on Medicaid and the Uninsured, State Health Facts, "Certified Nursing Facility Occupancy Rates," Menlo Park, CA: Henry J. Kaiser Family Foundation, Kaiser Commission on Medicaid and the Uninsured, 201, www.kff.org.

47. There is a question, however, as to whether the "Nursing Home Compare" scoring system accurately portrays the quality of care provided to residents. A 2014 investigation by the *New York Times* indicates how easily the rating system can be gamed. Of the three foremost measures, only the annual health inspection information relies on independent state surveys; staffing levels and quality of care criteria

mainly depend on the facility's self-reported figures that the government does not verify. Overall quality itself is based on the other three indicators.

The study found that nursing homes with a long history of substandard care generally rate well in the categories that use self-reported information. And some places inflate staffing during periods leading up to the annual inspection. Furthermore, the rating system does not take into account state penalties, resident complaints to local agencies or lawsuits against a facility. Thus, the Nursing Home Compare website can be seriously misleading. www.nytimes.com/2014/08/25/business/medicare-star-ratings-allow-nursing-homes-to-game-the-system.html?_r=0.

In February 2015, CMS slightly revised the system to ensure that five-star nursing homes are not inflating their scores with the self-reported data. The changes are intended to render it more difficult for a nursing home to earn a quality measure rating of two or more stars or to obtain an overall staffing rating of four or more stars. Consequently, the overall ratings of roughly 30 percent of institutions plummeted. The new measures will continue to rely on self-reported quality information but in 2016 the government will utilize an electronic system that can verify staffing levels through payroll records. Editorial Board, "Is that Really a Five-Star Nursing home?" *New York Times* (February 25, 2015).

As just one example of such manipulation, in 2014 Hollywood Hills received an overall four-star, above average rating although the facility was owned and operated by the same cast of characters. Given the horrendous conditions at the time my mother was a resident, it seems unlikely that the facility was so dramatically upgraded. Almost certainly, the owners played the system with unverified and erroneous self-reported data. Indeed, after CMS instituted slightly more stringent regulations for earning a quality measure rating of two or more stars, along with other revisions, Hollywood Hills' overall rating fell to one star (well below average).

48. Gracedale is the English translation of Gnadenthal.

49. Interview with Millard D. Freeman, Administrator, Gracedale Nursing Home, March 25, 2015.

50. By 2014 the deficit reached $6.7 million. It is projected that operating losses will increase $1.4 million annually, costing Northampton County $12.1 million in subsidies by 2018. Matt Assad, "Can Northampton County Taxpayers Afford to Keep Gracedale?" *Morning Call*, February 28, 2015.

In May 2016, the County Council must decide whether to attempt another privatization of the facility.

51. In 2014, Gracedale added a 27-bed post-acute services wing that Medicare reimburses at a daily per patient rate of $450 to $500, as compared to $220 for Medicaid residents. The intension is to expand the post-acute care capacity to 60 beds and eventually to 80 beds. While this would improve the financial state of the facility, there is concern about reducing available places for low-income, Medicaid-reliant people requiring long-term care. Currently, about 80 percent of the residents

(or 550 individuals) are subsidized partly or fully through Medicaid. According to Mr. Freeman, any initiatives that he undertakes have to be approved by the Northampton County Council. Freeman interview, March 25, 2015.

52. Of the $69 million in annual operating expenses, wages, and benefits represent $43.6 million or 63 percent of the total. As county employees, the staff is entitled to health care coverage with only minimal out-of-pocket expenses; a defined benefit retirement pension, based on a percentage of pay and years of service (which averages $8,400 a year per worker); and other fringe benefits such as paid sick days and vacation. As agreed to by their union (The American Federation of State, County and Municipal Employees—AFCME), subsequent to the referendum, the administration slightly increased workday hours and cut vacation time. Ibid.

Starting salaries for certified nursing aides ranges from $13.65 to $16.75, depending on the shift and whether it's a weekend or holiday; Corresponding figures for LPNs and RNs are from $20.18 to $24.53 and $25.45 to $30.78, respectively. Ibid.

There are roughly 600 full-time and 150 part-time workers at the facility. Unlike proprietary nursing homes, because of the relatively better wages and benefits, staff positions are relatively easy to fill and turnover is minimal.

53. According to Mr. Freeman, Gracedale will require at least $14 million in capital improvements over the next several years, mostly because of the age of its buildings. Ibid.

54. Dorie Seavey and Abby Marquand, *Caring in America: a Comprehensive Analysis of the Nation's Fastest-growing Jobs, Home Health and Personal Care Aides*, Paraprofessional Healthcare Institute (PHI), Bronx, New York, December 2011, www.phinational. org/policy.

55. In 2012, Medicare outlays for home health agencies amounted to $21 billion or 4 percent of its total expenditures, mostly for post-acute services. Terence Ng, Charlene Harrington, Mary Beth Musumeci, and Erica Reaves, *Medicaid Home and Community-Based Service Programs: 2010 Date Update*, March 27, 2014 (Menlo Park, CA: Henry J. Kaiser Family Foundation, March 27, 2014), http://www.kff.org.

56. Natalie Moyle and Thomas Day, *Using Professional Home Care Services*, National Care Planning Council (NCPC), Centerville, UT, 2014, www.longtermcarelink. net/eldercare/personal-care-home-care.htm.

57. Seavey and Marquand, *Caring in America.*

58. Ng, Harrington, Musumeci, and Reaves, *Medicaid Home and Community-Based Service Programs.*

59. In Ohio, for example, an investigation by *The Columbus Dispatch* found that there were many unscrupulous operators engaging in fraudulent activities, including the provision of low-quality care. Rita Price and Ben Sutherly, "Regulation of Ohio home health care lax," Special Investigation Series on Home Care: Families on Their Own in Trying to Find Reliable Home Health Care, *The Columbus Dispatch*,

December 16, 2014, www.dispatch.com/content/stories/local/2014/12/16/on-your-own.html.

60. Seavey and Marquand, *Caring in America*.

61. Rita Price and Ben Sutherly, "Regulation of Ohio Health Care Lax: Dispatch Special Investigation Series on Home Care, "*The Columbus Dispatch* (December 16, 2014), www.dispatch.com/content/stories/local/2014/12/16/on-your-own.html.

62. *The Columbus Dispatch* reporters similarly found that the website does not offer valuable information or cover the full range of agencies in an area. Ibid.

63. Onex, Inc. manages two private equity units, one of which is the large-cap Onex Partners fund.

64. In 2010, Onex Partners 111, LP and in 2004, private investment firm Onex Partners 1, LP (both Onex Corporation Partners) each purchased shares in the company, totaling roughly 78 percent. Onex, Inc., the parent company, has a 20 percent interest.

65. Their subdivisions include electronics manufacturing services, insurance, building products, commercial vehicles, health care, and aircraft leasing.

66. Doug Alexander and Laura Marcinek, "Onex CEO Gerry Schwartz $85.3 million pay trumps Disney, Coca-Cola and Visa CEOs rewards combined," *Bloomberg News*, April 11, 2–14, www.blooberg.com.

67. www.forbes.com/profile/gerald-schwartz/.

68. U.S. Securities and Exchange Commission (SEC), Form 10-K, Annual Report pursuant to Section 13 or 15 (d) of the Securities and Exchange Act of 1934, for the fiscal year ended December 31, 2013, Res-Care, Inc., 39, www.rescare.com/wp-content/uploads/2014/03/ResCare-10-K-Reports.pdf.

69. Hoovers, Inc., *Rescare, Inc., profile*, www.hoovers.com, accessed June 2, 2014.

70. Ralph G. Gronefeld (President and CEO) received $541,000; Patrick Kelley (Chief Operating Officer), $460, 000; D. Ross Davidson (Chief Financial Officer), $1.5 million; Roderick Purdy (Chief Human Resources Officer), 487,200; and Steven Reed (Chief Legal Officer and Corporate Secretary), $265,100. SEC Report, *Rescare, Inc.*, Profile: 55.

71. Ibid.

72. There are wide disparities across the states. For example, in 2013, the median hourly wage for the 13,260 personal care aides in Florida was $9.61 while earnings for comparable personnel in Pennsylvania (51,280 people) averaged $14.23. Dorie Seavey and Abby Marquand, *Caring in America*.

73. In Florida, 33 percent of aides have no health coverage at all, and another 31 percent rely on Medicaid for themselves and their families. The corresponding figures for Pennsylvania are 18 percent and 33 percent, respectively. Dorie Seavey and Abby Marquand, *Caring in America*; Annalyn Kurtz, *America's Fastest Growing Job Pays Poorly*, CNN money, March 11, 2013, http://www.money.cnn.com/2013/03/11/

news/economy/fastest-growing-job/; Harris-Kojetin, Sengupta, Park-Lee, and Valverde, *Long-term Care Services in the United States*, 2013.

74. See its website, www.gencap.com.

75. Hoover's, Inc., a subsidiary of Dun & Bradstreet, is a business research company that provides information on companies and industries in the U.S. See, Hoovers, I*nc., Univita Health Holdings, Inc. Profile*, www.hoovers.com, accessed June 28, 2014.

Univita's current CEO, Michael Muchnicki, is a former CEO of United Healthcare of Florida. Other executive leadership positions include Ben Lytle, Chairman; Hugh Lytle, Vice-Chairman; John Way, Chief Financial Officer; John Mach, President of Complex Case Management; and Michael O'Connor, President of Integrated Care.

76. Univita and their affiliates are subsidiaries of Univita Health Holdings, Inc., whose capital stock is held by its officers.

77. Hoovers, Inc., *Primary Medical Staffing Inc. Profile*, www.hoovers.com, accessed June 30, 2014.

78. Hoovers, Inc., *Affordable Rehab Services, Inc. Profile*, www.hoovers.com, accessed June 28, 2014.

79. Medicare Advantage constitutes 31 percent of total revenues for health insurance companies that offer these plans. "Is Market Competition Necessary or Sufficient for High Performance Health Systems?" Pauline Vaillancourt Rosenau. http://regulation.upf.edu/utrecht-08-papers/pvaillancourt.pdf.

80. Henry J. Kaiser Family Foundation, *Medicare Advantage Fact Sheet* (Menlo Park, CA: Henry J. Kaiser Family Foundation, Kaiser Commission on Medicaid and the Uninsured, May 1, 2014), http://kff.org/Medicare/fact-sheet/medicare-advantage-fact-sheet/.

81. In addition to Part A (Hospital Insurance) and Part B (Medical Insurance) coverage, MA Plans entice customers by offering various types of extra benefits. These can include vision services, hearing services, dental care, health and wellness programs, and Part D prescription drug coverage.

82. Service "gaps" include long-term supports, vision care, eyeglasses and lenses, dental services and dentures. Keith D. Lind, *Setting the Record Straight about Medicare*, AARP Public Policy Institute, fact sheet 249 (February, 2012).

83. Quoted in Jordan Rau, *Do Medicare Advantage Plans Skin Off the Healthiest Customers?* AARP, Kaiser Health News (February 4, 2013), http://blog.aarp.org/2013/02/04/do-medicare-advantage-plans-skim-off-the-healthiest-customers/.

84. With 2.8 million enrolled customers, Humana is tied for second place with Blue Cross/Blue Shield. United Healthcare, the largest, enrolls 19 percent of total Medicare Advantage customers.

85. These estimates are based on an analysis by Cowen & Co., New York, New York. It also found that UnitedHealth receives 25 percent if its revenues from Medicare Advantage plans. Alex Wayne and Alex Nussbaum, "UnitedHealth,

Humana May See Surge in Medicare Advantage," *Bloomberg News*, May 15, 2013, www.bloomberg.com/news/articles/2013-05-15/unitedhealth-humana-may-see-surge-in-Medicare-advantage-i38i8kan.

86. Ibid.; Humana Inc., "Income Statement Annual Report." http//csimarket.com/stocks/income.php?code=HUM.

UnitedHealth shares gained 14 percent in 2013.

87. This figure includes $8.9 million paid to Bruce D. Broussard, President and CEO; $4.9 million, Timothy S. Hural, Senior Vice-President and Chief Human Resources Officer; $4.1 million, James E. Murray, Executive Vice-President and Chief Operating Officer; $3.5 million, James H. Bloem, Senior Vice-President and Chief Financial Officer and Treasurer; and $3.1 million, Jody L. Bilney, Senior Vice-President and Chief Consumer Officer, www.salary.com/Executive-salaries-search-result.html?q=humana.

88. In line with the 2010 Affordable Care Act provisions, fees to Medicare Advantage insurance companies, including Humana, had been scheduled to be lowered by $206 billion over ten years. Faced by intense industry lobbying, the Obama Administration thus far has failed to implement the cuts. If it does not backpedal again, there will be a 4 percent reduction in 2015. Their elderly and disabled customers, however, will ultimately pay the greatest price. According to Medicare actuaries, in order to maintain high executive compensation packages and elevated company profit levels, these firms most likely will raise out-of-pocket beneficiary costs, reduce benefits, and abandon less profitable regions. Alex Wayne and Caroline Chen, "UnitedHealth, Humana Take a Cut on Medicare Advantage Plans, *Bloomberg News*, April 8, 2014, www.bloomberg.com/news/articles/2014-04-08/unitedhealth-humana-take-cut-in-Medicare-advantage-plans.

89. Although Assisted Living Facility is the most common term, similar accommodations are known as residential care facility, enriched housing program, community residence, personal care home, and shared housing establishment, depending on the state. Karl Polzer, *Assisted Living State Regulatory Review*, National Center for Assisted Living (NCAL), Washington, DC, March 2013, www.ahcancal.org/ncal/resources/Documents/2013-reg-review.pdf.

90. Fewer than 20 percent are nonprofit facilities, with only a tiny percentage government-owned. Roughly 40 percent of total ALFs are part of a chain. Eunice Park-Lee, Christine Coffrey, Manisha Sengupta, Abigail Moss, Emily Rosenoff, and Lauren D. Harris-Kojetin, *Residential Care Facilities: A key Sector in the Spectrum of Long-Term Care Providers in the United States*, NCHS Data Brief, No. 78, Hyattsville, MD: National Center for Health Statistics, December 2011. www.ahcancal.org/ncal/Documents/11 NCHSIssueBriefonRCFs.pdf.

91. According to one source, however, about 20 percent of ALFs have at least one Medicaid-funded resident. Polzer, *Assisted Living State Regulatory Review*.

92. Myra A. Aud and Marilyn J. Rantz, "Quality Improvement in Long-term Care," *Journal of Nursing Care Quality*, 19, No. 1, 2004: 8–9.

93. Harris-Kojetin, Sengupta, Park-Lee, and Valverde, *Long-term Care Services in the United States*, 2013.

Chapter 15

1. Terence Ng, Charlene Harrington, MaryBeth Musumeci, and Erica L. Reaves, *Medicaid and Community-Based Services Programs: 2011 Data Update.* Menlo Park, CA: Henry J. Kaiser Family Foundation, Kaiser Commission on Medicaid and the Uninsured, December 2014, http://files.kff.org/attachment/report-medicaid-home-and-community-based-services-programs-2011-data-update.

2. The program ends in September 2015, and is limited to a total of $3 billion.

3. The income threshold increased from 150 percent of the FPL to 300 percent of SSI, similar to waiver programs. Nevertheless, each state still determines the criteria. Edward Alan Miller, "The Affordable Care Act and Long-Term Care: Comprehensive Reform or Just Tinkering Around the Edges?" *Journal of Aging and Social Policy*, 2012, 24 (2): 101–17.

4. Charlene Harrington, Terence Ng, Mitchell LaPlante, and H. Stephen Kay, "Medicaid Home-and Community-Based Services: Impact of the Affordable Care Act, *Journal of Aging and Social Policy*, 2012, 24 (2): 169–87.

5. Assisted-living and HCBS agency-based providers "have been subject to far less scrutiny than nursing homes." Miller, "The Affordable Care Act and Long-Term Care," 106.

6. Catherine Hawes, Darcy M. Moudouni, Rachel Edwards, and Carles D. Phillips, "Nursing Homes and the Affordable Care Act: A Cease Fire in the Ongoing Struggle Over Quality Reform," *Journal of Aging and Social Policy*, 2012, 24 (2): 206–20.

7. For-profit facilities are represented by the American Health Care Organization (AHCA) and multi-facility chains and PI firms by The Alliance for Quality Nursing Home Care (AQNHC). Catherine Hawes, Darcy M. Moudouni, Rachel Edwards, and Carles D. Phillips, "Nursing Homes and the Affordable Care Act: A Cease Fire in the Ongoing Struggle Over Quality Reform," *Journal of Aging and Social Policy*, 2012, 24 (2): 206–20.

8. Ibid.

9. Ibid.

10. Robyn I. Stone and Natasha Bryant, "The Impact of Health Care Reform on the Workforce Caring for Older Adults," *Journal of Aging and Social Policy*, 2012, 24 (2): 188–205.

11. Annual staff turnover in home care agencies ranges from 40 to 60 percent and in some cases is as high as 65 percent. Miller, "The Affordable Care Act and Long-Term Care."

12. Several researchers point out that direct care workers will gain from ACAs health coverage provisions: the insurance exchanges, federal subsidies, and the Medicaid expansion. Nevertheless, their wages are so low that the premiums on the exchanges most likely won't be affordable for most of them, even with the subsidies. Moreover, because a significant number of states have opted out of the expansion, large numbers of direct-care workers won't be eligible for Medicaid.

13. The national minimum for certified nurses' aides is only 75 hours of pre-employment training. States are responsible for setting requirements in other settings and where regulations do exist, they tend to be even less rigorous. Robyn I. Stone and Natasha Bryant, "The Impact of Health Care Reform on the Workforce Caring for Older Adults," *Journal of Aging and Social Policy*, 2012, 24 (2): 188–205.

14. Dually eligible people represent 21 percent of Medicare beneficiaries but account for 31 percent of program outlays; For Medicaid, they are 15 percent of participants but fully 39 percent of total program costs. Randall Brown and David R. Mann, "Medicare Policy: Issue Brief," Kaiser (October 2012), https://kaiserfamilyfoundation.files.wordpress.com/2013/01/8353.pdf.

15. David C. Grabowski, "Care Coordination for Dually Eligible Medicare-Medicaid Beneficiaries Under the Affordable Care Act," *Journal of Aging and Social Policy*, 2012, 24 (2): 221–32.

16. Miller, "The Affordable Care Act and Long-Term Care."

17. Andrea Louise Campbell, *Trapped in America's Safety Net: One Family's Struggle* (Chicago, IL: The University of Chicago Press, 2014), xii.

18. Federal Interagency Forum on Aging-Related Statistics. *Older Americans: Key Indicators of Well-Being*. Federal Interagency Forum on Aging-Related Statistics, Washington, DC: U.S. Government Printing Office, July 2012.

19. Henry J. Kaiser Family Foundation, Kaiser Commission on Medicaid and the Uninsured, *Five Key Facts About the Delivery, Number and Financing of Long-Term Services and Supports*, Menlo Park, CA: Henry J. Kaiser Family Foundation, Kaiser Commission on Medicaid and the Uninsured, September 13, 2013, http://kff.org/medicaid/fact-sheet/five-key-facts-about-the-delivery-and-financing-of-long-term.

20. The CLASS Act was rescinded by the American Taxpayer Relief Act of 2012.

21. As Edward Alan Miller explains, the least healthy individuals or those at risk of disability would be the most likely to enroll. In turn, that would lead to escalating costs and ever-increasing premiums, rendering the scheme unattractive to the vast majority of eligible people. He estimated that only 3.5 percent of adults were expected to enroll. Edward Alan Miller, "Flying Beneath the Radar of Health Reform: The Community Living Assistance and Supports (CLASS) Act," *The Gerontologist*, 2011, 51 (2): 145–54.

22. Under CLASS, workers would have been vested after paying into the system for five years. Premium levels varied based only on age; there were no lifetime limits,

elimination periods, or cost-sharing requirements; and the benefit could supplement other federal or state assistance.

Beneficiaries would have received a minimum cash benefit of $50 per day (linked to the consumer price index) with an average of roughly $75, depending on functional ability. Miller, "Flying Beneath the Radar of Health Reform."

23. Less than 8 percent of Americans have purchased private LTC insurance.

24. Tara Siegel Bernard, "Fine Print and Red Tape in Long-Term Care Policies," *New York Times* (June 8, 2013), B1.

25. Miller, "Flying Beneath the Radar of Health Reform."

26. The medical loss ratio (MLR) is the percentage of premium dollars utilized for direct health services as opposed to expenses for marketing, profits, executive salaries and bonuses, administration, agent commissions, and the like.

Bibliography

Alexander, Doug, and Laura Marcinek. "Onex CEO Gerry Schwartz $85.3 Million Pay Trumps Disney, Coca-Cola and Visa CEOs Rewards Combined." *Bloomberg News*, April 11, 2014, Available at http://business.financialpost.com/executive/leadership/onex-ceo-gerald-schwartzs-85-3-million-pay-trumps-disney-coca-cola-and-visa-ceos-rewards-combined?_lsa=5737-f246.

American Association of Retired Persons. *Caregiving in the U.S.* Washington, DC: National Alliance for Caregiving and AARP, 2009. Available at www.caregiving.org/Caregiving_in_the_US_2009_full_report.pdf.

Amirkhanyan, Anna A. "The Smart-Seller Challenge: Exploring the Determinants of Privatizing Public Nursing Homes." *Journal of Public Administration Research and Theory* 17, no. 3 (July 2007): 501–27.

Amirkhanyan, Anna A., Hyun Joon Kim, and Kristina T. Lambright. "Does the Public Sector Outperform the Nonprofit and For-Profit Sectors?: Evidence from a National Panel Study on Nursing Home Quality and Access." *Journal of Policy Analysis and Management*, 27, no. 2 (2008): 326–53.

Appelbaum, Eileen, and Rosemary Batt. *Private Equity at Work*. New York: Russell Sage Foundation, 2014.

Assad, Matt. "Can Northampton County Taxpayers Afford to Keep Gracedale?" *Morning Call*, February 28, 2015.

Aud, Myra A., and Marilyn J. Rantz. "Quality Improvement in Long-term Care." *Journal of Nursing Care Quality* 19, no. 1 (2004): 8–9.

Bernard, Tara Siegel. "Fine Print and Red Tape in Long-Term Care Policies." *New York Times*, June 8, 2013.

Brown, Randall, and David R. Mann. *Medicare Policy: Issue Brief*. Menlo Park, CA: Henry J. Kaiser Family Foundation, Kaiser Commission on Medicaid and the Uninsured, October 2012. Available at https://kaiserfamilyfoundation.files.wordpress.com/2013/01/8353.pdf.

Campbell, Andrea Louise. *Trapped in America's Safety Net: One Family's Struggle*. Chicago, IL: The University of Chicago Press, 2014.

Casson, Joseph E., and Julia McMillen. "Protecting Nursing Home Companies: Limiting Liability Through Corporate Restructuring." *Journal of Health Law* 36, no. 4 (Fall 2003): 577–613.

The Center on Budget and Policy Priorities. *Policy Basics: An Introduction to Medicaid.* Washington, DC: The Center on Budget and Policy Priorities, May 8, 2013. Available at htpp: cbpp/files/policybasics-medicaid.pdf.

Chari, A. V., John Engberg, Kristin Ray, and Ateev Mehrotra, *The Opportunity Costs of Informal Elder-Care in the United States.* Santa Monica, California: Rand Corporation, October 27, 2014. Available at www.rand.org/pubs/external_pub-lications/EP66196.html.

Coontz, Stephanie. *The Way We Never Were: American Families and the Nostalgia Trap.* New York: Basic Books, 2000.

CSI Market Company. *Humana Income Statement Annual Report, 2014.* Coral Springs, Florida: CSI Market Company. Available at http//csimarket.com/stocks/income. php?code=HUM.

Federal Interagency Forum on Age-Related Statistics. *Older Americans 2012: Key Indicators of Well-Being.* Washington, D.C.: Federal Interagency Forum on Age-Related Statistics, August 16, 2012.

Feinberg, Lynn, Susan Reinhard, Ari Houser and Rita Choula. *Valuing the Invaluable: 2011 Update, The Growing Contributions and Costs of Family Caregivers.* AARP Public Policy Institute, Washington, DC: American Association of Retired Persons, 2011. Available at http://assets.aarp.org/rgcenter/ppi/ltc/isl-caregiving.pdf.

Florida Agency for Health Care Administration, Department of Elder Affairs. *Medicaid Long-Term Care in Florida, Conference on Aging: New Game, New Rules,* August 20, 2012. Available at http//ahca.myFlorida.com/Medicaid/recent_presenta-tions_Medicaid_Long_Term_Care_in_Florida_FCOA_082012.pdf.

Forbes, *The World's Billionaires: #118 Gerald Schwartz,* 2014. Available at http://www. forbes.com/profile/gerald-schwartz/. Accessed May 20, 2014.

"GE Healthcare Financial to Buy 186 Nursing Homes." *McKnight's,* June 27, 2006. Available at www.mcknights.com.

Grabowski, David C. "Care Coordination for Dually Eligible Medicare-Medicaid Beneficiaries Under the Affordable Care Act." *Journal of Aging and Social Policy* 24, no. 2 (2012): 221–32.

Gray, Bradford H. ed., *For-Profit Enterprise in Health Care.* Institute on Medicine (US) Committee on Implications of For-Profit Enterprise in Health Care. Washington, DC: National Academies Press, 1986.

Gross, Jane. *A Bittersweet Season: Caring for Our Aging Parents—And Ourselves.* New York: Vintage Books, 2012.

Harrington, Charlene, Terence Ng, Mitchell LaPlante, and H. Stephen Kay. "Medicaid Home-and Community-Based Services: Impact of the Affordable Care Act, *Journal of Aging and Social Policy* 24, no. 2 (2012): 169–87.

Harrington, Charlene, Steffie Woolhandler, Joseph Mullen, and David U. Himmelstein, "Does Investor Ownership of Nursing Homes Compromise the Quality of Care?" *American Journal of Public Health* 91, no. 9 (September 2001): 1452–55.

Harris-Kojetin, Lauren, Manisha Sengupta, Eunice Park-Lee, and Roberto Valverde. *Long-Term Care Services in the United States: 2013 Overview.* Hyattsville, MD: National Center for Health Statistics, 2013.

Hawes, Catherine, Darcy M. Moudouni, Rachel Edwards, and Carles D. Phillips. "Nursing Homes and the Affordable Care Act: A Cease Fire in the Ongoing Struggle Over Quality Reform." *Journal of Aging and Social Policy,* 24, no. 2 (2012): 206–20.

Henry J. Kaiser Family Foundation, Kaiser Commission on Medicaid and the Uninsured. *Medicare Advantage Fact Sheet.* Menlo Park, CA: Henry J. Kaiser Family Foundation, Kaiser Commission on Medicaid and the Uninsured, *Medicare Advantage Fact Sheet*, May 1, 2014. Available at http://kff.org/Medicare/fact-sheet/Medicare-advantage-fact-sheet/.

Henry J. Kaiser Family Foundation, Kaiser Commission on Medicaid and the Uninsured. *The Facts on Medicare Spending and Financing*, Menlo Park, CA: Henry J. Kaiser Family Foundation, Kaiser Commission on Medicaid and the Uninsured, July 28, 2014. Available at http://kff.org/medicare/fact-sheet/Medicare-spending-and-financing-fact-sheet/.

Henry J. Kaiser Family Foundation, Kaiser Commission on Medicaid and the Uninsured. *Medicare Benefit Payments by Type of Service.* Menlo Park, CA: Henry J. Kaiser Family Foundation, Kaiser Commission on Medicaid and the Uninsured, July 15, 2013. Available at http://kff.org/?attachment_id=64757.

Henry J. Kaiser Family Foundation, Kaiser Commission on Medicaid and the Uninsured. *Five Key Facts About the Delivery, Number and Financing of Long-Term Services and Supports.* Menlo Park, CA: Henry J. Kaiser Family Foundation, Kaiser Commission on Medicaid and the Uninsured, September 13, 2013. Available at http://kff.org/medicaid/fact-sheet/five-key-facts-about-the-delivery-and-financing-of-long-term.

Henry J. Kaiser Family Foundation, Kaiser Commission on Medicaid and the Uninsured, State Health Facts. *Certified Nursing Facility Occupancy Rates.* Menlo Park, CA: Henry J. Kaiser Family Foundation, Kaiser Commission on Medicaid and the Uninsured, 2012. Available at http://kff.org/other/state-indicator/nursing-facility-occupancy-rates/.

Hoovers, Inc. *Affordable Rehab Services, Inc. Profile.* Austin, TX: Hoovers, Inc. Available at http://www.hoovers.com/company-information/cs/company-profile.Affordable_Rehab.3582147df84f8241.html. Assessed June 28, 2014.

Hoovers, Inc. *Primary Medical Staffing Inc. Profile.* Austin, Texas: Hoovers, Inc. Available at http://www.hoovers.com/company-information/cs/company-profile.Primary_Medical_Staffing_Inc.00be7094850a98fb.html. Assessed June 30, 2014.

Hoovers, Inc. *Rescare, Inc., profile.* Austin, TX: Hoovers, Inc. Available at http://www.hoovers.com/company-information/cs/company-profile.RES-Care_Inc.ff51bf-ca8e64f4cc.html. Assessed June 2, 2014.

Hoovers, Inc. *Univita Health Holdings, Inc. Profile.* Austin, TX: Hoovers, Inc. Available at http://www.hoovers.com/company-information/cs/company-profile.Univita_Health_Holdings_Inc.b5f7ffd95c72eb00.html. Assessed June 28, 2014.

"Is that Really a Five-Star Nursing home?" *New York Times,* February 25, 2015.

Kurtz, Annalyn. "America's Fastest Growing Job Pays Poorly." *CNN money,* March 11, 2013. Available at http://www.money.cnn.com/2013/03/11/news/economy/fastest-growing-job/.

Lind, Keith D. *Setting the Record Straight about Medicare,* AARP Public Policy Institute, fact sheet 249, Washington, DC: American Association of Retired Persons, February 2012. Available at www.aarp.org/content/dam/aarp/research/public_policy_institute/health/Setting-the-Record-Straight-about-Medicare-fact-sheet-AARP-ppi-health.pdf.

The McArthur and Pew Foundations. *State Health Spending on Medicaid: a 50-State Study of Trends and Drivers of Cost.* Washington, DC: the Pew Charitable Trusts and the McArthur Foundation, July 1014. Available at www.pewtrusts.org/~/media/Data-visualizations/Interactives/2014/Medicaid/downloadables/state_health_care_spending_on_Medicaid.pdf.

Metlife Mature Market Institute. *Miles Away: The Metlife Study of Long-Distance Caregiving: Findings from a National Study by the National Alliance for Caregiving International.* Westport CT: Metlife Mature Market Institute, July 2014. Available at www.caregiving.org/data/milesaway.pdf.

Miller, Edward Alan. "The Affordable Care Act and Long-Term Care: Comprehensive Reform or Just Tinkering Around the Edges?" *Journal of Aging and Social Policy* 24, no. 12 (2012): 101–17.

———. "Flying Beneath the Radar of Health Reform: The Community Living Assistance and Supports (CLASS) Act." *The Gerontologist* 51, no. 2 (2011): 145–54.

Mor, Vincent, Jacqueline Zinn, Joseph Angelelli, Joan Teno, and Susan Miller. "Driven to Tiers: Socioeconomic and Racial Disparities in the Quality of Nursing Home Care." *Milbank Quarterly* 82, no. 2 (2004): 227–,56.

Moyle, Natalie and Thomas Day. *Using Professional Home Care Services,* Centerville, UT: National Care Planning Council (NCPC), 2014. Available at www.long-termcarelink.net/eldercare/personal-care-home-care.htm.

Napili, Angela, and Kristen J. Colello. *Funding for the Older Americans Act and Other Aging Services Programs.* Congressional Research Service, Report for Congress. Washington, DC: Congressional Research Service, February 22, 2013. Available at http://fas.org/sgp/crs/misc/RL33880.pdf.

Ng, Terrence, Charlene Harrington, Mary Beth Musumeci, and Erica C. Reaves. *Medicaid and Community-Based Services Programs: 2011 Data Update.* Menlo Park, CA: Henry J. Kaiser Family Foundation, Kaiser Commission on Medicaid and the Uninsured, December 14 2014. Available at http://kff.org/report-section/

medicaid-home-and-community-based-services-programs-2011-data-update-medicaid-hcbs-participants-and-expenditures/.

Ng, Terence Charlene, Harrington, Mary Beth Musumeci, and Erica Reaves. *Medicaid Home and Community-Based Service Programs: 2010 Date Update*. Menlo Park, CA: Henry J. Kaiser Family Foundation, Kaiser Commission on Medicaid and the Uninsured, March 27, 2014. Available at https://kaiserfamilyfoundation.files.wordpress.com/2014/03/7720-07-medicaid-home-and-community-based-services-programs_2010-data-update1.pdf.

O'Dell, Carol. *Mothering Mother: A Daughter's Humorous and Heartbreaking Memoir*. Largo, FL: Kunati Inc. Book Publishers, 2007.

Olson, Laura Katz. *The Politics of Medicaid*. New York: Columbia University Press, 2010.

O'Neill, Ciaran, Charlene Harrington, Martin Kitchener, and Debra Saliba. "Quality of Care in Nursing homes: An Analysis of Relationships Among Profit, Quality and Ownership." *Medical Care* 41, no. 12 (2003):1318–30.

Park-Lee, Eunice, Christine Coffrey, Manisha Sengupta, Abigail Moss, Emily Rosenoff, and Lauren D. Harris-Kojetin. *Residential Care Facilities: A Key Sector in the Spectrum of Long-Term Care Providers in the United States*. NCHS Data Brief, No. 78. Hyattsville, MD: National Center for Health Statistics, December 2011. Available at www.ahcancal.org/ncal/Documents/11 NCHSIssueBriefonRCFs.pdf.

Polzer, Karl. *Assisted Living State Regulatory Review*, National Center for Assisted Living (NCAL), Washington, DC: NCAL, March 2013, Available at www.ahcancal.org/ncal/resources/Documents/2013-reg-review.pdf.

Price, Rita, and Ben Sutherly, "Regulation of Ohio home health care lax," Special Investigation Series on Home Care: Families on Their Own in Trying to Find Reliable Home Health Care, *The Columbus Dispatch*, December 16, 2014. Available at www.dispatch.com/content/stories/local/2014/12/16/on-your-own.html.

Rau, Jordan. *Do Medicare Advantage Plans Skin Off the Healthiest Customers?* AARP, Kaiser Health News. AARP Public Policy Institute, Washington, DC: American Association of Retired Persons, February 4, 2013. Available at http://blog.aarp.org/2013/02/04/do-Medicare-advantage-plans-skim-off-the-healthiest-customers/.

Rosenau, Pauline Vaillancourt. *Is Market Competition Necessary or Sufficient for High Performance Health Systems?* August 2008. Available at http://regulation.upf.edu/utrecht-08-papers/pvaillancourt.pdf.

The Scan Foundation, *Who Pays for Long-Term Care in the U.S.?*, Fact Sheet. Long Beach, CA: The Scan Foundation, January 2013. Available at www.TheSCANFoundation.org.

Seavey, Dorie, and Abby Marquand. *Caring in America: a Comprehensive Analysis of the Nation's Fastest-growing Jobs, Home Health and Personal Care Aides*. Bronx, NY: Paraprofessional Healthcare Institute (PHI), December 2011. Available at www.phinational.org/policy.

Stevenson, David G., and David C. Grabowski. "Private Equity Investment and Nursing Home Care: Is it a Big Deal?" *Health Affairs* 27, no. 5 (September 2008):1399–1408.

Stone, Robyn I., and Natasha Bryant. "The Impact of Health Care Reform on the Workforce Caring for Older Adults" *Journal of Aging and Social Policy* 24, no. 2: 188–205.

Thomas, Katie. "Medicare Star Ratings Allow Nursing Homes to Game the System," *New York Times*, August 24, 2014. Available at www.nytimes.com/2014/08/25/business/medicare-star-ratings-allow-nursing-homes-to-game-the-system.html?-r=0.

Thorndike, John. *The Last of His Mind*. Athens, OH: Swallow Press/Ohio University Press, 2009.

Tinsley, Molly Best. *Entering the Blue Stone*. Ashland, OR: Fuze Publishing LLC, 2012.

U.S. Bureau of the Census. *Median Value of Assets for Households, by Type of Asset Owned and Selected Characteristic: 2011*. Table 1. Washington, DC. Available at www.census.gov/people/wealth/data/dtables.html.

U.S. Department of Health and Human Services (HHS), Administration on Aging, Administration for Community Living. *A Profile of Older* Americans (2012). Available at www.aoa.gov/Aging_statistics/Profile/2012/docs/2012profile.pdf.

U.S. Department of Health and Human Services (HHS), Center for Medicare and Medicaid Services (CMS). *Nursing Home Data Compendium 2013 Edition*, Washington, DC: U.S. Government Printing Office, 2013. Available at www.cms.gov/Medicare/Provider-Enrollment-and-Certification/Certificationand Complianc/downloads/nursinghomedatacompendium_508.pdf.

U.S. General Accountability Office (GAO). *Nursing Home Complexity of Private Purchases Demonstrates Need for CMS to Improve the Usability and Completeness of Ownership Data*. Washington, DC: U.S. Government Printing Office, September 2010.

U.S. Securities Exchange Commission, "Res-Care, Inc. Annual Report, fiscal year 2013," form 10-K. Washington, DC: U.S. Exchange Commission, Available at http://www.rescare.com/wp-content/uploads/2014/03/ResCare-10-K-Report.pdf.

U.S. Social Security Administration, Office of Research and Disability Policy, Office of Research, Evaluation and Statistics, SSA publication no. 13-11727. *Income of the Aged Chart Book, 2012*. Washington, DC: U.S. Government Printing Office, April 2014.

U.S. Social Security Administration, Office of Retirement and Disability Policy, Office of Research, Evaluation, and Statistics, SSA Publication No. 13-11785. *Fast Facts and Figures About Social Security, 2013*. Washington, DC: U.S. Government Printing Office, August 2013.

Wayne, Alex, and Caroline Chen. "UnitedHealth, Humana Take a Cut on Medicare Advantage Plans." *Bloomberg News*, April 8, 2014. Available at www.bloomberg.com/news/articles/2014-04-08/unitedhealth-humana-take-cut-in-Medicare-advantage-plans.

Wayne, Alex, and Alex Nussbaum. "UnitedHealth, Humana May See Surge in Medicare Advantage." *Bloomberg News*, May 15, 2013. Available at www.bloomberg.com/news/articles/2013-05-15/unitedhealth-humana-may-see-surge-in-Medicare-advantage-i38i8kan.

West, Loraine A., Samantha Cole, Daniel Goodkind, and Wan He. *65+ in the United States: 2010*. U.S. Department of Health and Human Services, U.S. Department of Commerce, U.S. Census Bureau, Current Population Reports. Washington, DC: Government Printing Office, June 2014.

31192021636350